THE
CROSS-STITCHER'S
COMPLETE COMPANION
500 MOTIFS FOR EVERY OCCASION

THE CROSS-STITCHER'S COMPLETE COMPANION

500 MOTIFS FOR EVERY OCCASION

Sterling Publishing Co., Inc.
New York

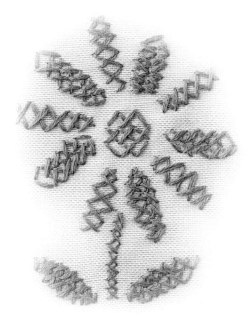

Designed and edited by Eaglemoss Publications Ltd

Library of Congress Cataloging-in-Publication Data Available

2 4 6 8 10 9 7 5 3 1

Published in 2004 by Sterling Publishing Co., Inc.
387 Park Avenue South, New York, NY 10016
Based on *Needlecraft Magic*, © 2003 by Eaglemoss Publications Ltd
Published in arrangement with BOOKSPAN
Distributed in Canada by Sterling Publishing
c/o Canadian Manda Group, One Atlantic Avenue, Suite 105
Toronto, Ontario, Canada M6K 3E7

Sterling ISBN 1-4027-1381-9

Contents

Introduction

Cross stitch, one of the oldest and simplest forms of embroidery, has in recent years become more and more popular. For some it is a lifetime's passion, for others a relaxing craft to enjoy in a spare moment. As you look through the wealth of beautiful designs in this book, you will begin to understand why this simple technique has given so much pleasure to needleworkers through the generations and continues to do so today. The aim of *The Cross-Stitcher's Complete Companion* is to give clear and straightforward instruction on the craft itself and to provide a comprehensive range of projects and patterns for all levels of expertise.

How to use this book

Counted cross stitch is closely related to needlepoint, and cross stitch and half cross stitch are often worked on canvas. Therefore, designs worked on canvas as well as the more usual evenweave fabric are included. Each of the projects has a list of the items you will need to carry out the work, but be sure also to have some embroidery scissors and pins on hand. A sewing machine is useful, too, though not essential for many of the projects.

For easy reference, the book is divided into six chapters. **Before You Start** takes you step-by-step through the essential techniques, with clear instructions on how to cross-stitch, read charts, and handle your work. The simple instructions will show you how to achieve professional results, even if you have never tried cross stitch before.

The next four chapters of wonderful projects for all occasions include ideas for embellishing household linen, furnishings, accessories, and clothes. In **Nature's Delights** you will find designs featuring flowers, plants, animals, and friendly pets. **Gifts and Celebrations** includes a Valentine's set, greeting cards, a sampler, and festive decorations. **For Babies and Children** has projects that make delightful presents for youngsters of all ages, and **Around the World** includes motifs from ancient Egypt, France, and Mexico.

Finishing and Making Up shows you the various techniques you will need to complete the projects including piping, hemming, and mitering; and how to make the various items on which the cross stitch is displayed including drawstring bags, double-fold cards, pillowcases, and cushion covers. Each project is explained in easy-to-follow steps, illustrated with clear color photographs.

It is easy to become proficient in cross stitch and with this clear and wide-ranging book you can develop your skill as you make beautiful gifts and items for your home, family, and friends.

Chapter 1
Before You Start

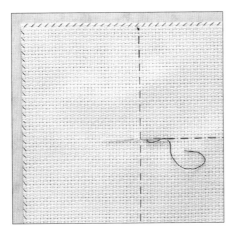 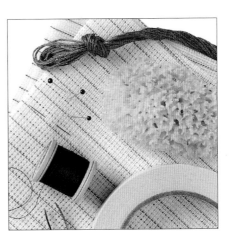

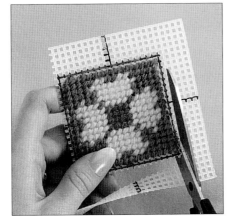 

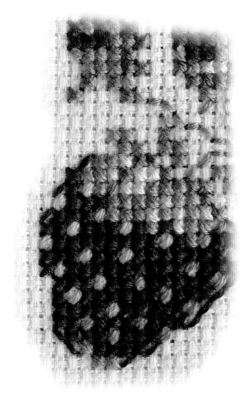

Counted Cross Stitch

The appeal of counted cross stitch is that you can recreate a design exactly and achieve perfect results. The designs are worked from charts printed on squared paper, each square representing one cross stitch. The stitches are worked on evenweave fabric, which has easily countable threads that form a grid, like the squares on the chart.

What is evenweave?

The distinguishing feature of even-weave fabrics is that they have the same number of vertical (warp) threads and horizontal (weft) threads over a given measurement. The fabric is graded according to the number of threads or blocks of threads per 1 in. (2.5 cm). This is called the count, or thread count. The lower the count, the larger the weave and the bigger the stitches.

There are three main types of evenweave: single-thread; Hardanger, woven with pairs of threads; and aida (pronounced "aid-a"), with blocks of threads. Aida is the most popular of these, as the thread blocks are easy to see, count, and stitch—you just slip the needle through the gaps between the blocks.

Aida has blocks of threads that are easy to see and count. Popular counts are 11, with 11 thread blocks per 1 in. (2.5 cm), and 14, with 14 thread blocks per 1 in. (2.5 cm).

Threads and needles

You can use many types of thread for counted cross stitch; the most versatile is stranded embroidery floss. You can separate it into different numbers of strands to suit the fabric count, and it comes in a huge range of colors. Work with lengths of no more than 15 in. (38 cm) to avoid tangles.

Tapestry needles are ideal for evenweaves. They have large, easy-to-thread eyes, and their blunt points slide between the fabric threads without splitting them.

Getting started

Before you start to stitch, cut the fabric at least 2 in. (5 cm) larger all around than the motif, and overcast the edges to prevent fraying. Mark the center with basting, as shown below, using contrasting sewing thread.

With larger cross-stitch projects, work with the fabric in an embroidery frame or hoop (see page 12).

Stranded floss has six strands which you split and then recombine to suit the fabric and the design. Unless stated otherwise, use two strands on 14-count fabric and three on coarser 11-count.

Preparing the fabric

1 Cut the fabric at least 2 in. (5 cm) larger all around than the motif. Overcast the raw edges as shown, or machine-stitch using zigzag.

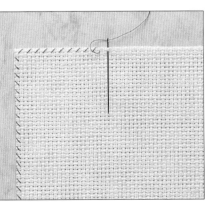

2 Find the center of two adjacent edges, and baste across the fabric from those points to mark the fabric's center (a tapestry needle slips easily between fabric threads).

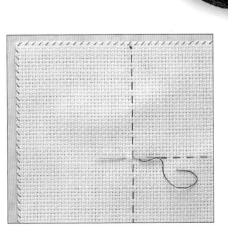

Mounting the fabric in a hoop

You'll always get better results if you use an embroidery hoop than if you do not. It holds the fabric taut, so you stitch more evenly, and it reduces fabric distortion.

Embroidery hoops consist of an inner ring which fits inside an adjustable outer ring. They are made of wood or plastic and range in size from 4 to 12 in. (10 to 30 cm) in diameter. Before cutting the fabric for a project in this book, make sure that the specified size is not too small for your hoop; if necessary, use a larger piece of fabric. For large projects, move the fabric around in the hoop as you finish each section.

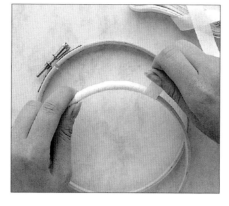

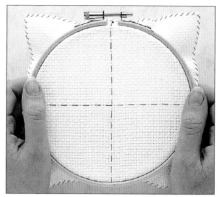

1 To prevent the fabric from slipping, remove the smaller ring from the hoop and bind it with cotton tape. Secure the ends with a few stitches.

2 Center the fabric over the smaller ring. Ease the larger ring in place, making sure the fabric is taut and even. Tighten the screw on the outer ring.

Using counted cross stitch charts

Using a counted cross stitch chart is just a matter of matching the squares on the chart with the grid of threads on your evenweave fabric. There are several kinds of charts.

Color charts show each stitch as a square of the appropriate color and are used for simple designs in clearly contrasting colors.

Black and white charts show each stitch as a symbol.

Color symbol charts (see below) show each stitch as a symbol drawn in a square of the appropriate color. The key (below right) shows which color thread to use for each symbol and the number of skeins required. Most of the charts in this book are of this type.

Small symbols or **colored triangles** on some charts show fractional, or three-quarter, stitches.

Heavy lines indicate outlines and

special details. These are worked in backstitch, and are usually added after the cross stitching is complete.

Arrows at the center of each edge enable you to find the center of the design, so that you can relate it to the center of the fabric. To find the center, join the arrows with a pencil and ruler. Always start stitching in the center, working outward from the center of the design to prevent distortion.

Fractional stitches appear as smaller symbols on symbol charts.

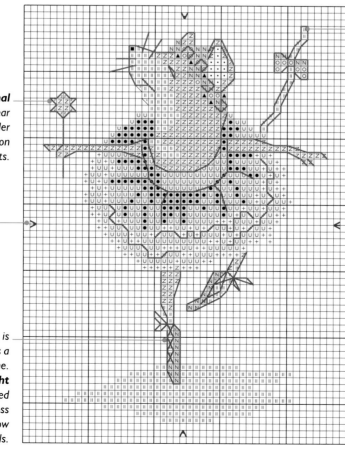

Arrows mark the centers of the edges.

Backstitch is shown as a heavy line.
Long straight stitches worked over cross stitches show details.

A symbol in a colored square indicates a single cross stitch. The correct thread color for each symbol is shown in the color key below.

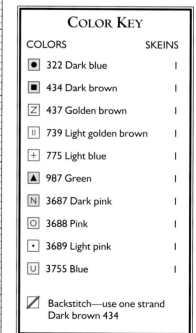

COLOR KEY		
COLORS		**SKEINS**
● 322 Dark blue		1
■ 434 Dark brown		1
Z 437 Golden brown		1
II 739 Light golden brown		1
+ 775 Light blue		1
▲ 987 Green		1
N 3687 Dark pink		1
O 3688 Pink		1
· 3689 Light pink		1
U 3755 Blue		1
⧄ Backstitch—use one strand Dark brown 434		

Cross Stitches

A cross stitch forms a diagonal cross on the front of the fabric; each cross is composed of two diagonal stitches worked one on top of the other. It is one of the easiest embroidery stitches to learn and use.

Cross stitch, front

Counted cross stitch is worked from charts on evenweave fabrics (see page 11). Begin with some aida cloth, which is the easiest to use. Then practice on single-thread evenweave.

You can use rows of cross stitches to form blocks of color, or work individual stitches. Always make sure to work all the lower diagonals slanting in one direction and all the top diagonals slanting in the other. This produces a neat, smooth effect.

Two other stitches are often shown on charts. **Fractional stitches (three-quarter stitches)** are a variation of normal cross stitch; they consist of a full diagonal and a half diagonal stitch. A single three-quarter stitch fills half the space of a full cross stitch, while a double three-quarter stitch takes up the space of a full cross stitch. These stitches are used to create smooth outlines around curved shapes and to add details. They are shown on charts as a small symbol or a colored triangle.

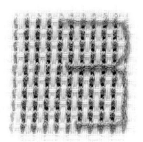

Cross stitch, back

Backstitch, shown as a heavy line, is used to create outlines around blocks of cross stitch and to add line details, also to seam fabrics if a sewing machine is not available.

Starting and fastening off

For a professional finish, always weave the loose ends of the thread into the back of the work. Do not tie a knot in the thread—the knot will make a lump on the right side and may eventually work loose, so that your stitching unravels.

1 Close to your starting point, push the needle through to the back of the fabric, leaving a 2-in. (5-cm) thread end at the front. You will secure this later, when you have finished stitching the length of thread.

2 When you have about 2 in. (5 cm) of thread left, or you have finished the color block, take the needle through to the back and darn the thread end under several stitches. Then pull the loose thread end at the start of your stitching through to the back, and darn it in.

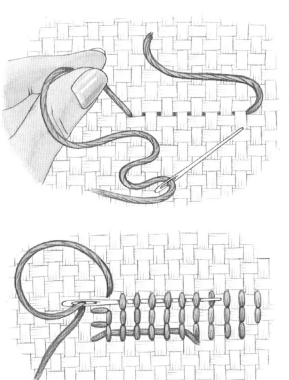

BRIGHT IDEAS

COMPLETING A COLOR AREA

Always fasten off the thread after completing each stitched area. Do not be tempted to carry a length of thread between two stitched areas on the wrong side. The floating thread will show through on the right side and spoil your work.

Joining in a new thread

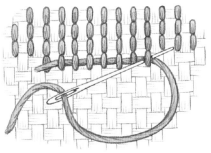

On the back of the fabric, run the new length of thread under the back of several stitches close to where you are working. Then take a small backstitch over the last stitch and bring the needle out in the correct place at the front of the fabric.

Working individual cross stitches

Bring the needle out at the front of the fabric and insert it one hole down and one hole to the right. Pull the thread through. Bring the needle out one hole to the left and insert it one hole up and one to the right.

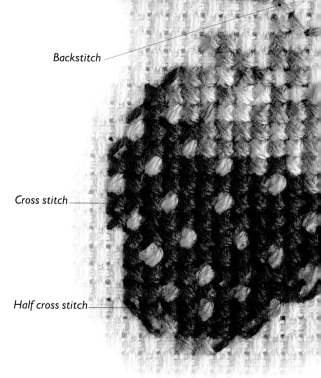

Backstitch

Cross stitch

Half cross stitch

Working a row of cross stitches

Each row of counted cross stitch is worked in two horizontal journeys. It does not matter in which direction you start stitching, so long as all the bottom stitches and all the top stitches slant in the same direction.

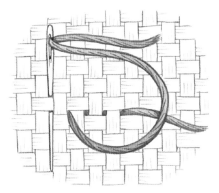

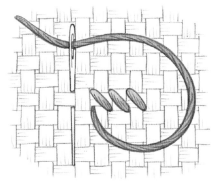

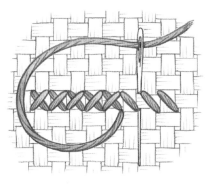

1 Bring the needle out to the front at the start of the work—this will usually be at the center of the design. To start working from right to left, insert the needle one hole up and one hole to the left, to make a diagonal stitch, and bring it out one hole down.

2 Insert the needle one hole up and one hole to the left, then bring it out one hole down. Continue working like this to form a row of upward diagonal stitches.

3 Work from left to right to complete the crosses. Bring the needle out directly below the top of the last diagonal. Insert it one hole up and one to the right, and bring it out one hole down. Continue like this to the end of the row.

Working fractional (three-quarter) stitches

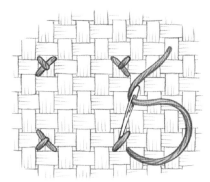

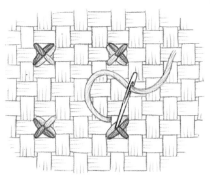

Working backstitch

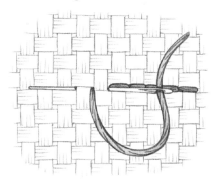

Single three-quarter stitch
This fills half the space of one whole cross stitch. Work a full-sized diagonal. Bring the needle out at the corner of the fabric block, then push it down in the center, over the full diagonal.

Double three-quarter stitch
This fills the space of one whole cross stitch. Work two three-quarter stitches back to back; the full diagonals share the same holes and the half stitches share the same center point.

Bring the needle out on the right side of the fabric and take a backward stitch, horizontally, vertically, or diagonally. Bring the needle out again, one stitch length from the start of the first stitch. Continue in this way.

14

Cross Stitch Variations

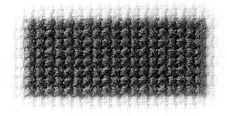

Two-sided cross stitch

Alternate cross stitch

Half cross stitch

Cross stitch is very versatile—there is a method to suit any design and virtually any fabric, whether you are working large areas or intricate details, or stitching lightweight or heavyweight fabrics.

As with basic cross stitch (see pages 13–14), it is important to work so that all the bottom diagonal stitches slant one way and the top diagonals the other.

Two-sided cross stitch looks exactly the same on the back and front of the fabric. Use it to work monograms and borders where both sides of the item are visible, and on semitransparent fabrics, such as voile, organdy, and fine linens. This stitch uses up more thread than ordinary cross stitch.

Alternate cross stitch produces a neat, well-tensioned surface. It is ideal for large background areas, but it uses up much more thread than ordinary cross stitch.

Half cross stitch is the first stage of a cross stitch, used alone. It can be used on evenweave fabrics to give a light texture to areas of a cross-stitch design, and it is also used as a needlepoint stitch, to cover canvas (see page 260). Plastic or interlock canvas should be used for this, as half cross has a tendency to distort an ordinary canvas weave. When used along with cross stitch, it is usually worked slanting from bottom left to top right, irrespective of the top slant of the cross stitches, although you can bend this rule for a less formal effect.

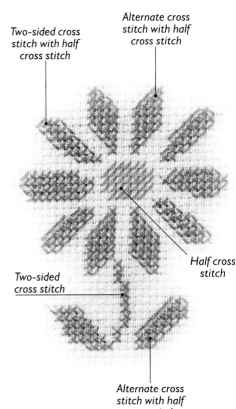

Two-sided cross stitch with half cross stitch

Alternate cross stitch with half cross stitch

Two-sided cross stitch

Half cross stitch

Alternate cross stitch with half cross stitch

Working two-sided cross stitch

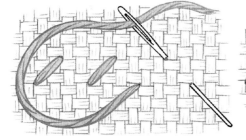

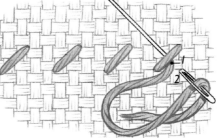

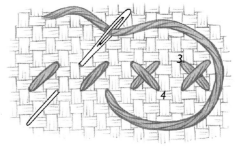

1 Working from left to right and over pairs of fabric blocks, work evenly spaced diagonal stitches slanting from bottom left to top right and covering alternate pairs of blocks.

2 At the end of the row, bring the needle through at 1 at the center of the last diagonal stitch. Insert it at 2 and bring it through at 1, again under the slanting stitch.

3 Insert the needle at 3 and bring it out again at 4. Then work back along the row, from right to left, making diagonal stitches to complete the alternate cross stitches.

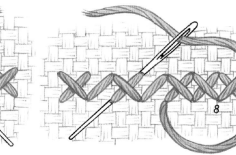

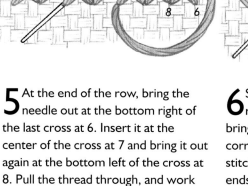

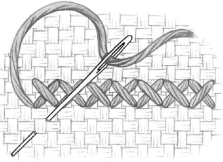

4 At the end of the row, insert the needle at 5, at the point where the thread emerged previously. Pull the thread through and work back along the row, working diagonal stitches slanting from bottom left to top right. (Note that the right-hand stitch breaks the rule about uniform slant.)

5 At the end of the row, bring the needle out at the bottom right of the last cross at 6. Insert it at the center of the cross at 7 and bring it out again at the bottom left of the cross at 8. Pull the thread through, and work back along the row from right to left to complete the crosses.

6 Start the second and subsequent rows by making a half stitch, bringing the thread through in the correct position to work the first stitch. Take care to secure the thread ends neatly to avoid spoiling the neatness of the wrong side.

Working alternate cross stitch

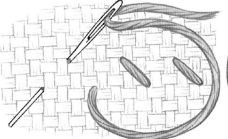

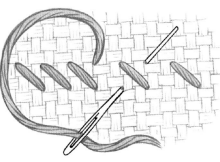

Alternate cross stitch

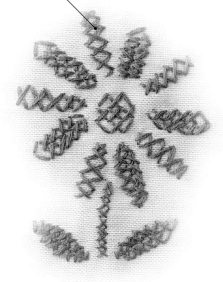

1 Work a row of evenly spaced alternate diagonal stitches, following step 1 (page 15), but slant the stitches from bottom right to top left, and work from right to left.

2 Work from left to right, making diagonal stitches between the alternate stitches to complete the row.

Working half cross stitch

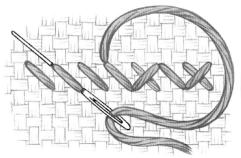

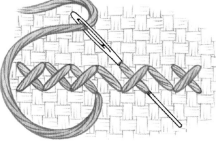

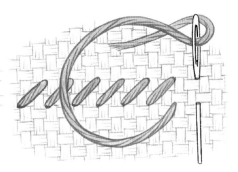

3 Work from right to left, working a row of alternate diagonal stitches slanting from top right to bottom left to complete alternate crosses.

4 Working from left to right, complete the remaining crosses. Work the next and subsequent rows below the first and previous until the block of stitching is complete.

Working from left to right, make a row of diagonal stitches slanting from bottom left to top right.

Other Useful Stitches

Counted cross-stitch designs are often embellished with other embroidery stitches, called "free-style," "free embroidery," or "surface embroidery" stitches, which are usually worked on non-evenweave fabric. Some of these can be worked in a regular, even formation, to harmonize with the grid structure of cross-stitch designs, and included here are instructions for those of these stitches that are used in the projects in this book.

Curly cross stitch is a textured variation of ordinary cross stitch, and is worked in rows over two horizontal journeys. It can be worked solidly so that all the rows touch, or be spaced out in a checkerboard fashion. On a non-evenweave fabric, it can be worked irregularly but it can also be worked as part of a counted cross-stitch design.

French knots are small, circular knotted stitches that stand out from the fabric. They are used alone or in small groups to highlight a particular feature of a design, such as an eye or a flower center. French knots should always be worked with the fabric held taut in a frame.

Blanket stitch is a looped stitch with many variations. Also called buttonhole stitch, it is often used as a surface embroidery stitch; but it can be used to edge a piece of fabric, preventing it from fraying and serving as a decoration at the same time. The stitches can be worked spaced apart or close together, as appropriate. When worked as an edging, the loops sit on the fabric edge.

Satin stitch is sometimes included in cross-stitched designs in lines or motifs. The stitch consists of parallel threads placed close together, creating a solid satiny effect. If you want to enhance the sheen, use a light-reflecting embroidery thread, such as stranded floss. The stitch is often worked on a diagonal, but it can also be worked vertically. On evenweave fabric it is easy to keep the stitches parallel because the weave forms a regular grid, but make sure that the thread is at least as thick as the fabric threads for adequate coverage.

Starting and finishing French knots

When you are working widely spaced French knots, fasten off the thread after each knot. When working groups of closely spaced knots, you can carry the thread across the back of the fabric between knots.

To start, work two or three tiny stitches at the back of the fabric, positioning them where they will be covered by the embroidery stitch. To finish, fasten off the thread in the same way, directly beneath the knot.

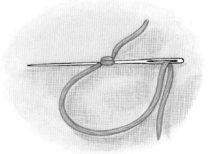

Working a French knot

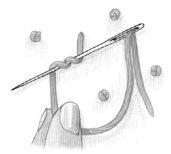 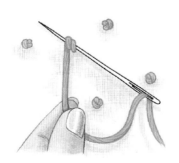 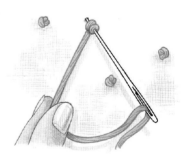

1 Bring the thread through to the front of the fabric. Holding the thread taut with one hand, wrap it twice around the needle. (For a flatter effect, wrap the thread only once around the needle.)

2 Pull the thread gently to tighten the twists around the needle. Do not overtighten, or you will find it difficult to slide the needle through in the next step.

3 Still holding the thread taut with one hand, insert the needle into the fabric close to the point where it originally emerged. Pull the needle and thread through to the back.

Working blanket stitch as fabric edging

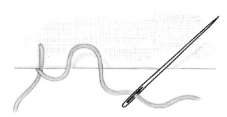

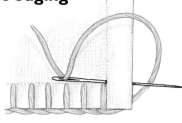

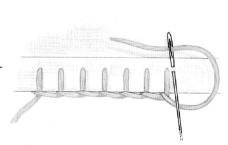

1 To start, insert the needle at the top edge of the stitching line, leaving a tail of thread at the front. Take the working thread over the loose thread, ready to work the next stitch.

2 Work as for surface blanket stitch, placing the loops on the fabric edge. To turn a corner, insert the needle where it last emerged and bring it out on the adjacent edge, taking the thread underneath the corner.

3 To fasten off, take the thread to the back. Make two or three tiny stitches on top of each other, next to the last upright, taking the needle through the background fabric only. Fasten off the thread starting in the same way.

Working blanket stitch for surface embroidery

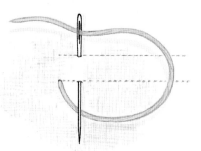

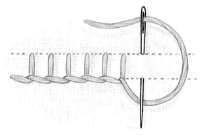

1 Leaving a tail of thread on the wrong side, bring the needle to the front on the lower line and insert it at the top, a little way to the right. Bring it out directly below, keeping the thread under the tip of the needle .

2 Pull the thread through the fabric, over the top of the working thread. Gently pull the thread to form a firm loop at the lower line. Continue working in this way along the line. To fasten off, weave the starting and ending threads under the stitches on the wrong side.

Working curly cross stitch

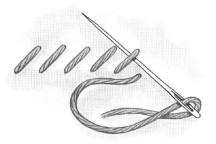

1 Work from left to right to make a row of diagonal stitches slanting from bottom left to top right. Turn and bring the needle through at the bottom right-hand corner of the row as if to complete a cross, but slip the needle under the diagonal stitch.

Working a basic satin-stitched line

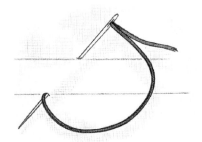

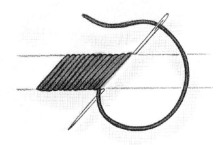

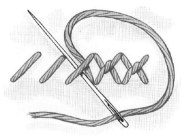

1 Bring the needle out at the front of the fabric at the lower marked line. Take the thread upward and insert the needle on the top row, at the desired angle to the marked line; bring it out again next to where you started.

2 Work parallel, closely spaced stitches along the row, keeping them at exactly the same angle and placing the needle precisely on the marked lines to create even edges.

2 Pull the thread through, then slip the needle under the diagonal stitch again. Pull the thread through gently to tighten, and then insert the needle at the top left-hand corner to complete the cross and bring it through ready to make the next stitch. Repeat along the row.

Running stitch is the simplest of all stitches. It is used for many purposes, including basting, joining seams (where little strength is required), quilting, and adding simple decorative lines to embroidered designs. It produces a broken line on the fabric. Double running stitch is simply two lines of running stitch, worked one on top of the other to produce a solid line, similar in appearance to backstitch (see page 14).

Straight stitches are often used as repeat patterns or accents in counted cross stitch embroidery. They may be placed side by side to make a spaced border design, or worked in a radiating formation to suggest a flower, or worked so that they radiate from a single point, suggesting a star. Avoid carrying the thread from one such motif to another, which might show through the fabric or cause it to pucker.

Stem stitch, although rarely used in cross stitch embroidery, can be useful for adding script-style lettering to a design. In the illustrations on page 20, the stitches are of uniform size; however, when working on evenweave fabric you will need to follow the fabric grid (see the chart on pages 114–115), which may result in slight variations in stitch length. An alternative is to use a sharp-pointed needle, which will pierce the fabric threads.

Hemstitching is another useful stitch for your repertoire. It is basic to the technique known as drawn threadwork and, as the name suggests, is often used as a decorative way of securing a hem.

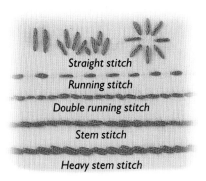

Straight stitch

Running stitch

Double running stitch

Stem stitch

Heavy stem stitch

Begin by removing the chosen number of threads along the position for the hemstitching, using a tapestry needle to pull them out gently. Or, if using the stitch for hemming, turn up a double hem and baste it in place; then draw out the threads just above the hem fold. Work from the right side if the stitch is purely decorative, from the wrong side if stitching a hem (see page 20).

Working running stitch

Working from right to left, bring the needle out to the front at your starting point. Pass the needle in and out of the fabric along the stitching line. Work several stitches at a time, keeping the length and tension even. This is easy on an evenweave fabric.

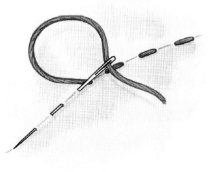

Working straight stitch

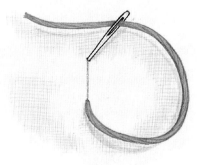

To work an individual straight stitch, bring the needle out to the front. Push it through to the wrong side to make a single stitch of the required length.

Double running stitch

Work a row of evenly spaced running stitches along the stitching line. Turn the work around. Work another set of running stitches, filling in the spaces left by the first and using the same holes.

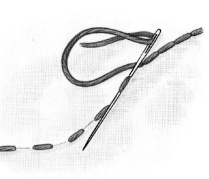

To create a simple straight-stitch flower, make as many straight stitches as desired, working outward from a central circle or point.

Stem stitch

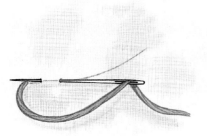 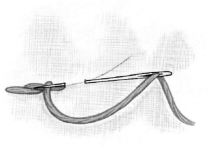 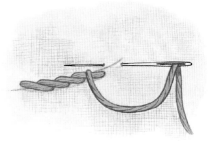

1 Work from left to right, keeping the working thread under the needle. Bring the needle out to the front and insert it a little way from your starting point. Bring it out again, half a stitch length back.

2 Insert the needle half a stitch length from the end of the previous stitch. Bring it out at the end of the previous stitch, through the same hole in the fabric. Continue in this way.

For a heavy stem stitch line, angle the needle slightly as you insert it, and work smaller stitches.

Working single hemstitch

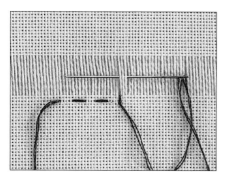 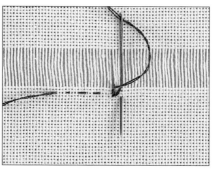 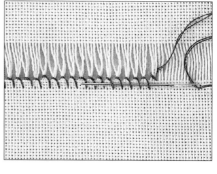

1 Secure the thread temporarily with a few running stitches close to the starting point, leaving a short tail. Anchor it with a small vertical stitch, then pass the needle under two, three, or more of the vertical strands and pull it through.

2 Make a small vertical stitch under two or three horizontal threads to the right of the cluster. Continue working in this way across the border, keeping the stitches even.

3 At the end of the border, secure the thread under several stitches on the wrong side of the fabric, and cut off the end. Pull out the running stitches at the other end of the border and secure the thread in the same way.

Securing thread ends

When working linear stitches, such as running, double running, and backstitch (see page 14), start and fasten off the thread as shown here, which produces a neat effect on the wrong side and, unlike a knot, is unlikely to pull free.

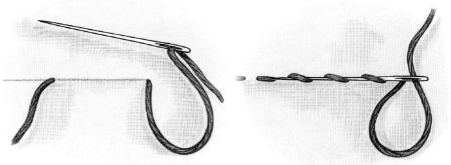

1 To begin, take the needle to the back of the fabric, a little way from your starting point, leaving a short tail of thread at the front. Bring the needle up at your starting point. As you work along the line, stitch over the thread to secure it. Pull the loose thread end to the back, and snip it off.

2 To secure the thread end when you have finished, take the needle to the back of the fabric. Weave the thread into the back of several stitches, and trim it off close to the fabric.

Plastic Canvas

7-mesh red plastic canvas

14-mesh semi-transparent canvas

Pearl cottons

Ribbon

Preformed circle

Persian yarn

Preformed lozenge

Plastic canvas is a relatively new material for cross stitch and needlepoint, and it opens up all sorts of possibilities. It consists of a plastic sheet, punched with a regular grid of holes, which you stitch in exactly the same way as any ordinary canvas. Plastic canvas is easy to handle—the mesh does not distort, so there is no need to use a frame, and the edges do not fray. It is quite rigid, so it is ideal for making mats or hanging items such as earrings. It can be cut and shaped to make useful three-dimensional objects such as trinket boxes. It can also be used as a backing to stiffen other embroidered fabrics.

Types of plastic canvas

The most widely available plastic canvas is 7-mesh. It comes in sheets of semitransparent plastic or opaque, colored plastic. You can also buy semitransparent, preformed shapes, to make into objects such as coasters, handbags and Christmas decorations. The finer 10- or 14-mesh plastic canvas is sold in small semi-transparent sheets.

Using plastic canvas

Threads Use any thread that you would use on ordinary canvas, or try a more unusual thread, such as narrow ribbon.

Stitches Either half cross or cross stitch can be used on plastic canvas (as, of course, can tent stitch, the most widely used needlepoint stitch).

Joining and finishing With pieces to be edged or joined (instead of framed) stitch them leaving one row of unworked holes all around the edge. Use either overcast or braided cross stitch to finish the edge, or to join two pieces (see page 22). Overcast stitch is the easier of the two stitches, although braided cross stitch gives an attractive, plaited finish.

Cutting and stitching plastic canvas

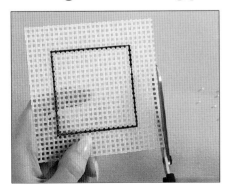

1 Mark out the shapes with a permanent marker—the ink from ordinary pens will rub off. Cut out, leaving a margin of at least five holes all around. Trim off the bumps of plastic extending along the edges.

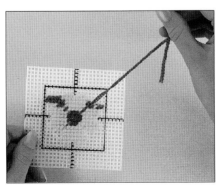

2 Using a ruler and permanent marker, measure and mark the center of each edge. Join each pair of opposite marks to find the center. Stitch the design, working outward from the center of the canvas.

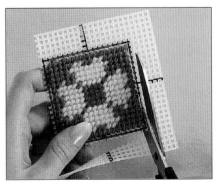

3 When the design is complete, trim the plastic canvas to size. For pieces that will be edged or joined, leave one row of unworked holes all around the stitching. For pieces that will be framed, leave at least five holes.

Edging plastic canvas with overcast stitch

1 Work overcast edging stitch from left to right. Bring the needle out to the front at your starting point. Bring the needle out to the front again one hole to the right, pulling the thread through so that it lies over the edge of the canvas. Continue in this way.

2 When you reach an inside corner, work one stitch into the corner hole. For an outside corner, work two or three stitches into the corner hole, so that the thread covers the corner. Take care not to force too many stitches through the corner hole, or you may tear the plastic mesh.

Edging plastic canvas with braided cross stitch

1 Work braided cross stitch from left to right. Bring the needle to the front through the first hole. Take the thread over the edge of the plastic canvas, and bring the needle through to the front through the third hole. Then bring the needle to the front through the first hole again.

2 To start the second stitch, bring the needle to the front through the fourth hole. Take the thread to the back, then bring it out to the front again through the second hole. Continue like this, using the fifth and third holes for the next stitch, then the sixth and fourth holes, and so on.

Joining plastic canvas

Making a hinge for a box lid

Place the two pieces together with wrong sides facing and edges and holes aligned. Secure the thread on the wrong side of one piece, close to your starting point. Working from the right side, overcast-stitch the two edges together as shown, taking the needle through both pieces in one movement. Alternatively, use braided cross stitch.

Edge both pieces with overcast stitch or braided cross stitch (see above). Secure a length of matching thread on the wrong side of one piece, close to where the hinge is required. Holding the pieces edge to edge, take a stitch between them. Work six more closely spaced stitches, then fasten off the thread end securely.

Waste Canvas

Using waste canvas makes it possible to stitch your favorite cross-stitch motifs on anything from T-shirts and towels to curtains and bedspreads, no matter what fabric they are made of.

Waste canvas is an evenweave, mesh-like fabric, woven from threads stiffened with starch. It is very easy to use; you simply baste it over the area you want to embroider and then work the design through the canvas onto the fabric, using the mesh as a stitching guide.

Contrasting threads are woven into the canvas at regular intervals to make it easy to place the design. The mesh is formed from pairs of threads—when you stitch, treat each pair as a single thread, and insert the needle through the

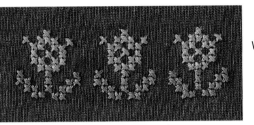

large holes where the pairs of threads intersect. When you have finished stitching the design, you dampen the waste canvas with just a little water to soften the starch, and then pull out the threads one by one, to leave a perfectly stitched design on your main fabric.

Waste canvas is sold by the yard or in pre-cut pieces. It comes in a range of mesh sizes, from 8 pairs of threads per 1 in. (2.5 cm) to 16 pairs of threads per 1 in. (2.5 cm). If you cannot find waste canvas in the mesh size you need, you can use an ordinary mono (single-thread) canvas instead. Do not try to use interlock or double canvas, as the threads will be difficult to remove.

For stitching, use a crewel or a chenille needle, both of which have sharp points that will easily penetrate the main fabric. Take care not to split the canvas threads.

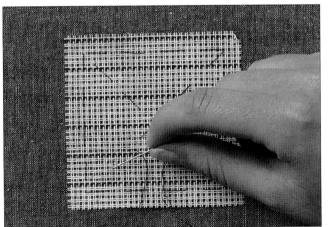

Sponge
Waste canvas
Crewel needle
Tweezers
Masking tape

Using waste canvas

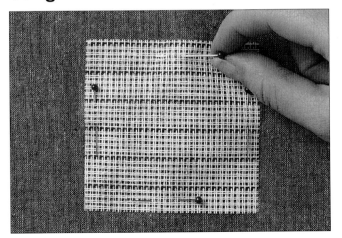

1 Cut a piece of waste canvas at least 1 in. (2.5 cm) larger all around than the finished design. Pin the waste canvas in position on the right side of the fabric, making sure that the fabric grain lines up with the canvas mesh.

2 Using a contrasting thread, baste around the edge of the canvas and from corner to corner. For a large piece, add more basting to hold the canvas flat. On stretchy fabrics, secure the canvas with masking tape.

3 Work the design, stitching through both the canvas and the fabric. Hold the needle at a right angle to the surface, and take it through the exact center of each hole.

4 Make sure that the thread ends are carefully secured on the wrong side of the work; otherwise they may pull loose when you remove the canvas threads.

5 When the design is complete, remove the basting threads. Then use small, sharp scissors to trim the waste canvas close to the design, leaving two or three double threads of canvas all around the embroidery.

6 Using a damp sponge or a cotton ball, moisten the work very slightly to dissolve the starch holding the canvas threads together. Use only a little water, as the starch may glue the canvas to the embroidery threads.

Messy motifs
Motifs stitched with waste canvas can look messy if the stitches are placed inaccurately. When two stitches share the same hole, make sure the needle enters the fabric below in exactly the same place each time. Use a stabbing motion, taking the needle down through the canvas and fabric, then up again.

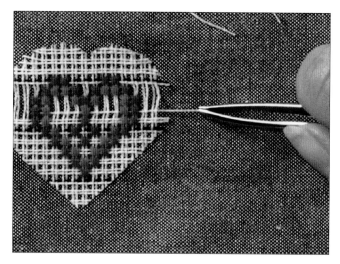

7 Using tweezers, pull out the canvas threads one by one. Remove all the threads lying in one direction first, then turn the work and pull out the threads lying the other way. Pull the threads straight out—do not pull at an angle—and hold the opposite edge firmly at all times.

Ribbon Weaving

This simple technique involves no sewing or special equipment. You can create beautiful and versatile fabrics from a wide variety of ribbons, as well as from bands of aida and other evenweave material. These can be embroidered with cross-stitch motifs and then woven to make intriguing designs (see page 216). Stitching can also be added after the ribbons are woven together, which, in the case of satin ribbons, will help to anchor the weave.

The steps here explain how to make a simple plainweave ribbon fabric. Once you have mastered the basic technique, you can experiment with a variety of designs, colors, and thicknesses of ribbon.

Use a piece of cork or insulation board as a base for the weaving—make sure that you can push the pins into it easily. The ribbons are woven together and pinned to the board over a layer of lightweight, fusible interfacing. When the weaving is complete, you can iron straight over the finished weave to bond it to the interfacing. The interfacing helps to hold the woven ribbons in place, providing a firmer, more stable fabric for assembling into your chosen article than would otherwise be the case.

When you pin the ribbons onto the board, angle the pins away from the work to make the ironing easier when the weaving is complete.

Cross stitches added after satin ribbons have been woven together will help to stablize the weave.

You Will Need

* Cork or insulation board
* Ribbon
* Lightweight fusible interfacing
* Ruler
* Pencil
* Pins
* Scissors
* Small safety pin

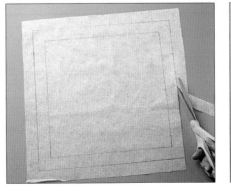

1 On the interfacing use the ruler and the pencil to draw a square or rectangle the size of the finished piece, then add on 1 in. (2.5 cm) all around. Cut out along the outer drawn line.

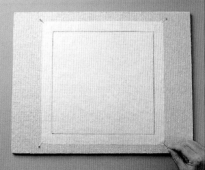

2 Center the interfacing, adhesive (shiny) side up, on the cork or insulation board. Pin it in place at the corners, angling the pins away from the interfacing.

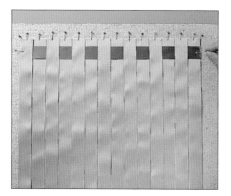

3 Cut the required number of vertical (warp) ribbons the finished depth of the piece plus 2 in. (5 cm). Pin them over the interfacing, side by side, starting at the left-hand edge.

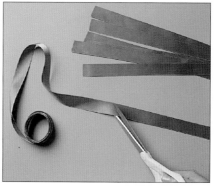

4 Cut the required number of horizontal (weft) ribbons the finished width of the piece plus 2 in. (5 cm).

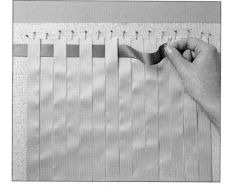

5 Insert the safety pin at one end of the first horizontal ribbon. Weave the ribbon under the first vertical ribbon and over the next. Continue weaving it under, then over, the remaining vertical ribbons.

6 Remove the safety pin and push the woven ribbon carefully up to the top. Make sure that it is straight and taut, then pin it at each end.

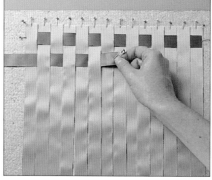

7 Insert the safety pin at one end of the next horizontal ribbon. Weave it through the vertical ribbons, but this time take it over, then under, then over, then under, and so on.

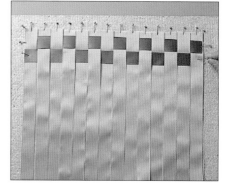

8 Push the second ribbon up as close as possible to the first ribbon; check that it is straight and pin it in place at each end. Continue in this way to complete the ribbon weaving.

Choose ribbons in contrasting colors to highlight the design of the weave.

9 Lightly press the ribbons with a dry iron to bond them to the interfacing. Take out the pins and turn the work over carefully. Press it again using a steam setting.

Chapter 2
Nature's Delights

TULIPS AND DAFFODILS

RICH ORANGE TULIPS AND
BRIGHT GOLDEN DAFFODILS
ADD A DASH OF
SPRING COLOR TO
A DINING ROOM.

TABLECLOTH AND CHAIR PANELS

Panels of tulips and daffodils on fabric covers give a bright new look to an old table and chair.

Varying the size of motifs adds interest to cross-stitch designs. On the chair cover, the large tulip is worked over four linen threads using four strands of floss; the tablecloth tulips are worked over two threads, using two strands.

If your table stands against a wall, make just one panel for the front edge; for a freestanding table, make panels for two or all four sides. The tablecloth panel is 7¾ in. (19.5 cm) deep, and the chair panel is 16 x 10¼ in. (41 x 26 cm). To make the chair cover, follow the instructions given on pages 309–310.

The fabric quantities given are enough to make one chair panel and a tablecloth panel with seven flowers.

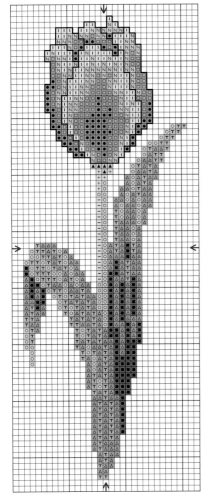

STITCHING THE TABLECLOTH PANEL

1 Mark the center of the fabric with basting and overcast the edges. Working out from the vertical center, mark the vertical centers of the other motifs, at 3½–4-in. (9–10-cm) intervals. Make the outer vertical lines at least 3 in. (7.5 cm) from the short fabric edges. Mount the center of the fabric in the hoop; move the fabric along in the hoop as required.

2 Work a daffodil in the center of the fabric, referring to the chart (below) and the color key. One square on the chart represents one stitch worked over two fabric threads. Use two strands of floss for the cross stitch and one strand for the backstitch.

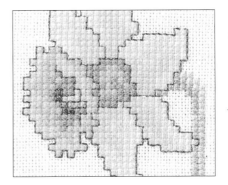

On the daffodil, cleverly shaded colors bring the trumpet to the foreground, creating a naturalistic effect.

3 In the same way, work a tulip on either side of the daffodil, then add more daffodils and tulips, alternating the flowers across the panel. Stitch as many panels as required.

4 Take the finished work out of the hoop and press it lightly on the wrong side. Trim the top and lower edges 1½ in. (4 cm) above and below the stitching.

5 Press ⅝ in. (1.5 cm) to the wrong side all around the panel. Pin it in place on the tablecloth; stitch all around. Press lightly on the wrong side.

STITCHING THE CHAIR COVER PANEL

1 Mark the center of the fabric with basting, overcast the edges, and mount it in the hoop. Work the tulip or daffodil from the center out using four strands of floss for cross stitch and two for backstitch. Work each stitch over four fabric threads.

2 With the flower centered, trim the fabric to measure 17¼ x 11½ in. (44 x 29 cm). Press under ⅝ in. (1.5 cm) all around, and topstitch to the back of the chair cover in the desired position. Press lightly from the wrong side.

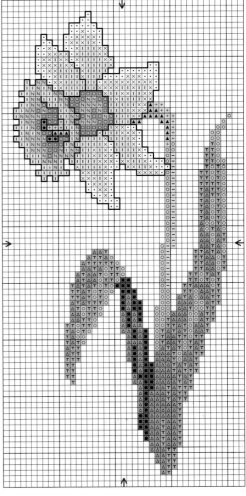

FLOWER FRAME

The diamond-patterned frame is stitched on plastic canvas and mounted on foam board. It is decorated with freestanding flowers, also stitched on plastic canvas. The finished frame is 7½ x 5½ in. (19.5 x 14 cm). For detailed instructions on using plastic canvas, see pages 21–22.

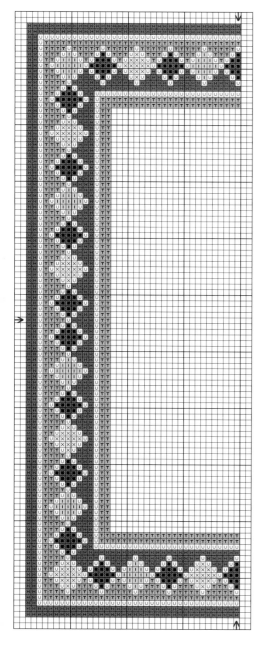

1 From plastic canvas: cut an 8¼ x 6¼-in. (21 x 16-cm) piece for the frame, and cut an 8 x 4-in. (20 x 10-cm) piece for each motif. Mark the center of each piece.

2 Stitch the frame following the chart (left), starting at the center of one inner edge. Use three strands of floss, and work over one mesh. Work the other half of the chart to match the first.

3 Work the flowers as for the frame, following the charts and key on pages 30–31; use one strand for backstitch. Trim the stitched pieces, leaving one row of unworked holes all around the stitching.

4 From foam board: cut a frame slightly smaller than the plastic canvas frame, and a backing rectangle to match. Cut a stand traced from the template on page 160.

5 Use double-stick tape to stick the stitched frame to the foam-board frame. Butt together the short top edges of the frame and backing; stick with masking tape to make a hinged joint.

6 Cut the stand along the dashed line through one layer of paper and the foam; trim away from the flap to leave one layer of paper. Fold back the flap and use double-stick tape to stick it to the center of the frame back, with the sloping edge at the bottom edge.

7 To attach the motifs with blocks of foam board, follow the instructions on page 160.

YOU WILL NEED

* 14-count plastic canvas, at least 8½ x 14½ in. (21 x 37 cm)
* DMC stranded floss as listed in the color key on page 30
* Tapestry needle, size 24
* Foam board, same size as plastic canvas
* Permanent marker
* Tracing paper and pencil
* Double-stick tape
* Masking tape
* Sharp scissors, utility knife, and metal ruler

COUNTRY PIGS

A FRIENDLY BROWSING PORKER JOINS
FAVORITE COUNTRYSIDE MOTIFS IN THIS
CHARMING SAMPLER PICTURE AND
MATCHING ACCESSORIES.

KITCHEN PIGS

Pig and piglets, stars and hearts, and apples and pears can be combined in a country sampler or used separately to decorate towels and napkins.

PIG NAPKIN

Baste the waste canvas diagonally across one corner of the napkin. Cross-stitch a single small pig motif using two strands of floss for the cross stitch and working over one pair of threads. Backstitch using one strand of floss. Remove the waste canvas with tweezers, and press from the wrong side.

PIG KITCHEN TOWEL

1 Fold the band in half widthwise and mark the center with basting. Working out from the center, use two strands of floss to stitch the lower border on the chart. Work over two fabric threads, and repeat the pigs and flowery border to make up the required length. Backstitch using one strand of floss.

Snuffling farmyard pigs make cheerful motifs for kitchen accessories. Work the curly tail in cross stitch, and define the curls in backstitch.

2 Trim the border to fit the towel, allowing ⅜ in. (1 cm) extra at each end. Slip-stitch the border in place, turning under the raw ends.

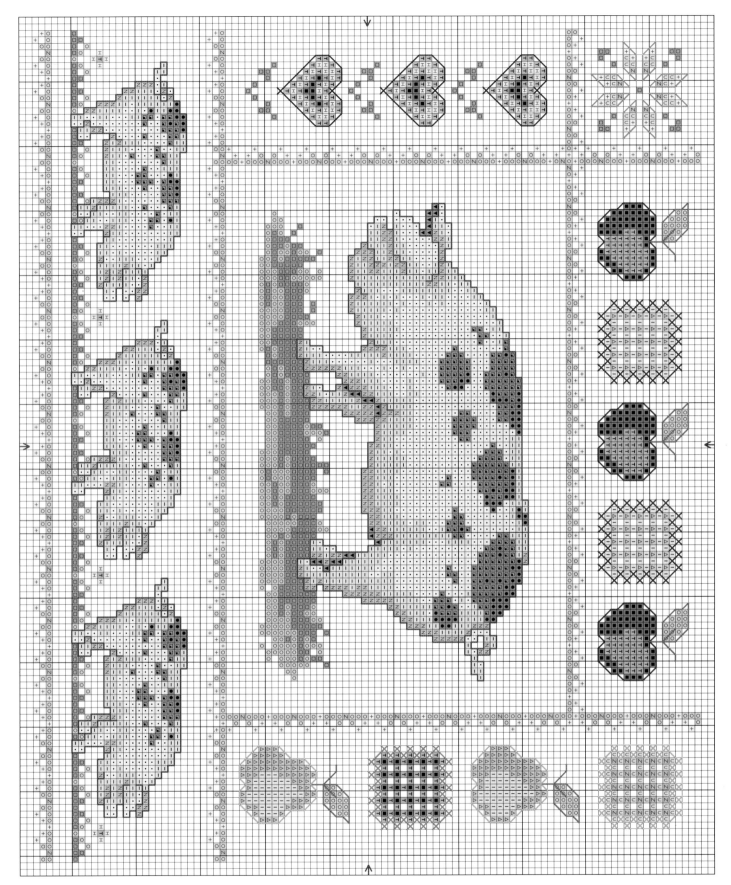

PIG SAMPLER

This sampler chart shows the complete country pigs design. The finished stitched area measures 9¼ x 7½ in. (23.5 x 19 cm).

1 Mark the center of the aida with basting, and mount it in the hoop. Cross-stitch the design using two strands of floss and working each stitch over one thread block. Use one strand for backstitch.

2 Take the finished work out of the hoop and press it carefully on the wrong side. Take the piece to a professional framer or frame it yourself (see pages 297–298).

35

FRUITY EXTRAS

The small motifs from the country pigs design can be used to decorate a whole range of kitchen accessories, such as the shelf edging and the matching jam-jar band shown here. Follow the sampler chart on page 35, and refer to the color key on page 34 to select the threads you need.

YOU WILL NEED

For both items:
- ❋ DMC stranded floss as in the color key on page 34
- ❋ Tapestry needle, size 26
- ❋ Thread for basting
- ❋ Double-stick tape

For the shelf edging:
- ❋ 2-in. (5-cm) wide 14-count cream aida band, to fit across the shelf plus 2 in. (5 cm)

For the jam-jar band:
- ❋ 2-in. (5-cm) wide 14-count cream aida band, to fit around the jar plus 2 in. (5 cm)
- ❋ Sewing needle and thread

SHELF EDGING

1 Fold the band in half widthwise, and mark the foldline with basting. Referring to the chart and the color key, cross-stitch the top border from the center out using two strands of floss. Make each stitch over one thread block. Use one strand for the backstitch. Repeat the design as required to fit across the band, and stop stitching at least 1 in. (2.5cm) from each end.

2 Press the finished work from the wrong side with a warm iron, taking care not to crush the stitching. Use the double-stick tape to secure the band to the front edge of the shelf.

JAM-JAR BAND

1 Fold the band in half widthwise and baste along the foldline. Cross-stitch the design from the center out, referring to the chart and color key. Make each stitch over one thread block. Use two strands for cross stitch and one for backstitch.

2 Press the finished work. Pin the stitched band around jam jar, wrong side out. Slip the band off the jar and stitch the ends together. Trim the seam, turn right side out, and slip the band onto the jar again.

BRIGHT IDEAS

PEAR TAG

Give a jar of jam or preserves a special label with this pretty pear tag. Stitch a pear motif in the center of a 2¾ x 2¼ in. (7 x 5.5 cm) piece of 14-count aida. Use two strands of floss for cross stitch and one for backstitch. Fuse a piece of interfacing ¼ in. (5 mm) smaller than the aida to the wrong side. Attach a grommet, and fringe the edges of the aida up to the interfacing. Tie the tag in place with twisted cord.

GREEN LEAVES

FRESH SPRING LEAVES WITH
GRAPHIC SILHOUETTES AND INTRICATE
SURFACE DETAIL ARE SOFTLY SHADED IN
MYRIAD GREEN HUES.

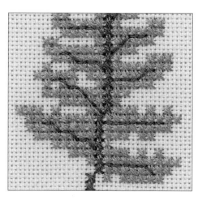

The delicate fern frond is stitched in leaf green with dark avocado veins.

LEAF TABLECLOTH

A square border of informally arranged leaves brings a breath of woodland freshness to summer table linen.

The border is stitched in the center of the tablecloth so that it appears in full view on the tabletop, where the details can be fully appreciated. The leaves are stitched in a delicate range of greens with hints of gold-lime and terracotta. The stitching is worked using two strands of floss, and the tracery of veins is worked in both cross stitch and backstitch. The stitched border is 16½ in. (42 cm) square, and the cloth measures approximately 46 in. (117 cm).

1 Mark the center of the fabric with basting, and overcast the fabric edges to prevent fraying. Mount the fabric in the hoop or the frame.

2 Work the first half of the design from the center out, referring to the color key (left) and the chart (below). Use two strands of floss for cross stitch and backstitch, and work each stitch over two fabric threads.

3 Complete one leaf before moving on to the next; count the threads between carefully, remembering that each square represents two threads. Rotate the chart 180 degrees to work the second half of the border.

4 Take the completed work off the hoop or frame, and press it lightly on the wrong side. Press under a double ⅜-in. (1-cm) hem all around, mitering the corners. For instructions in these finishing techniques, see pages 277–278.

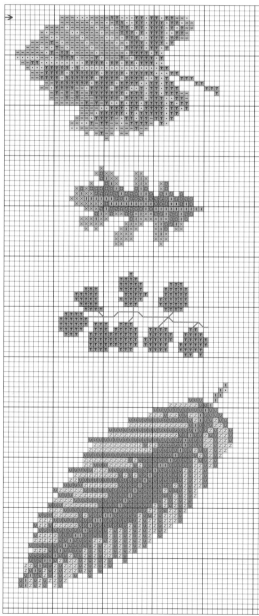

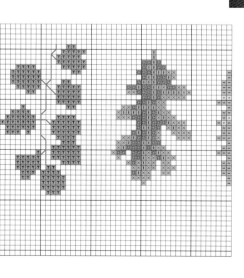

The larger leaves are positioned diagonally at the corners to complete the square border.

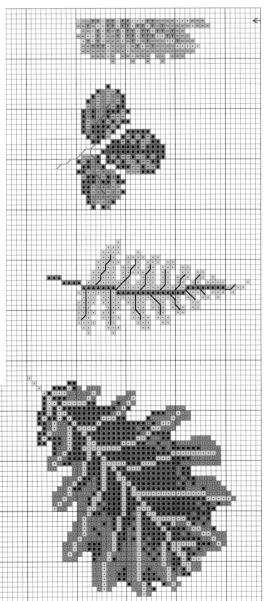

LEAF LINE-UP

In this graphic panel, fresh green leaves form an elegant line on white linen, imitating the look of a collection of pressed leaves.

The stitched area measures 14¼ x 4¼ in. (36 x 11 cm), and the area of fabric in the frame is 19¼ x 8 in. (49 x 20 cm).

YOU WILL NEED

❋ 28-count antique white evenweave fabric, 26 x 14 in. (66 x 36 cm)

❋ DMC stranded floss as listed in the color key

❋ Tapestry needle, size 26

❋ Sewing needle and thread for basting

❋ Large embroidery hoop or rectangular frame (see page 12)

COLOR KEY

COLORS	SKEINS
⊞ 356 Medium terracotta	1
▲ 469 Dark avocado	1
U 470 Medium avocado	1
Z 472 Spring green	1
I 734 Gold-lime	1
✕ 3053 Pale gray-green	1
● 3345 Hunter green	1
T 3346 Medium hunter green	1
– 3347 Pale hunter green	1
• 3348 Leaf green	1
■ 3362 Dark antique green	1
▣ 3363 Antique green	1

Backstitch

◥ 469 Dark avocado

◥ 3345 Hunter green

◥ 3346 Medium hunter green

1 Mark the center of the fabric with basting and overcast around the fabric edges to prevent fraying. Mount the fabric in the frame or embroidery hoop.

2 Work the design from the center out, referring to the color key (left) and the chart (below). Use two strands of floss for cross stitch and backstitch, and work each stitch over two fabric threads.

3 Complete one leaf at a time. Count the threads very carefully before starting the next leaf, remembering that each square on the chart represents two threads of the fabric.

4 When the work is complete remove it from the frame and press lightly on the wrong side. Take the work to a professional framer, or frame it yourself, following the instructions on pages 297–298.

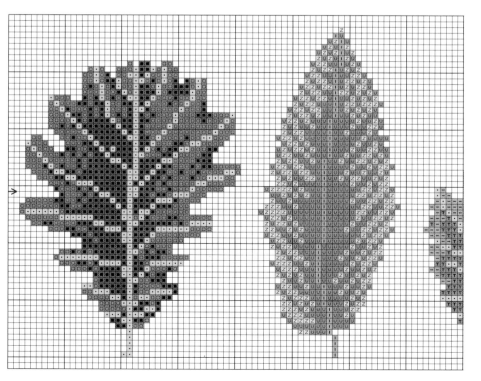

40

The rounded blackberry leaflets are stitched in medium hunter green.

The fine tracery of veins on the maple leaf is stitched in leaf green.

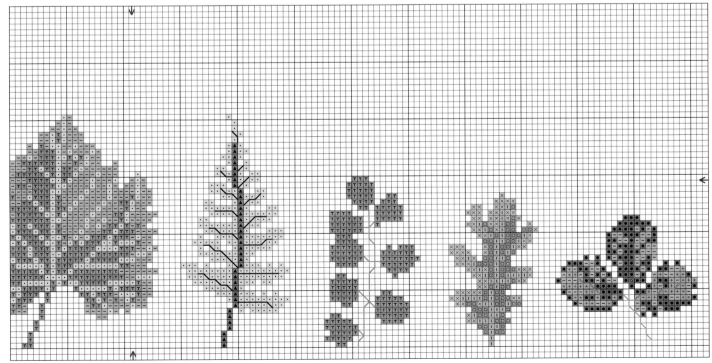

41

LEAF NAPKIN RINGS

The smallest leaf is a perfect size to work on a pair of linen napkin rings to complement the tablecloth and picture. Each ring is 2¼ in. (6 cm) wide.

YOU WILL NEED

* 28-count antique white evenweave fabric and white polyester-cotton fabric: 6 x 5½ in. (15 x 14 cm) of each
* Tapestry needle, size 26
* DMC stranded floss as listed in the color key
* Sewing needle and thread for basting and hand-stitching

COLOR KEY

COLORS		SKEINS
✛	356 Medium terracotta	1
●	3345 Hunter green	1
▬	3347 Pale hunter green	1
Backstitch		
◹	3345 Hunter green	1

1 Cut both pieces of fabric in half lengthwise to make two 6 x 2¾ in. (15 x 7 cm) pieces. On the chart on page 41, mark the vertical and horizontal center of the right-hand leaf. Mark the center of the evenweave fabrics with basting, and overcast the fabric edges to prevent fraying.

2 Work the design from the center out, with the long edges of the fabric at the sides. Refer to the color key (above) and the chart on page 41. Work a leaf on each piece of evenweave, using two strands of floss throughout. Work each stitch over two fabric threads.

3 When complete, press lightly on the wrong side. Stitch an evenweave and a plain fabric piece together with right sides facing, leaving an opening in one edge.

4 Turn ring right side out and press. Tuck in the raw edges along the opening, and hand-stitch closed. Slip-stitch the short edges together to make a circle. Make the other napkin ring in the same way.

BRIGHT IDEAS

PRESSED LEAF COASTER

Imitate the look of pressed leaves with a single specimen laid flat within a clear coaster. Choose any of the four smaller leaves from the chart on page 41, and stitch the design in the same way as the napkin rings.

PUPPY POWER

PLAYFUL PUPPIES SCAMPER
OVER A SPLENDID SET OF
ACCESSORIES FOR A
TOP DOG.

TOP DOG SET

Add to the pleasure of looking after your pet with a personalized mat, a trimmed jar for tasty treats, and a special bag for grooming kit.

The pampered pet's set features a cute Scottie, an inquisitive spaniel, and a cheeky Jack Russell. The jar trim shown is 4½ in. (11.5 cm) deep; if you wish to make it deeper simply adjust the fabric depth. For the length, measure around the jar and add on 1¼ in. (3 cm). The feeding mat measures 16 x 12 in. (41 x 30 cm) and the bag approximately 11 x 9½ in. (28 x 24 cm).

JAR TRIM

1 Overcast the raw edges of the evenweave fabric, and mark the center with basting. Mount the fabric in the embroidery hoop.

2 Working from the center out, stitch the Scottie dog from the chart (opposite top right); refer to the color key (left). Use two strands of floss for cross stitch and one for backstitch, and work each stitch over two fabric threads. When work is complete, remove from the hoop and press the stitching lightly.

3 Trim the long edges 1 in. (2.5 cm) outside the stitching. Press under the long edges ⅜ in. (1 cm) from the stitching. Secure the hems with running stitch, worked four threads in from the top and bottom edges: use two strands of dark brown, and work each stitch over four fabric threads.

4 Fold ⅝ in. (1.5 cm) to the wrong side on one short edge, and stick in place with double-stick tape. Wrap the band around the jar, lapping the finished edge over the raw edge, and stick in place with double-stick tape.

The Scottie is worked in three shades of gray with dark brown outlines.

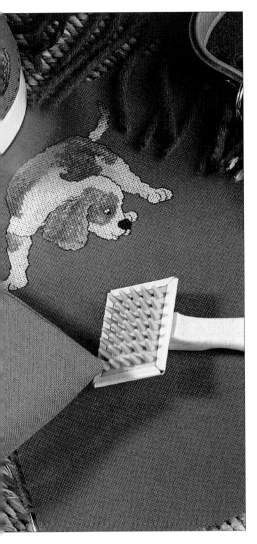

FEEDING MAT

Overcast the edges of the evenweave. With the short edges at the sides, use basting to mark the center of the design 4 in. (10 cm) in and down from the top left-hand corner. Stitch the dog from the chart on page 46 as for the Jar Trim, step **2** (opposite). Fuse the interfacing to the wrong side of the fabric. Trim away the holes from the plastic pocket. Trim the fabric to fit in the plastic pocket and slip it in the pocket.

GROOMING BAG

Lay one piece of evenweave flat with the long edges at the sides. Mark the vertical center with basting, then mark the horizontal center 4½ in. (11.5 cm) above the bottom. Referring to the Jar Trim step **2** (opposite), stitch the Jack Russell from the chart (below right). Make the stitched piece into a drawstring bag with eyelets, referring to the instructions on pages 283–284. Use the other evenweave piece for the back.

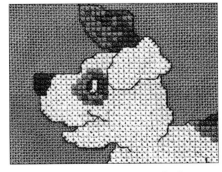

The cheeky Jack Russell has a dark eye patch worked in gray and dark gray.

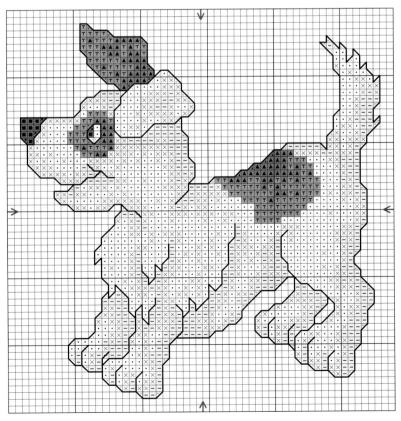

PUPPY BLANKET

The inquisitive spaniel is worked over waste canvas on a warm blanket to make a basket cozy for a new puppy. The motif is 6 in. (15 cm) from paw to paw and nose to tail.

YOU WILL NEED

❋ Blanket

❋ 10-count waste canvas, 7 in. (18 cm) square

❋ DMC stranded floss as listed in the color key on page 44

❋ Crewel needle, size 6

❋ Thread for basting

❋ Tweezers

---

1 Mark the center of the waste canvas with basting. Baste it to the blanket so that its center is about 12 in. (30 cm) from one corner.

2 Referring to the chart (right) and the color key on page 44, work the design from the center out. Work each stitch over a pair of canvas threads. Use four strands of floss for cross stitch and two for backstitch.

3 When work is complete, dampen the waste canvas and remove the canvas threads with tweezers. Place the work face down on a soft towel, and press it gently from the wrong side, taking care not to crush the blanket fabric.

The spaniel is stitched in white, beige, and ecru, with large patches worked in tan and golden brown.

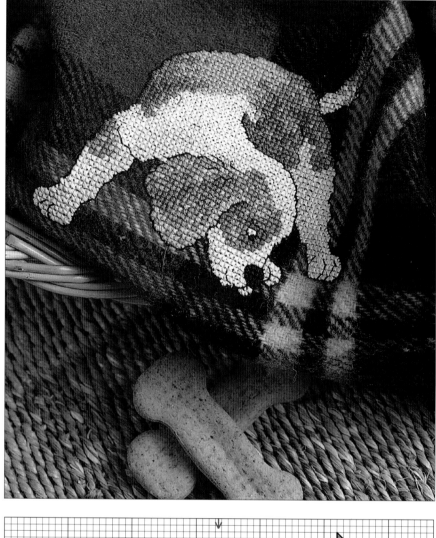

DANCING DRAGONFLIES

GLISTENING BLUE AND GREEN DRAGONFLIES
FLUTTER AROUND MINIATURE FLOWERS, CREATING
BEDROOM LINENS OF SHIMMERING BEAUTY.

DRAGONFLY BED LINEN

Scatter dragonflies and flowers on a fine white pillowcase
and sheet to create a beautiful set of coordinating bed linen.

It is easy to create beautiful designs with these dragonfly and flower motifs. Here, the dragonflies are shown scattered around the edges of a crisp white pillowcase and along the top edge of a sheet. They would look just as good on a duvet cover, plain throw, or towel.

Bed linen is usually made from fine non-evenweave fabric, so you need to stitch the designs over waste canvas. Use a new, sharp crewel needle to pierce the weave of the linen.

When you are stitching the pillowcase or duvet cover, mount the layer of the fabric that you wish to work in an embroidery hoop, so you are less likely to stitch through both layers by mistake.

If you are embroidering on brand-new bed linen, wash it first to remove the manufacturer's sizing, making it softer and easier to handle.

YOU WILL NEED

* White cotton sheet and pillowcase
* 14-count waste canvas, 16 x 15 in. (40 x 38 cm)
* DMC stranded floss as listed in the color key
* Crewel needle, size 9
* Embroidery hoop (see page 12)
* Sewing thread and needle
* Tweezers

COLOR KEY

COLORS	SKEINS
913 Jade green	1
955 Pale green	1
800 Pale blue	1
809 Blue	1
Backstitch	
913 Jade green	
809 Blue	

STITCHING THE MOTIFS

1 Cut the waste canvas into twelve pieces, each measuring 5 x 4 in. (13 x 10 cm). Mark the center of each piece with basting. Pin the squares in the desired positions on the right side of the sheet and pillowcase. Baste them in place. Mount the bed linen in the embroidery hoop. ▼

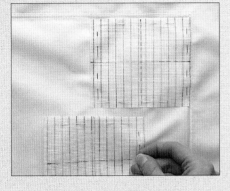

2 Stitch the dragonflies from the center out, following the chart (right) and color key on page 48. Use two strands of floss for the cross stitch and one strand for the backstitch, and work each stitch over one pair of canvas threads. Add a sprinkling of flowers around each motif.

3 When you have completed the embroidery, pull out the basting, and, using the tweezers, remove the waste canvas carefully, thread by thread. Press the work from the wrong side with a warm iron.

With their transparent wings and gleaming bodies, these naturalistic dragonflies appear to hover over a pool of water.

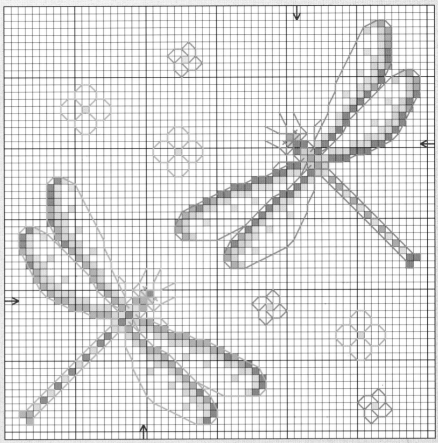

BRIGHT IDEAS

GLOWING IN THE DARK

The dragonflies look almost luminous when they are stitched on a darker background—on this silky royal blue scarf, a single dragonfly shimmers as though it is sitting in a patch of moonlight. To copy this idea, use 14-count waste canvas and a size 9 crewel needle. Cross-stitch the motif using two strands of floss over one pair of canvas threads. Work the backstitch in one strand of floss over one pair of canvas threads.

BONBON BOLSTER

YOU WILL NEED

❋ Bolster pillow form,
   18 in. (46 cm) long by
   6½ in. (17 cm) in diameter

❋ White voile, 42 x 28 in.
   (105 x 71 cm)

❋ DMC stranded floss as
   listed in the color key on
   page 48

❋ Tapestry needle, size 20

❋ White sewing thread

❋ 2¾ yd. (2 m) coordinating
   ribbon

❋ Air-erasable fabric
   marker

❋ Magnifying glass (optional)

❋ Embroidery hoop
   (optional; see page 12)

Sheer fabrics make an ideal background for delicate cross-stitch motifs. Try scattering dragonflies across a floaty muslin curtain, or make this filmy voile cover for a bolster pillow. Once embroidered, the fabric is hemmed, then simply wrapped around the bolster pillow and tied in place with silky ribbon.

If you cannot find a suitable pillow form, make one by rolling up a strip of polyester batting and sewing the end in place. Cover this with white cotton, then make the outer cover. Voile is an evenweave fabric, so you can stitch directly on it. Choose a loosely woven fabric, and use a magnifying glass if necessary.

1 Wrap the voile around the bolster pillow and decide where to position the dragonflies. Mark the positions with the air-erasable fabric marker.

2 Stitch a dragonfly at each marked position, adding a couple of flowers close by. Use two strands of floss for the cross stitch and one strand of floss for backstitch. Work each stitch over four threads of the voile.

3 Turn under ¼ in. (5 mm), then ¾ in. (2 cm) all around the edges. Fold the hems into neat miters at the corners (see page 278), and clip away the excess fabric so that they lie flat. Hand or machine-stitch.

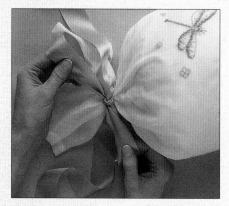

4 Cut the ribbon in two. Wrap the voile around the bolster pillow. Wrap a length of coordinating ribbon around each end and tie it in a big floppy bow. ▲

BLOSSOM TIME

SPRAYS OF APPLE BLOSSOM AND DAINTY
SINGLE FLORETS, IN SOFT SPRING
SHADES OF WHITE AND PINK, BURST
INTO BLOOM ON A TRIO OF
PASTEL CUSHIONS.

REPEAT FLOWERING

Delicate sprigs of blossom are repeated to make a central spray or a pastel border for fresh spring cushions.

On the lilac cushion, the white sprays alternate with the pink-flowered sprays, positioned with their corners toward the center. On the white cushion, the sprays of white flowers are positioned with their corners away from the center. The finished cushion covers are 14 in. (36 cm) square.

LILAC CUSHION

1 Overcast the edges of the lilac linen square and mark the center with basting. Mount it in the embroidery hoop.

2 Stitch the first half of the design from the center out, using two strands of floss for cross stitch and one for backstitch. Refer to the color key (above) and the chart (opposite). Work each stitch over two fabric threads.

3 When the first half of the design is complete, rotate the chart 180 degrees and stitch the second half of the design.

4 Take the work out of the hoop and press it lightly on the wrong side. Using the backing fabric for the cushion back, make the cover with a cord trim, following instructions on pages 307–308.

The pink flowers are stitched in three shades of pink, with dark dusty mauve backstitching.

WHITE CUSHION

Work the first quarter of the design as in step **2** (opposite), but stitch just the white motif, and treat the bottom right-hand corner of the chart as the center of the design. Rotate the chart 90 degrees to work the next quarter; repeat twice more. Complete the cushion as in step **4** (opposite).

SCATTERED FLOWERS

Complete the trio with this sky blue linen cushion cover decorated with attractive florets.

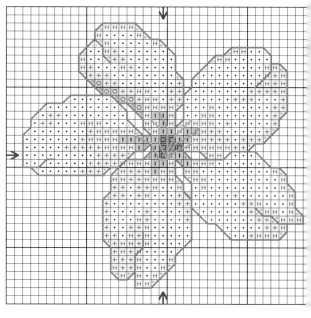

1 Overcast the edges of the linen square, and baste a 14-in. (36-cm) square in the center. Decide where to stitch the flowers within the square, and mark their centers with safety pins. Mount the fabric in the hoop.

2 Stitch the first flower, referring to the chart (right) and the key (above). Use two strands for cross stitch and one for backstitch. Work each stitch over two fabric threads.

3 Stitch the remaining flowers in the same way, turning the chart so that they face in different directions. Finish the cushion as in step 4 on page 52.

The white flower petals are tinged with pale baby pink around the edges and toward the center. Deep ice pink is worked at the center, with pale dusty mauve shadows.

CARROT PATCH

WITH THEIR DELICATE GREENERY AND CRISP ORANGE
SHAPE, IMAGES OF CARROTS ARE EXCELLENT FOR
BRIGHTENING UP KITCHEN LINENS, GIVING A
DISTINCTIVE GARDEN LOOK.

KITCHEN COORDINATES

With waste canvas in different mesh sizes, you can use carrots to create bold or dainty designs to suit any kitchen item.

STITCHING THE APRON

The complete carrot design makes a bold contrast on the pocket of a rich blue apron.

1 Cut a 6-in. (15-cm) square of 14-count waste canvas and mark the center with basting. Center the canvas on the pocket and baste in place around the edges, taking care to stitch through the front of the pocket only.

2 Using two strands of floss, and the size 8 crewel needle, stitch the design from the center out, referring to the chart (opposite) and color key (above). Work each stitch over one pair of canvas threads. Dampen the waste canvas and remove the threads.

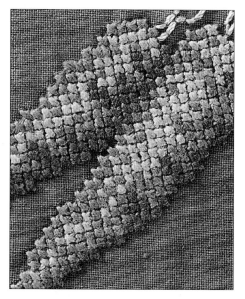

Buttermilk highlights and vivid shades of orange and yellow depict the plumpness of fresh carrots. ◄

STITCHING THE TABLECLOTH AND TABLE MAT

Mix and match carrot motifs to create your own unique designs. The large carrot at the center of the tablecloth is taken from the chart (right)—the foliage has been trimmed to make the carrot stand out. The mini carrots in each corner of the tablecloth, and on the table mat pictured on page 55, are taken from the small carrot chart on page 58.

1 For a single large carrot, cut a 6-in. (15-cm) square of 10-count waste canvas. For a mini carrot, cut a 4-in. (10-cm) square of 10-count waste canvas. Mark the center and baste in place.

2 Use the size 7 crewel needle and three strands of floss. For the large carrot, follow the chart (right), omitting the stitches above the blue line. Follow the chart on page 58 for the small carrot.

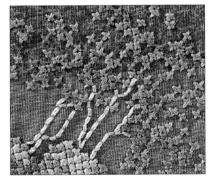

Widely spaced cross stitches in two shades of green suggest the ferny carrot tops. ▲

The higher the mesh count of the waste canvas, the smaller the carrots. For 5-in. (13-cm) long carrots, use 10-count. For 4-in. (10-cm) long carrots, use 14-count waste canvas. ▲

OVEN SET

This single carrot motif can be used to decorate a matching oven glove and pot holder. Stitch just one motif, or use a finer waste canvas for a border of smaller carrots.

1 For the single carrot, cut a 5 x 3-in. (12.5 x 7.5-cm) piece of 10-count waste canvas. For the border, cut a 6 x 3-in. (15 x 7.5-cm) piece of 10-count waste canvas. Mark the center with basting and baste the canvas in the desired position on the holder.

2 Refer to the chart (below) and the key on page 56. For the single motif, use three strands of floss and the size 7 crewel needle. For the border, use two strands of floss and the size 8 crewel needle. Work the central carrot first, then count 20 threads to the right or left to find the center of the next carrot.

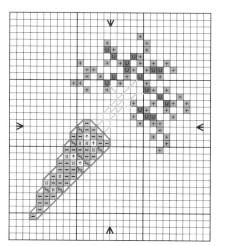

COLOR KEY	
COLORS	**SKEINS**
V B5200 Brilliant white	I
▣ 320 Gray green	I
⊠ 347 Dark red	I
⋂ 350 Red	I
S 471 Pale olive green	I
+ 989 Green	I
− 3341 Pink	I
↑ 3822 Pale gold	I
O 3823 Cream	I
Backstitch	
╱ 320 Gray green	
╱ 347 Dark red	
╱ 350 Red	
╱ 471 Pale olive green	
╱ 729 Gold	I
╱ 989 Green	
╱ 3822 Pale gold	

BRIGHT IDEAS

CLEVER COMBINATIONS

Combine motifs to create your own exciting designs—like this carrot and strawberry shelf strip. To copy this idea, you will need some aida band at least 30 thread blocks wide. Use the charts shown here (right), spacing the motifs evenly, and the color keys for the strawberry (left) and the carrot (page 56).

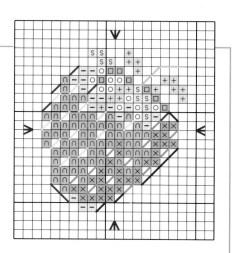

SUMMER FRUITS

A DESIGN OF CRISP APPLES AND JUICY BLACKBERRIES ENHANCES PURE WHITE LINEN, PERFECT FOR SUMMER LIVING.

FRUIT TABLE LINEN

The dark fruits of the blackberry bush contrast with green apples and leaves in two exquisite designs for a tablecloth and napkins.

YOU WILL NEED

For both items:

❋ DMC stranded floss as listed in the color key

❋ Tapestry needle, size 26

❋ Sewing needle and thread for basting and stitching

❋ Embroidery hoop (see page 12)

For the tablecloth:

❋ 1⅝ yd. (1.4 m) of 55-in. (140-cm) wide 25-count white evenweave linen

For each napkin:

❋ 25-count white evenweave linen, 16 in. (40 cm) square

COLOR KEY

COLORS	SKEINS
⊙ 320 Medium green	1
Ⅰ 336 Navy	1
⊟ 368 Soft green	1
▲ 471 Lime green	1
⊞ 472 Light lime green	1
▣ 550 Dark violet	1
⊡ 772 Pale green	1
Ⓝ 839 Brown	1
◼ 939 Dark navy	1
⊠ 988 Grass green	1

Backstitch

◪ 839 Brown	
◣ 890 Dark green	1

These beautiful apple and blackberry designs give a light summery look to pure white table linens. The tablecloth shown here measures about 54 in. (138 cm) square, but the circular design would look just as good on a smaller or larger cloth, or even a circular cloth; simply adapt the fabric quantities to suit your requirements. The matching napkins measure 15 in. (38 cm) square.

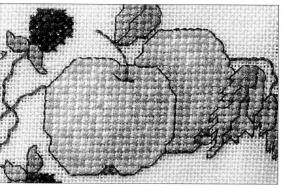

Fractional (three-quarter) stitches worked at the edges of the leaves and apples help to give them a lifelike shape.

TABLECLOTH

1 Mark the center of the tablecloth linen with lines of basting about 12 in. (30 cm) long. Mount the fabric in the embroidery hoop.

2 Counting out carefully from the center, work the design following the color key (opposite) and the chart (right). Use two strands of floss for cross stitch and the brown backstitch; use one strand only for the dark green backstitch. Work each stitch over two linen threads.

3 When you have completed the first quarter of the circle, rotate the chart 90 degrees and repeat step **2**. Repeat twice more to complete the circle.

4 Take the work out of the hoop and press lightly from the wrong side. Trim away the selvages, and trim the fabric if necessary to make a square, with the design centered. Turn a double ¼-in. (5-mm) hem all around and machine-stitch in place.

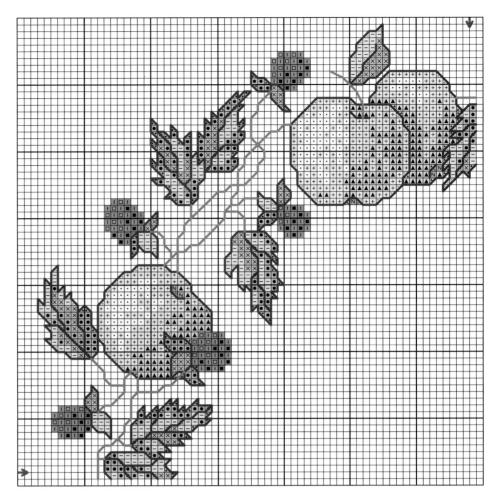

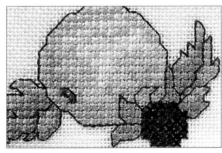

Pale green cross stitches at the center of the apple suggest sunlight reflecting off its shiny green skin, giving the fruit an almost three-dimensional quality.

MAKING THE NAPKIN

Baste lines 4 in. (10 cm) from the left edge of the napkin, and 3 ¼ in. (8 cm) above the lower edge—the basting lines cross at the center of the design. Following the chart (below), work the design. Hem the edges as for the Tablecloth, steps **2** and **4** (above).

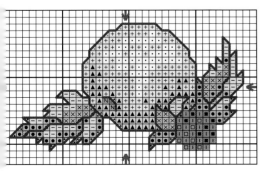

Cutlery Roll

Keep your silverware neat in this unusual roll, cross-stitched with a simple design of blackberries, taken from the tablecloth design.

1 Mark the center of the fabric, and overcast the edges. Work the design following the chart (below right) and the color key on page 60. Use two strands of floss for cross stitch and one for backstitch. Work each stitch over two linen threads.

2 When the design is complete, remove the basting and press the work lightly from the wrong side.

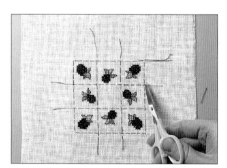

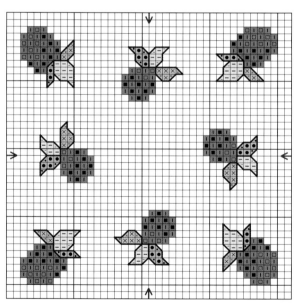

Dark violet and two shades of navy give the blackberries texture.

3 Baste a 3⅜-in. (8.5-cm) square around the design. Baste lines 1⅛ in. (8.4 cm) apart to divide it into nine small squares; trim the thread ends. Center the batting, then the interfacing on the wrong side. Pin, then machine-stitch along the basted lines. ▲

4 Press ⅜ in. (1 cm) to the wrong side along three edges. Fold the unpressed edge to the back, and fold the opposite edge over it, as shown; pin and slip-stitch. Stitch the Velcro to the short sides to fasten the roll. ►

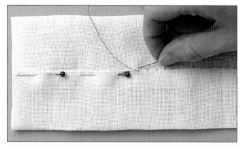

Rose Romance

Shades of lilac and white combine with soft greens in this romantic rose collection for lingerie and bed linen.

Lilac Satin Lingerie

A white rose in bloom and white rosebuds add luxurious detail to a silky lingerie set.

The motifs are worked over waste canvas, which is dampened and removed after stitching. A single open rose is stitched on the front of the kimono, and the nightgown has three rosebuds around the hem. The rose is 3⅜ in. (8.5 cm) long; the rosebuds, 2⅛ in. (5.5 cm).

You Will Need

- ❋ Kimono
- ❋ Nightgown
- ❋ 14-count waste canvas, 5 x 4 in. (13 x 10 cm) for the kimono, three pieces 3½ x 2½ in. (9 x 6 cm) for the nightgown
- ❋ DMC stranded floss as listed in the color key except 340, 341, and 3746
- ❋ Crewel needle, size 6
- ❋ Sewing needle and thread for basting
- ❋ Tweezers

Color Key

COLORS		SKEINS
▢	Blanc	1
▬	340 Deep lilac	1
•	341 Lilac	1
▲	503 Sea green	1
⊠	504 Pale sea green	1
◼	3746 Rich lilac	1

Backstitch using one strand

◩	333 Purple	1
◩	502 Pale jade	1

Backstitch using two strands

◩	502 Pale jade	

64

STITCHING THE KIMONO

1 Mark the center of the waste canvas with basting. Decide on the position for the motif on the kimono. Center the waste canvas over the motif position with the shorter edges at the top and bottom; baste.

2 Cross-stitch the motif from the center out, referring to the chart (right) and color key (opposite). Use two strands of floss and work over each pair of canvas threads.

3 When all the cross stitch is complete, work the backstitches around the petals, bud, and leaves, using one strand of floss over one pair of threads. Finally, backstitch the stems using two strands of floss.

4 When the stitching is complete, dampen the canvas and remove the threads with the tweezers. Press the motif lightly from the wrong side at a temperature suitable for the fabric.

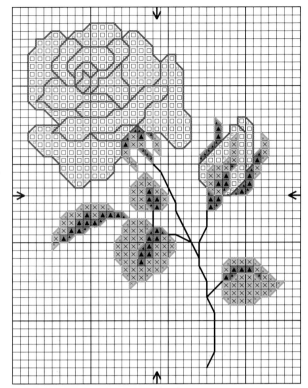

The beautiful open rose on the kimono is worked entirely in white cross stitch and then outlined in purple backstitching to show the layers of soft petals.

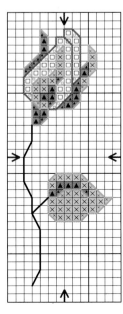

The white rosebud is partially encased by its calyx, worked in sea green and pale sea green with pale jade outlines.

STITCHING THE NIGHTGOWN

Mark the center of the waste canvas pieces with basting, and lay the nightgown skirt out flat. Place a piece of waste canvas diagonally on the center front, with its center 3½ in. (9 cm) above the hem edge; baste in place. In the same way, baste the second piece 8 in. (20 cm) to the left of the center piece, and the third 8 in. (20 cm) to the right. Work the rosebuds following the chart (left), and remove waste canvas, referring to Stitching the Kimono, steps **2–4**.

ROSE PILLOWCASE

Continue the romantic theme by stitching rose motifs on white bed linen. Here, a lilac rose and rosebud decorate a pillowcase with a frothy, ruffled eyelet lace edging, threaded with lilac ribbon. If you prefer colored bed linen, use the white rose and rosebud motifs from page 65. The lilac motif is 3⅜ in. (8.5 cm) long.

YOU WILL NEED

❀ Fabric for pillowcase as given on page 279

❀ Pre-gathered eyelet lace edging and ribbon to fit around pillowcase (optional)

❀ 14-count waste canvas, 5 x 4 in. (13 x 10 cm)

❀ DMC stranded floss as listed in the color key on page 64 except blanc

❀ Embroidery and sewing equipment as listed on page 64

The petals of the rose are stitched in three shades of lilac with purple backstitching around the edges.

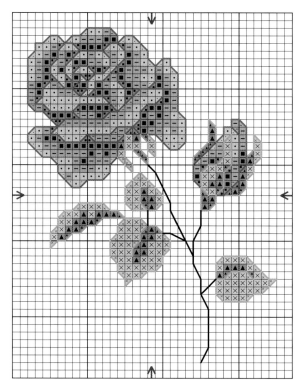

1 Cut out the pillowcase front, referring to the instructions for a housewife pillowcase on pages 279–280. Mark the center of the waste canvas, and baste it to the right side of the pillowcase front at the desired position.

2 Stitch the rose motif following steps **2–4** of Stitching the Kimono (page 65), but refer to the chart (left). Complete the pillowcase following the instructions on pages 279–280.

3 If desired, trim the pillowcase with the pre-gathered eyelet lace edging. Thread the ribbon through, and tie the ends in a bow at one corner.

TROPICAL FISH

THE VIBRANT COLORS AND EXOTIC FORMS OF
FISH FROM THE SOUTHERN SEAS ADD
CHEERFUL NOTES TO COSMETICS BAGS, A ROLL
FOR MAKE-UP BRUSHES, AND A SWIM SET.

<table>
<tr><td>

YOU WILL NEED

For all items:

❋ DMC stranded floss as listed in the color key

❋ Tapestry needle, size 26

❋ Embroidery hoop (see page 12)

❋ Pencil

❋ Sewing needle and thread for basting and stitching

For the bags:

❋ 14-count orange aida and 22-count navy Hardanger fabric

❋ Materials for making box bags as listed on page 287

For the brush holder:

❋ 14-count orange aida: two 9 x 8¼-in. (23 x 21-cm) pieces

❋ ¾ yd. (70 cm) of narrow elastic

❋ Two snaps

COLOR KEY

COLORS	SKEINS
✓ Blanc	1
T 304 Dark red	1
● 310 Black	1
Z 413 Dark pewter	1
• 414 Light pewter	1
✕ 415 Pearl gray	1
▽ 666 Flame red	1
■ 740 Bright tangerine	1
+ 742 Pale tangerine	1
→ 744 Medium yellow	1
↑ 762 Pale pearl gray	1
▲ 796 Royal blue	1
△ 798 Medium French blue	1
− 799 Deep blue	1
▨ 902 Burgundy mauve	1
H 995 Deep turquoise	1
I 996 Turquoise	1

Backstitch

◥ 310 Black

</td></tr>
</table>

BAGS AND POUCH

Decorate cosmetics and toiletries bags and a make-up brush holder with colorful tropical fish.

The toiletries bags can be made to any size you wish, and finished with your favorite selection of fish from the charts (right and on page 70.) The small yellow fish is the perfect size for the pouch.

Choose bright orange aida or navy Hardanger, and work out roughly how large each fish will be when you are planning the design for the front of the bag—fish stitched on the Hardanger will be slightly larger than the same fish stitched on the aida.

The bags shown here are about 10¼ x 7 in. (26 x 18 cm) and 7 x 4¾ in. (18 x 12 cm). The make-up brush roll is 7 in. (18 cm) long.

STITCHING THE BAGS

1 From the aida or Hardanger: cut out the bag front 1½ in. (4.5 cm) larger all around than needed; for details see page 287. Overcast the raw edges, and baste a rectangle on the center of the fabric to show the finished area of the front.

2 Select one or more fish from the charts (right and on page 70) and mark their centers with the pencil. Decide where to stitch them on the bag front, and use basting to mark the centers. Mount the fabric in the embroidery hoop.

3 Work each fish from the center out, referring to the charts (right and on page 70) and the color key (left). Use two strands of floss for cross stitch and one for backstitch. Work each stitch over one aida block or two pairs of Hardanger threads.

4 Take the finished piece out of the hoop, and press it lightly on the wrong side. Trim the fabric ⅝ in. (1.5 cm) outside the basted rectangle, then complete the bag following the instructions on pages 287–288.

68

The African peacock cichlid is worked in bold blues with golden highlights on the fins and eye.

MAKING THE POUCH

1 Mark the center of the small yellow fish on the chart (above). Overcast the edges of one aida piece, and mark its center with basting. Placing the short edges at the sides, stitch the fish, as in Stitching the Bags, step **3** (opposite). When complete, remove from the hoop and press lightly on the wrong side.

2 Cut the elastic into three pieces. Pin them across the plain aida, parallel to the long edges and 1 ¼ in. (3 cm) apart. Stitch across the elastic with rows of stitching ¾ in. (2 cm) apart to make pockets for the brushes.

3 Stitch the aida pieces right sides together taking ⅝ in. (1.5 cm) seams; leave an opening. Turn right side out and slip-stitch the opening. Roll up the holder with the elastic on the inside and attach snaps to fasten it as shown above. ▲

SWIM SET

DUFFLE BAG

1 From the Hardanger: cut a 29½ x 17-in. (75 x 43-cm) rectangle and a 10¼-in. (26-cm) circle for the base. Overcast the edges of the rectangle. With the short edges at the sides, stitch your chosen fish, following Stitching the Bags, steps **2–3** (page 68).

2 When complete, remove from the hoop and press. Interface the wrong side of the Hardanger pieces. Complete the bag following the instructions on pages 285–286.

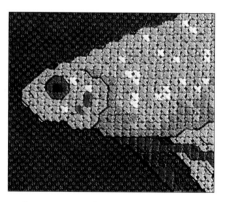

The Siamese fighter fish is worked in blues with bright red accents on the fins.

WORKING THE TOWEL

Mark the center of the band. Refer to the chart (below) and step **3** of Stitching the Bags (page 68) to work as many fish as required, leaving six blocks between each pair. Finish at least 2 in. (5 cm) from the ends.

Press the band lightly. Stitch the band in place, turning in the ends.

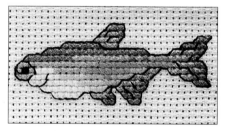

The tiny neon tetra fish has a turquoise face, iridescent stripes, and a silvery belly.

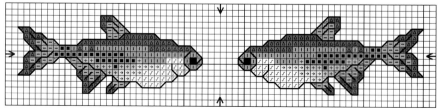

CACTUS SET

USE THE DISTINCTIVE SHAPES AND
SPECTACULAR SPINES AND FLOWERS OF
THESE DESERT PLANTS TO CREATE AN UNUSUAL
SET OF ACCESSORIES FOR THE HOME.

PICTURE AND TRIM

Images of these unmistakeable plants with their characteristic prickles can be used to make a stylish picture or a trim for a plain container.

French knots make an interesting textural alternative for the cactus flowers although you may prefer to stay with simple cross stitch.

YOU WILL NEED

* 14-count blue aida: 9 x 8 in. (23 x 20 cm) for the picture; a 4¾-in. (12-cm) deep strip for the trim
* DMC stranded floss as listed in the color key
* Sewing thread for basting
* Tapestry needle, size 26
* Embroidery hoop (optional; see page 12)
* Fabric adhesive (for the trim)

COLOR KEY

COLORS	SKEINS
209 Violet	1
335 Pink	1
435 Golden brown	1
437 Light brown	1
666 Red	1
725 Yellow	1
727 Pale yellow	1
895 Dark green	1
904 Green	1
906 Pale green	1
3326 Pale pink	1

Backstitch

300 Dark brown	1
335 Pink	
666 Red	
725 Yellow	
895 Dark green	
907 Lime green	1

CACTUS PICTURE

1 Overcast the edges of the aida to prevent them from fraying. Mark the center with basting. Mount the fabric in a hoop, if desired.

2 Using two strands of floss and working from the center out, cross-stitch the design. Refer to the chart and color key, and make each stitch over one thread block.

3 Cross-stitch the flowers or work them as French knots, using two strands of floss and referring to the key for colors.

4 Backstitch the outlines around the pots and the cacti, using one strand of floss. Work each stitch over one thread block, unless the chart indicates two thread blocks, as on the spines of the cacti.

5 Finally, cross-stitch the border using two strands of floss. Press the finished piece on the wrong side with a warm iron. Take the embroidery to a professional to have it framed, or see pages 297–298.

CACTUS TRIM

1 Cut the strip of aida to fit around the container plus 1½ in. (4 cm). Overcast the edges to prevent fraying, fold the strip in half lengthwise, and baste along the foldline.

2 Plan your design, marking the center of each motif with a vertical line of basting. As a guide, allow 1⅜ in. (3.5 cm) for each motif.

3 Stitch the cacti as for the picture. Work the border three thread blocks above the cacti and then the same distance below.

4 Trim excess fabric from the long edges of the aida. Glue the strip around the container, turning under the short ends and butting them together.

When stitching the spines of the cacti, make single, extra-long, straight stitches at sharp angles for a really spiky effect.

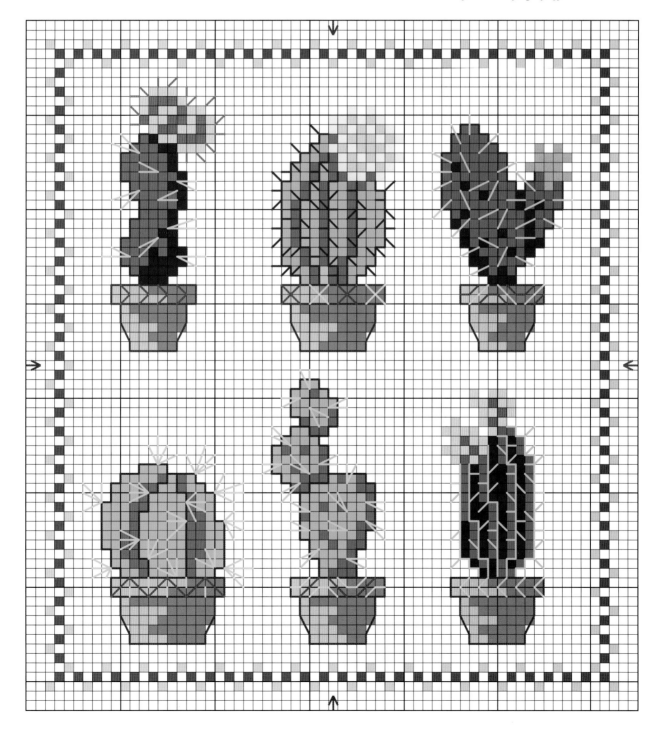

CACTUS MAGNETS

The weird shapes of the cactus plants and their chunky pots make wonderful cutouts to scatter around the kitchen. Fix tiny magnets to the back and you can attach your cacti to metal surfaces, such as the refrigerator door.

For the best results, stitch the designs onto a stiff fabric, such as plastic canvas or the latest vinyl weave which is available in special refrigerator magnet kits. These contain a self-adhesive magnetic strip and enough vinyl to stitch two cactus motifs. You can buy them in needlecraft stores or by mail order.

YOU WILL NEED

For two cactus magnets:

❋ Refrigerator magnet kit, including self-adhesive magnet and vinyl canvas

❋ Permanent marker

❋ Tapestry needle, size 22

❋ Selection of DMC stranded floss as listed on page 72

1 Cut the vinyl canvas in half widthwise to give two 3½ x 2-in. (8 x 5-cm) pieces. Referring to the instructions on page 21, mark the center of each piece with the permanent marker.

BRIGHT IDEAS

NAPKINS

Stitch your favorite cactus motif onto the corner of a rich blue linen napkin. Use 14-count waste canvas and a size 9 crewel needle. Work the cross stitch with three strands of floss over one pair of threads, and use one strand for the backstitch details.

2 Using two strands of floss, cross-stitch a cactus motif on each piece of canvas. Work from the center out, and make each stitch over one pair of threads, following the chart and key on pages 72–73. Work the flowers and backstitch the outlines and the spines following steps **2–4** of Cactus Picture on page 72.

3 Trim carefully around the cactus, leaving one pair of threads as a border. Cut a piece of magnetic strip to the approximate size of the cactus, then trim it to fit neatly on the wrong side of the embroidery. Peel off the paper backing and stick the magnetic strip onto the back of the cactus.

MAGNOLIAS

MAGNIFICENT MAGNOLIA FLOWERS,
WITH THEIR LARGE GLOSSY LEAVES,
MAKE A STRIKING DESIGN TO USE IN
THE BEDROOM.

PINK MAGNOLIAS BED SET

The pink magnolia flowers, growing on woody stems, can be repeated to create a flowering branch or worked individually.

The flowering branch on the sheet consists of three repeats from the chart. It is worked over 8-count waste canvas to create a life-size image measuring 27 x 6 in. (68 x 15 cm). The single motif on the pillowcase is worked over 10-count waste canvas and measures 7¾ x 5¼ in. (19.5 x 13.5 cm). An English-style pillowcase is ideal, but an ordinary one will do.

For a more delicate effect, the magnolia on the bedside table overcloth is stitched on fine linen; it measures 5¾ x 3½ in. (14.5 x 9 cm).

STITCHING THE SHEET

1 Work two lines of basting to mark the center of the 8-count waste canvas, then mark the vertical center of the fold-back area of the sheet with a pin.

2 Position the waste canvas on the right side of the fold-back area of the sheet, with the horizontal center 3½ in. (9 cm) above the hem stitching and the vertical centers matching. Baste the waste canvas in place around the edge.

3 Mount the layers in the hoop. Work the design from the center out, referring to the chart (below) and the key (opposite). Use four strands for cross stitch and two for backstitch. Work each stitch over one pair of canvas threads.

4 Complete the first motif, then repeat it on each side so that the branches join up. Remove the work from the hoop and dampen the waste canvas. Remove the threads with the tweezers.

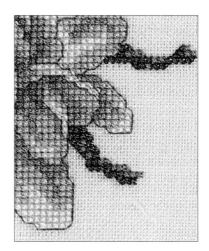

Use dark fawn and light fawn to cross-stitch the bare woody stems.

Outline and define the curling petals with dark pink and backstitch.

STITCHING THE PILLOWCASE

1 Mark the center of the 10-count waste canvas with basting. Baste it to the top right corner of the pillowcase, in the desired position, allowing for the curvature of the pillow.

2 Work a single motif following step **3** (above). When the work is complete, dampen the canvas and remove it with tweezers.

MAKING THE CLOTH

Mark the center of the linen with basting and mount it in the hoop. Work the motif from the center out, following the chart (above) and the key (opposite). Use two strands for cross stitch and one for backstitch. Work each stitch over two threads.

Remove the work from the hoop and steam-press it gently from the wrong side. Press ¼ in. (5 mm) then ⅝ in. (1.5 cm) to the wrong side, mitering the corners (see page 278); stitch the hem in place.

CREAM MAGNOLIA DUVET SET

These magnolia flowers, with their glossy, dark green leaves add an elegant floral touch to a neutral color scheme. The flowers are stitched randomly on the duvet cover over 8-count waste canvas and measure 10 x 6¼ in. (25 x 16 cm). The single bloom on the pillowcase is stitched on slightly finer 10-count waste canvas and measures 8 x 5 in. (20 x 13 cm). You can substitute an ordinary pillowcase for the English-style one shown here.

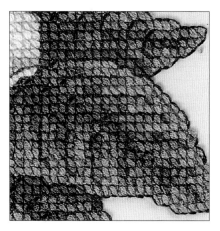

Pick out the leaf veins with two strands of gray and backstitch.

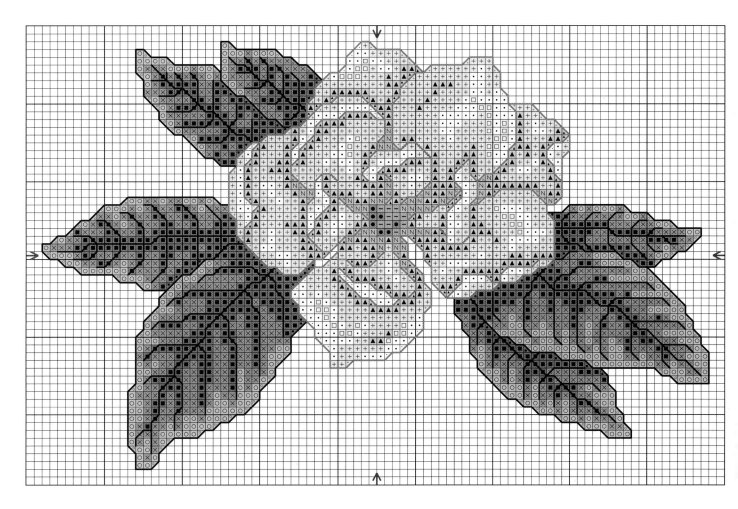

STITCHING THE COVER

1 Mark the center of each piece of 8-count waste canvas with basting. Baste the pieces randomly on the top of the duvet cover as desired; take care to stitch through one layer of the duvet cover only. Mount the fabric in the embroidery hoop.

2 Work one motif on each piece of waste canvas, referring to the chart (above) and the color key (opposite). One square on the chart represents one stitch worked over one pair of waste canvas threads. Work from the center outward, and use four strands of floss for the cross stitch and two strands of floss for the backstitch.

3 When you have finished all the cross stitch and the backstitch, indicate the flower centers with French knots (see page 17) using four strands of floss.

4 When the design is complete, remove the work from the embroidery hoop. Dampen the waste canvas and remove the threads with the tweezers. Press the cover gently from the wrong side, taking care not to crush the stitching.

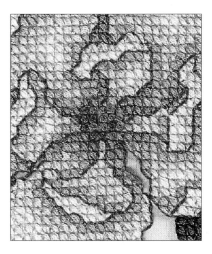

Create the prominent flower center with larger French knots worked using four strands of floss.

STITCHING THE PILLOWCASE

Mark the center of the piece of 10-count waste canvas with basting. Baste it to the top left corner of the pillowcase in the desired position, allowing for the curvature of the pillow. Take care to stitch through the top layer of fabric only.

Work the motif following Stitching the Cover, steps **2–3** (left). When the work is complete, remove it from the hoop and dampen the waste canvas. Remove the threads with the tweezers. Press the work lightly from the wrong side.

PRETTY AS A PICTURE

A single cream magnolia stitched on natural linen makes an elegant picture for a contemporary room scheme and teams perfectly with the cream bed linen set.

The stitched area is 5½ x 3⅜ in. (14 x 8.5 cm) and the fabric area within the frame is 7½ x 5½ in. (19 x 14 cm).

YOU WILL NEED

❊ 32-count natural evenweave linen, 14 x 12 in. (35 x 30 cm)
❊ DMC stranded floss as listed in the color key on page 78, one skein of each
❊ Tapestry needle, size 26
❊ Thread for basting
❊ Embroidery hoop (see page 12)

---

1 Mark the center of the linen with two lines of basting, and overcast the raw edges to prevent them from fraying. Mount the fabric in the embroidery hoop.

2 Cross-stitch the design from the center outward, referring to the chart and the color key on pages 78–79. One square on the chart represents one stitch worked over two linen threads. Use two strands of floss for the cross stitch and French knots, and one strand of floss for the backstitch.

3 When the motif is complete, remove the work from the hoop and steam-press it gently from the wrong side with a warm iron. Take it to a professional framer; or frame it yourself following the instructions on pages 297–298, adding a mat, if desired, or omitting it as shown here.

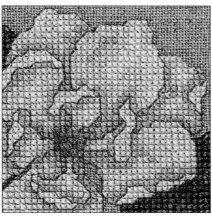

Soft shades of brown, fawn, and beige add depth and shadow at the base of the magnolia petals.

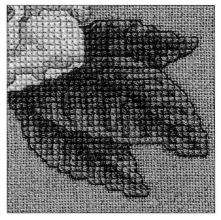

The large, glossy leaves are stitched in dark green at the center, fading into medium then light green at the edges.

WHALES AND DOLPHINS

THESE MARINE MAMMALS, LEAPING AND
DIVING ABOVE THE OCEAN, MAKE GREAT
MOTIFS ON SWIMMING GEAR.

FLYING DOLPHINS

Playful dolphins can be worked in a group along a border, or used as a single motif.

This border is worked on a towel with a 3¾-in. (9.5-cm) deep, 14-count aida border, which is especially made for counted thread embroidery. If you cannot find a towel of this type, use a separate aida band and sew it to the towel as described on page 231.

The pocket on the duffle bag is also worked on 14-count aida; the stitched dolphin motif is 3⅜ x 2¼ in. (8.5 x 6 cm). The dolphin on the jacket is worked over 10-count waste canvas and measures 4½ x 2¾ in. (11.5 x 7 cm).

YOU WILL NEED

For all items:
- ❀ DMC stranded floss as listed in the color key below and on page 86
- ❀ Thread for basting
- ❀ Embroidery hoop (see page 12)

For the towel:
- ❀ Towel with a 14-count aida band
- ❀ Tapestry needle, size 26

For the jacket:
- ❀ Purchased jacket
- ❀ 10-count waste canvas, 6½ x 5 in. (17 x 13 cm)
- ❀ Crewel needle, size 6
- ❀ Tweezers

For the duffle bag:
- ❀ 14-count royal blue aida, 10 in. (25 cm) square
- ❀ Tapestry needle, size 26
- ❀ 1 yd. (1 m) of white terry cloth
- ❀ Fabric and materials to make the duffle bag, substituting heavyweight interfacing for the batting (see page 286)
- ❀ Filler cord for piping (optional)
- ❀ Sewing needle and thread
- ❀ Sewing machine

COLOR KEY

COLORS	SKEINS
⊞ Blanc	1
⊠ 414 Pewter gray	1
⊡ 415 Pearl gray	1
◼ 796 Royal blue	1
⊙ 809 Delft blue	1
◼ 3799 Dark charcoal	1

Backstitch

◹ 3799 Dark charcoal

THE TOWEL

1 Mark the center of the aida panel with basting, and mount the central part of the panel in the embroidery hoop. Work the dolphin border from the center out. Move the hoop along as required, and refer to the chart (below) and the color key (opposite).

2 Use two strands of floss for the cross stitch and one strand for the backstitch. Work each stitch over one thread block. Work three repeats to complete the border, then remove the work from the hoop and press it lightly on the wrong side.

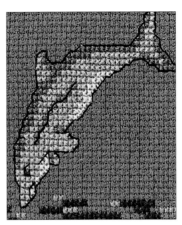

The graceful dolphins are worked in pewter and pearl gray with blanc on the underside.

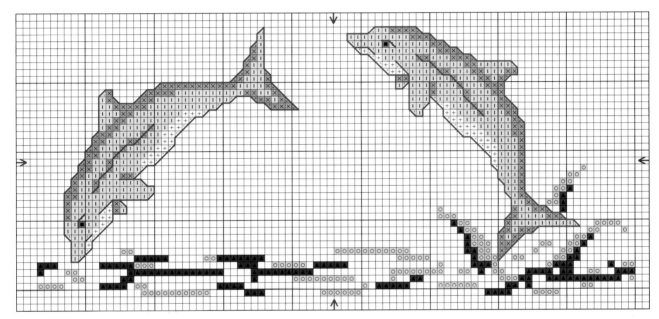

THE JACKET

1 Mark the center of the waste canvas, and baste it in position on the jacket. Mount the work in the hoop.

2 Refer to the color key and chart on page 86. Work the cross stitch first, using two strands of floss, then the backstitch using one strand. Work each stitch over one pair of canvas threads.

3 When the design is complete, take the work out of the hoop. Dampen the waste canvas and remove the threads with the tweezers. Press the work lightly from the wrong side, taking care not to crush the stitching.

The single flying dolphin is worked over waste canvas on the jacket with backstitched outlines in dark charcoal.

THE DUFFLE BAG

1 Overcast the edges of the aida. Work the design as for the Towel, step 1 (top), but refer to chart and key on page 86. Press on the wrong side. Trim the fabric to 9 x 7 in. (23 x 18 cm) with center of design ⅜ in. (1cm) below fabric center.

2 From the terry cloth, heavyweight interfacing, and lining fabric: cut a 10¾-in. (27-cm) diameter circle for the base and a 30¾ x 18½ in. (78 x 47 cm) rectangle for the side piece.

3 Cut out the tab and cord stay, and make the duffle bag, following the instructions on pages 286, but use the aida for the pocket, and replace the batting with heavyweight interfacing. If desired, pipe the edges of the circular base (see pages 275–276).

JUMPING WHALES

These are ideal for children's gear to be taken on trips to the seashore or the swimming pool. The towel has an aida band, which is decorated with a border of jumping whales. The duffle bag has an aida pocket with a single 3½ x 2½ in. (9 x 6.5 cm) motif. The larger whale on the top is worked over waste canvas and measures 4¾ x 3½ in. (12 x 9 cm).

THE TOP

Select an appropriate area on the top, and work the design in the same way as for The Jacket (page 83) but refer to the single whale chart (opposite) and the color key (left).

THE TOWEL

Work the design in the same way as for The Towel (page 83) but refer to the whale border chart (below) and color key (left). Work a jumping whale at the center, then a diving whale on either side, then add another jumping whale at each side.

The whales on the border jump from and dive into a band of ocean waves, which is stitched in lively splashes of royal and Delft blue.

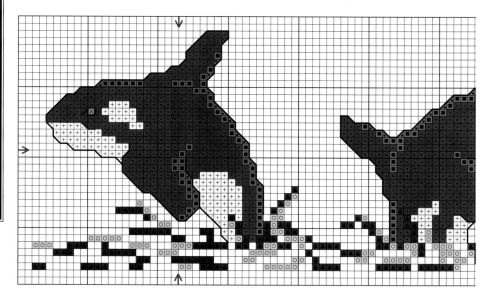

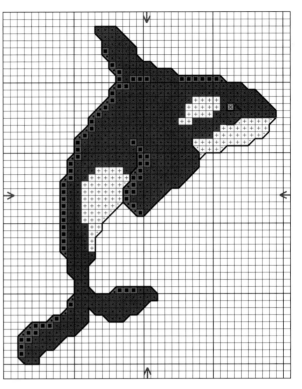

THE DUFFLE BAG

Stitch a single whale at the center of the aida fabric, following step **1** of The Duffle Bag (page 83) but using the single whale chart (above) and the color key (opposite). Make the duffle bag as on page 83, steps **2–3**, but use the gray corduroy fabric instead of white terry cloth.

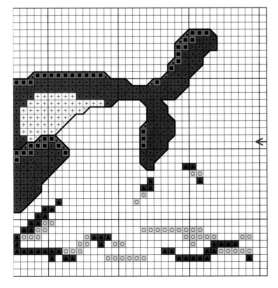

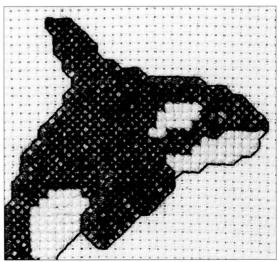

The whales are stitched in black with dark charcoal gray stitches to lighten the edges. The fins and body are outlined in black backstitching.

DOLPHIN PATCH

A single leaping dolphin worked on a patch of royal blue aida is an easy way to add extra appeal to swimming gear. The patch is shown here on a blue and white striped towel, but you could use it to decorate a bag or an item of clothing. The finished patch is 5½ x 4¾ in. (14 x 12 cm).

YOU WILL NEED

* 14-count royal blue aida, 8 in. (20 cm) square
* DMC stranded floss as listed in the color key
* Thread for basting
* Tapestry needle, size 26
* Towel
* Embroidery hoop (optional; see page 12)

COLOR KEY

COLORS	SKEINS
⊞ Blanc	1
⊠ 414 Pewter gray	1
I 415 Pearl gray	1
⊡ 761 Pink	1
■ 3799 Dark charcoal	1

Backstitch

◪ 3799 Dark charcoal

The smiling dolphin is worked with pink inside the mouth and gleaming white stitching on the underside.

1 Overcast the edges of the aida and mark the center with basting. The piece is small enough to work in your hand, but if you wish, mount it in an embroidery hoop.

2 Work the dolphin from the center out, referring to the chart (right) and the color key (left). Use two strands of floss for cross stitch and one for backstitch. Work each stitch over one thread block.

3 When the design is complete, remove the hoop, if used, and press lightly on the wrong side. With the dolphin centered, trim the aida to 5½ x 4¾ in. (14 x 12 cm).

4 Baste the patch diagonally near one corner of the towel, or on the chosen item. Backstitch all around, four blocks in from the edge, using two strands of white floss and stitching over one block. Fray the edges of the aida for three blocks all around.

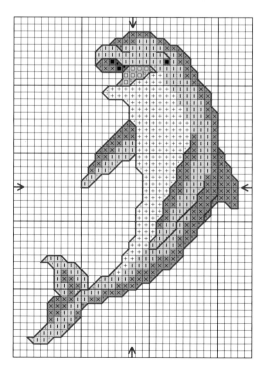

LAVENDER

SPRIGS OF FRAGRANT LAVENDER
FORM CORNERS AND BORDERS, AND
A BEADED BOUQUET ON A LAVENDER BAG
FOR A SWEET-SCENTED BEDROOM.

LAVENDER CORNERS

Stitched on pure white linen, lavender corners form central and corner motifs on the throw and a border on the cushion.

The corner motif creates three different effects on the throw and cushion. In each case, the chart is easier to follow if you start with the backstitched stems, rather than the cross-stitched flowers. On the throw, the lavender corners are 9 in. (23 cm) high and deep, and on the cushion, 6 in. (15 cm) high and deep. The finished lavender throw is 76 x 50 in. (193 x 127 cm), and the cushion cover is 14 in. (36 cm) square.

STITCHING THE THROW

1 Overcast the raw edges of the evenweave fabric to prevent fraying. Mark the center with basting; baste a 47-in. (120-cm) square in the center of the fabric. Mount the central area of the fabric in the embroidery hoop.

2 Starting with the stems, work the bottom left quarter of the central motif. Refer to the chart (opposite) and color key (left), and stitch from the center out. Use two strands for backstitch and three for cross stitch. Work each stitch over three threads.

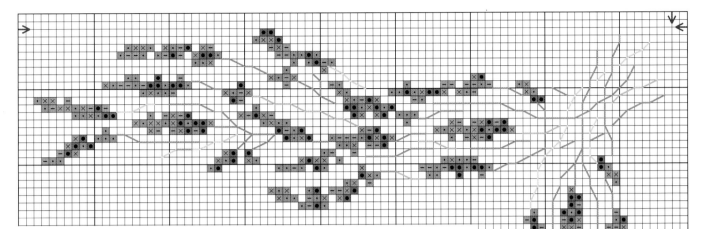

3 When the first quarter is complete, turn the chart 90 degrees to work the next quarter. Repeat twice more to complete the central motif.

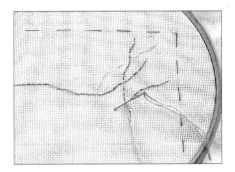

4 Next, stitch a motif in each corner of the basted square, matching the basted lines to the positions of the arrows on the chart. Take the work out of the hoop and press it gently. ▲

5 On two opposite sides of the evenweave, turn under and press a double ½-in. (1.2-cm) hem; stitch with matching thread. Hem the short edges of the mauve fabric pieces in the same way.

6 Placing right sides together, stitch a mauve piece to one raw edge of the evenweave, taking a ⅝-in. (1.5-cm) seam. Press the seam toward the mauve fabric. Stitch the other mauve piece to the other raw edge in the same way.

7 Placing wrong sides together, fold the outer edge of each mauve border up to the seam; press and slip-stitch in place. To finish, topstitch the sides of the mauve borders close to the edges.

STITCHING THE CUSHION

1 Cut a 17-in. (43-cm) square of evenweave. Baste a 13-in. (33-cm) square in the center of the fabric; overcast the edges, and mount it in the embroidery hoop.

2 Stitch an L-shaped motif in each corner of the square, as in Stitching the Throw, step **4** (above), using two strands throughout and working each stitch over two threads.

3 Take the finished piece out of the embroidery hoop and press it gently on the wrong side. Trim the fabric 1¼ in. (3 cm) outside the basted square.

4 Make the piece into a cushion cover with a cord trim, referring to the instructions on pages 307–308. Use the remaining evenweave for the overlapped back.

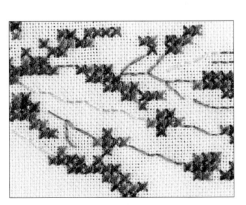

Cross stitch in purple, mauve, and violet depicts the tiny individual flowers growing on narrow stems.

LAVENDER BAG

A single lavender sprig proclaims the contents of a fragrant drawstring bag, designed to sweeten a lingerie drawer or the linen closet. For a charming touch and added texture, little mauve-colored seed beads replace some of the cross stitches.

YOU WILL NEED

- ❋ 28-count white evenweave fabric, 11 x 8 in. (28 x 20 cm)
- ❋ DMC stranded floss and embroidery materials as listed on page 88
- ❋ Mauve seed beads
- ❋ Lilac fabric, 12 x 8 in. (30 x 20 cm)
- ❋ 1⅝ yd. (1.5 m) of narrow cord
- ❋ White and mauve sewing threads
- ❋ Safety pin
- ❋ Dried lavender

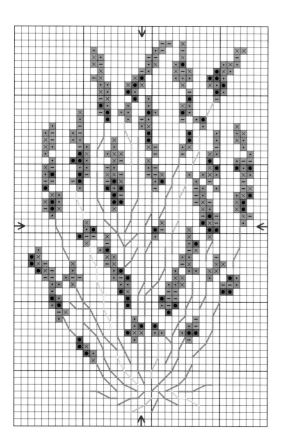

1 Overcast the edges of the evenweave, mark the center with basting, and mount it in the hoop. Work with the short edges at the sides.

2 Work the design from the center out, using two strands throughout. Refer to the chart (left) and the color key on page 88. Apply the beads where cross stitches in 340 (mauve) are shown. Work over two threads.

3 When work is complete, take it out of the hoop and press it lightly. Trim the fabric ⅝ in. (1.5 cm) below the design and 1⅜ in. (3.5 cm) above.

4 Cut a 10¾ x 1⅜-in. (27 x 3.5-cm) strip and a 10¾ x 5¾-in. (27 x 14.5-cm) piece of mauve fabric. Stitch the strip to the bottom of the evenweave and the other piece to the top. Take ⅜ in. (1 cm) seams.

5 Stitch the side edges of the bag, center the seam, and press. Stitch the bottom edge. At the top, press ⅜ in. (1 cm), then 2½ in. (6.5 cm) to the wrong side. Stitch the hem close to the top of the evenweave, then ⅜ in. (1 cm) above that.

6 Make the casing following the instructions on page 284 (top). Thread the cord through the casing, using it doubled, then fill the bag with dried lavender.

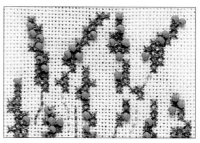

Secure each bead with 340 (mauve) and cross stitch; apply the bead as you work the final diagonal of the cross.

CURIOUS CATS

THE SINUOUS FORMS OF LUCKY BLACK
CATS MAKE LIVELY DECORATIONS
FOR STYLISH ACCESSORIES IN
THE LIVING ROOM.

ARMCHAIR SET

The perfect set for a cat lover combines playful cats with a paw-print border on a matching cushion and antimacassar.

STITCHING THE CUSHION

The cushion cover features five cats framed by a paw-print border. Copy the design shown here, or make up your own, arranging the cats as you wish. Whichever arrangement you choose, stitch the border first, then work the cats nearest to it, to make sure that you don't run out of space.

1 Mark the center of the fabric with basting, and overcast the edges. Measuring from the center outward, baste a 14-in. (36-cm) square to mark the area of the finished cushion front. Mount the fabric in the embroidery hoop.

2 Work the design referring to the charts (below and opposite below) and the color key (left). Each square on the charts represents one stitch worked over two fabric threads. Use three strands of floss for the cross stitch, and one strand for the backstitch.

3 Work the paw border in one corner, with the outer stitches ¾ in. (2 cm) in from the basting. Continue the border, turning the chart 90 degrees to work the next corner; repeat for the other two corners. Work the cats, starting with the outer cats; position them as desired.

4 Press the work lightly from the wrong side. Trim it ¾ in. (2 cm) outside the basted outline and remove the basting. Assemble cushion, following the instructions on pages 307–308.

YOU WILL NEED

For both items:
* DMC stranded floss as listed in the color key
* Tapestry needle, size 26
* Embroidery hoop (see page 12)
* Sewing needle, black and cream thread, and thread for basting

For the cushion:
* 28-count cream evenweave fabric, 18 in. (46 cm) square
* Cream fabric for cushion back, 22 x 16 in. (56 x 40 cm)
* Pillow form, 14–15 in. (36–38 cm) square
* 1⅝ yd. (1.5 m) cord trim

For the antimacassar:
* 28-count cream evenweave fabric, 30 x 20 in. (76 x 50 cm)
* ½ yd. (45 cm) of black fringe

COLOR KEY

COLORS	SKEINS
▨ 224 Dusky pink	1
■ 310 Black	7
Backstitch	
▢ Ecru	1
◩ 224 Dusky pink	
◩ 3740 Purple-pink	1

A cat dangles a ball of yarn from its paw, adding a touch of color to the monochrome scheme.

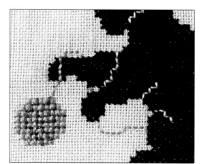

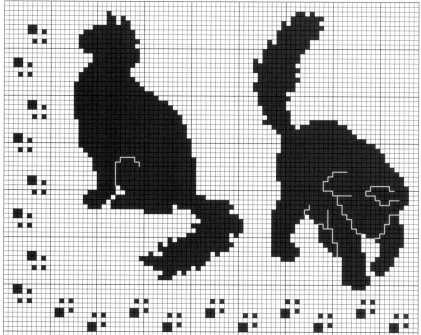

ANTIMACASSAR

The antimacassar features three of the cats and the paw-print border. One edge is finished with a silky black fringe. The finished item (without fringe) measures approximately 27 x 16 in. (70 x 42 cm).

1 Work the design from the chart (below), positioning the lower stitches on the paw-print border 3¼ in. (8 cm) above one short edge of the cloth. Then work the cats. Take the work out of the hoop and press it from the wrong side.

2 Trim the cloth evenly so that it measures 29 x 18 in. (74 x 46 cm). Press ¼ in. (5 mm) then ⅝ in. (1.5 cm) to the wrong side all around. At each corner, unfold the ⅝-in. (1.5-cm) hem and press it in diagonally, level with the hem fold. Trim the corner ¼ in. (5 mm) from the diagonal fold, then refold it to form a miter. Slip-stitch the hems. ▼

3 Place the fringe over the lower edge of the antimacassar. Stitch it in place, turning in the raw ends.

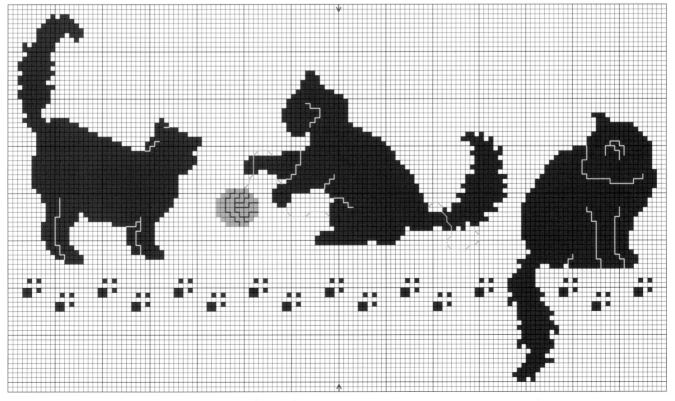

93

GLASSES CASE

The glasses case features a cat sitting between two paw-print borders. Make it to coordinate with the armchair set, using leftover evenweave and embroidery floss, or stitch one especially for a cat-loving friend.

Follow the chart (below) to work the design shown in the photograph, or use a cat from the charts on pages 92 and 93. The finished item measures 7 x 3¾ in. (18 x 9.5 cm).

YOU WILL NEED

❀ 28-count cream evenweave fabric, 10 x 6 in. (25 x 15 cm)

❀ DMC stranded floss, one skein each of ecru and 310 (black)

❀ Tapestry needle, size 26

❀ Embroidery hoop (see page 12)

❀ Cream backing fabric, 8¼ x 4¾ in. (21 x 12.5 cm)

❀ Fusible interfacing, 8¼ x 4¾ in. (21 x 12.5 cm)

❀ ¾ yd. (60 cm) cord trim

❀ Sewing needle, black and cream thread, and thread for basting

❀ Sewing machine

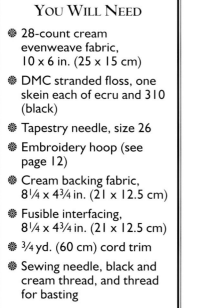

1 Mark the center of the evenweave fabric with basting, overcast the edges, and mount it in the embroidery hoop. Work the design from the center outward, following the chart (right) and referring to the color key on page 92. Work each stitch over two fabric threads. Use three strands of floss for the cross stitch and one strand for the backstitch.

2 Take the work out of the hoop and press it lightly from the wrong side. Trim the fabric evenly around the embroidery to measure 8¼ x 4¾ in. (21 x 12.5 cm). Fuse the interfacing onto the wrong side of the cloth.

3 Pin the evenweave to the backing fabric, right sides together. Stitch with cream thread, leaving the top edge open and taking ⅝ in. (1.5 cm) seams. Trim the seams and finish them by machine with zigzag stitch.

4 At the top edge, turn ⅝ in. (1.5 cm) to the wrong side and slip-stitch with cream thread. Turn the case right side out and press it. With black thread, slip-stitch the cord trim around the seamline, beginning at the top left corner and securing the end on the inside. Sew it around the case, then across the top edge of the front, and secure the end of the cord on the inside as before.

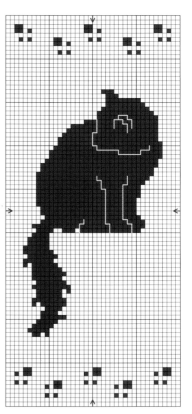

FORGET-ME-NOTS

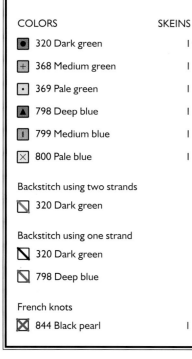
DESK SET

Embroidered forget-me-nots on these writing accessories make it a pleasure to make notes and send greetings to friends and family.

Clusters of dainty forget-me-nots are a favorite in many gardens. Their delicate shades of blue and their slender leaves add fresh notes to a writing set.

The border on the stationery folder is approximately 13½ x 3¼ in. (34 x 8 cm), the patch on the address book is 4½ in. (11.5 cm) square, and each stitched panel on the note holder is 3¾ x 3½ in. (9.5 x 9 cm).

STATIONERY FOLDER

1 Mark the center of the fabric with basting, and overcast the edges to prevent fraying. Mount the fabric in the embroidery hoop.

2 Cross-stitch the design from the center out, referring to the chart (opposite) and the color key (left). Use two strands of floss, and work each stitch over one thread block. Repeat the design until it is at least as deep as the folder front.

3 When all the cross stitch is complete, backstitch the stems using two strands of 320 (dark green) floss. Then backstitch the veins and the outlines using one strand of floss and referring to the chart and the color key.

4 Finally work the French knots using two strands of floss. Wrap the thread twice around the needle for the smaller knots and three times for the larger ones.

5 Remove the work from the hoop, and press it gently on the wrong side. On the long edges, trim the fabric ¾ in. (2 cm) outside the stitching, then press ½ in. (12 mm) to the wrong side. Stick the hems in place with fabric glue.

6 Place the border on the folder front; wrap the ends to the inside, and trim them as required. Stick the border in place using the fabric glue. Cover the inside of the folder with the paper or fabric to hide the ends of the aida, sandwiching a ribbon tie at the center of the edges.

ADDRESS BOOK

Choose a motif and mark its horizontal center on the chart (below). Stitch following steps **1– 4** of Stationery Folder (left). Trim six blocks outside the stitching. Fray the edges, and glue to the address book front.

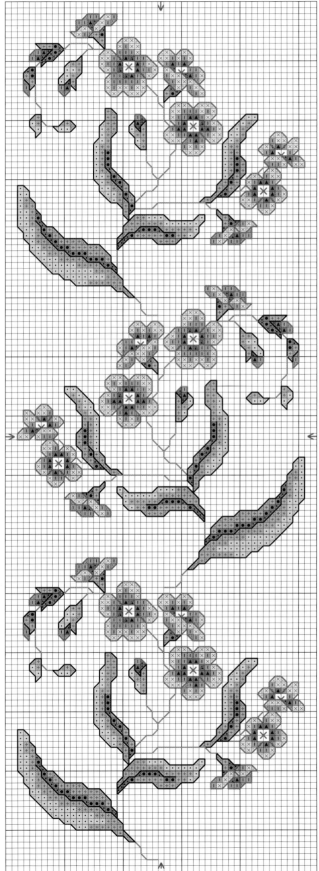

NOTE HOLDER

1 For each aida piece, mark the horizontal center of your chosen motif on the chart (right). Prepare the fabric and stitch the motifs following steps **1– 4** of Stationery Folder (left). Trim the aida to fit one panel of the note holder.

2 Take the inner plastic sleeve out of the note holder. Use small pieces of the double-stick tape to stick a stitched aida piece onto each section of the plastic sleeve. Then put the sleeve back in position in the note holder.

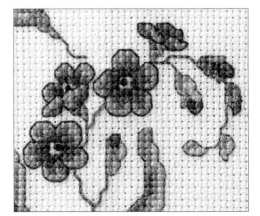

The flowers are stitched in three shades of blue, with the deepest near the center, radiating out through medium blue to pale blue. Deep blue backstitch, using one strand of floss, outlines the flowers and their petals.

FRIENDLY NOTES

A forget-me-not card is perfect for dropping a note to a distant friend or absent loved one, sometimes better than an e-mail. The card patches are about 2¼ in. (6 cm) square and the envelope patch is 1⅛ x 1 in. (3 x 2.7 cm).

YOU WILL NEED

❋ 18-count white aida, about 4 in. (10 cm) square for cards, 2 in. (5 cm) square for envelopes

❋ DMC stranded floss and embroidery materials as listed on page 96

❋ Single-fold plain cards and envelopes

❋ Contrasting card stock and pinking shears (optional)

❋ Fabric glue

1 For each card, choose a sprig or part of one from the charts (right and below). For each envelope, choose a flower. Stitch as in steps **1–4** of Stationery Folder on page 96; if you prefer, work four cross stitches in pale green at the flower centers instead of the French knots.

2 For a card with a plain forget-me-not patch, trim the aida nine blocks outside the stitching, and fray the outer three blocks all around. Glue onto the card front, centered across the width.

3 For a card with a contrasting mount, trim and fray the aida as in step **2**, then use the pinking shears to cut a square of contrasting card stock a little larger than the aida. Glue the square diagonally on the top half of the card front. Glue the forget-me-not patch on top.

4 For the envelopes, trim the aida five blocks outside the stitching, and fray the edges for one block. Glue the patch on the lower left-hand corner of the envelope front.

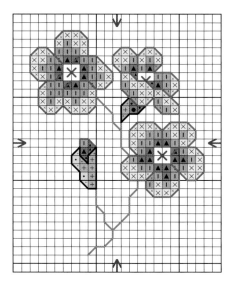

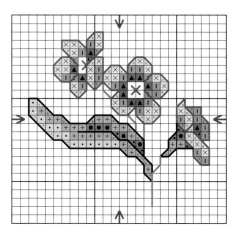

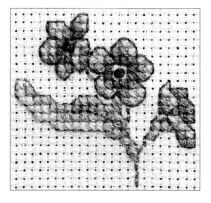

The French knots at the flower centers are worked in two strands of 844 (black pearl). Wind the floss around the needle twice for a small knot or three times for a larger one.

98

Chapter 3
Gifts and Celebrations

BLUE STITCHES

TRADITIONAL SAMPLER MOTIFS
STITCHED IN BLUE THREAD ON COARSE
NATURAL LINEN DECORATE A PORTABLE
SEWING SET FOR EMBROIDERERS.

SEWING SET

A roll-up travel sewing folder, a tiny needlecase, and a plump pincushion display floral borders, lovebirds, and hearts.

The sewing folder is a simple flap purse with a pocket divided into sections to hold a pair of scissors, threads, fabric scraps, and other needlecraft essentials. It measures 7¾ x 6½ in. (19.5 x 16.5 cm) and can be rolled up and secured with its rickrack tie for traveling. The little needlecase is 3¼ x 2 in. (8 x 5 cm), and the circular pincushion is 3½ in. (9 cm) in diameter.

SEWING FOLDER

1 Overcast the edges of the linen. Mark the vertical center of the design with a line of basting parallel to the long edges. Mark the horizontal center of the lovebirds motif (see page 104) 7⅝ in. (19.5 cm) above the short bottom edge. Baste lines 2⅜ in. (6 cm) above and below this to mark the horizontal centers of the borders. Mount the work in the hoop.

2 Stitch the birds from the center out, referring to the chart on page 104 and the color key (left). Use two strands of floss for cross stitch and one for backstitch. Work each stitch over two fabric threads.

3 In the same way, work the right-hand half of the top border, referring to the chart (opposite below), then stitch another repeat to the left. Turn the chart upside down; work the bottom border in the same way.

4 Take the work out of the hoop and press it lightly, then trim the long edges ⅝ in. (1.5 cm) from the stitching.

5 Make the flap purse with a 4-in. (10-cm) deep pocket and a 5½-in. (14-cm) deep flap. Take ⅜ in. (1 cm) seams, and refer to the instructions on pages 291–292. Divide the pocket into sections with vertical lines of stitching. For the tie, fold the rickrack in half and stitch it to one side edge.

NEEDLECASE

1 Overcast the edges of the linen. Use basting to mark the horizontal center parallel to the long edges. Mark the vertical center of the design 1 3/8 in. (3.5 cm) from the short right-hand edge.

2 Stitch the heart as for Sewing Folder step **2** (left), but refer to the chart (below left). Press lightly from the wrong side.

3 Baste a length of the rickrack 3/4 in. (2 cm) from each long edge. Make the needlecase following the instructions on page 306, but use 4-in. (10-cm) lengths of rickrack for the ties and omit the batting.

PINCUSHION

1 Mark the center of the linen with basting, then stitch the circle of flowers as for Sewing Folder step **2** (left) but refer to the chart (above). Press the work on the wrong side.

2 Trim the linen 5/8 in. (1.5 cm) outside the stitched design, and cut a circle of the backing fabric to match.

3 Fold the cord into a loop and place it on the wrong side of the stitched piece with the raw edges matching. Stitch the linen and the backing together with right sides facing, adding a rickrack trim; take a 3/8 in. (1 cm) seam, and leave a gap to turn through.

4 Turn right side out, fill with stuffing and slip-stitch the gap.

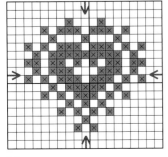

HEART

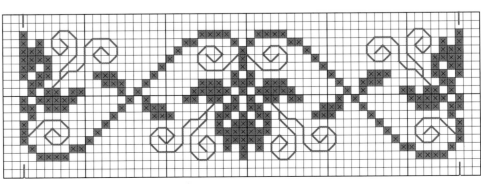

BORDER

THREAD BOX

YOU WILL NEED

❋ Specialist box with an oval lid, approximately 5½ x 4 in. (14 x 10 cm) for displaying embroidery

❋ DMC stranded floss and embroidery materials as listed on page 102

❋ 28-count oatmeal evenweave linen, 8 x 7 in. (20 x 18 cm) square (adjust fabric size for different size of box)

❋ Sewing needle and strong thread

❋ Sewing machine

1 Overcast the raw edges of the fabric, mark the center with basting, and mount it in the hoop.

2 Work the lovebirds from the center out, referring to the chart (below) and the color key on page 102. Use two strands of floss for cross stitch and one for backstitch. Work each stitch over two fabric threads.

3 Take the finished piece out of the hoop and press it lightly on the wrong side. Cut the fabric 1 in. (2.5 cm) larger all around than the lid, then finish the cut edges with machine zigzag stitch.

4 Take the fabric-covered pad out of the lid. Stretch the linen fabric, right side up, over the top of the pad with the design centered, and pin around the edges to hold.

5 Wrap the excess linen fabric around to the back of the pad, pulling it taut, and pin it to hold. Using a needle and the strong thread, lace the fabric edges together firmly (see page 222), then insert the pad in the lid.

LOVEBIRDS

Floral motifs and a heart unite the perfectly matched lovebirds.

DECORATIVE BANDS

STRIPS OF HEARTS, FLOWERS, SWAGS, AND
DIAMONDS FORM AN APPEALING ARRAY OF IDEAS
TO EMBELLISH YOUR HOME.

SAMPLER

Work all the bands together to create an attractive sampler in bright summer hues.

This unusual design for a sampler represents a twist on tradition. It combines bands of mini-motifs in a block formation, worked in pastel colors. The stitched area measures about 9¼ x 5½ in. (23.5 x 14 cm).

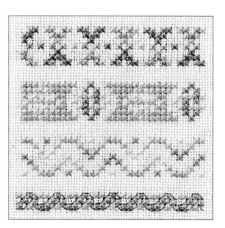

Repeating motifs create appealing bands of color on the sampler.

1 Overcast the edges of the fabric to prevent fraying. Mark the center with one vertical row and one horizontal row of basting. Mount the fabric in the embroidery hoop.

2 Cross-stitch the design from the center out, referring to the chart (opposite) and the color key (left). Use two strands of floss throughout, and work each stitch over two fabric threads.

3 When all the cross stitch is complete, work the backstitch using one strand of the color indicated in the key. Then work the straight-stitch details.

4 When the design is complete, take the work out of the embroidery hoop, and press it lightly on the wrong side. Take it to a professional framer, or frame it yourself, following the instructions on pages 297–298 and adding a mat if you wish.

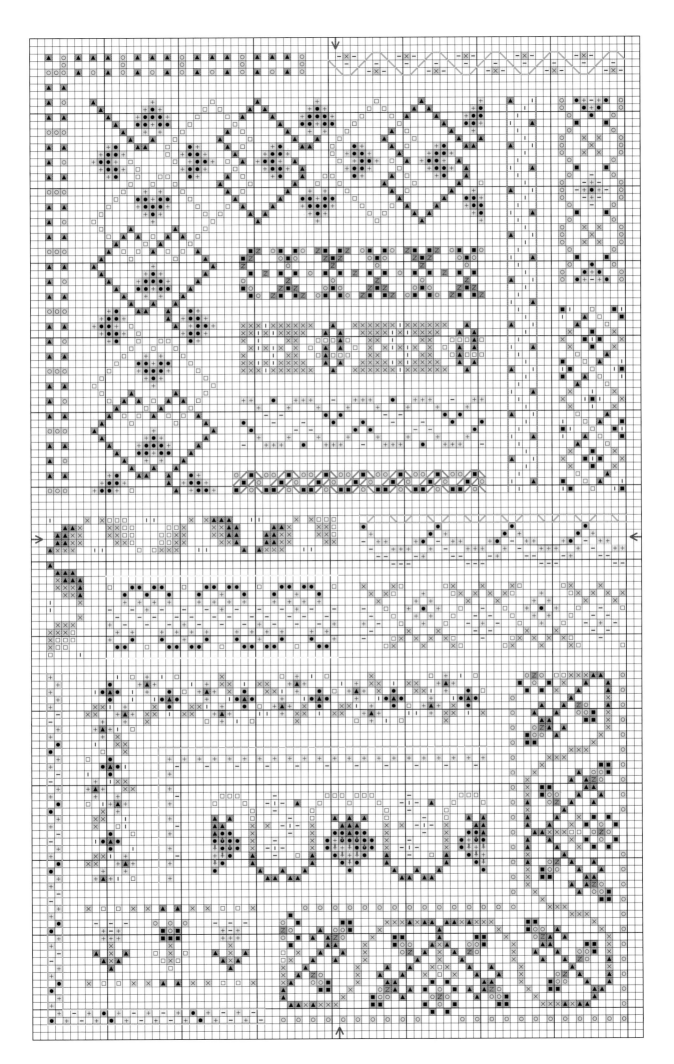

AIDA BANDS

The complete sampler design (pages 106–107) inspires a host of decorative ideas. The individual elements are perfect for stitching on ready-made aida bands, with either woven or scalloped edges. Stitch a wide band across the front of a large cosmetic bag, a medium band on a flat cosmetic bag, or use a narrow band to decorate a towel.

Start stitching the aida band at a short end, following the repeat lines on the chart. Note that on the largest chart (opposite below), the two design elements repeat at different points.

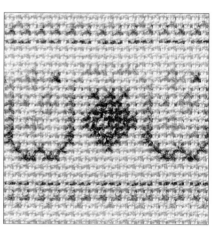

Tiny straight stitches in one strand of dark brown suggest the strawberry seeds.

COSMETIC BAG TRIMS

1 Mark the horizontal center of the band with basting. Mount it in the embroidery hoop.

2 Cross-stitch the border, referring to the appropriate chart (opposite above or below) and the color key on page 106. Follow the repeat lines and use two strands of floss. Work each stitch over one thread block.

3 When all the cross stitch is complete, work the backstitch and any straight stitch using one strand of floss.

4 When the work is complete, remove it from the hoop and press lightly. Press in ⅜ in. (1 cm) at each end, then slip-stitch the band across the front of the bag.

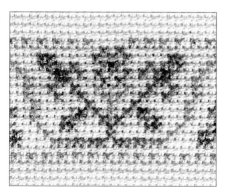

The small lavender-colored flowers are linked by swag-like, trailing green stems.

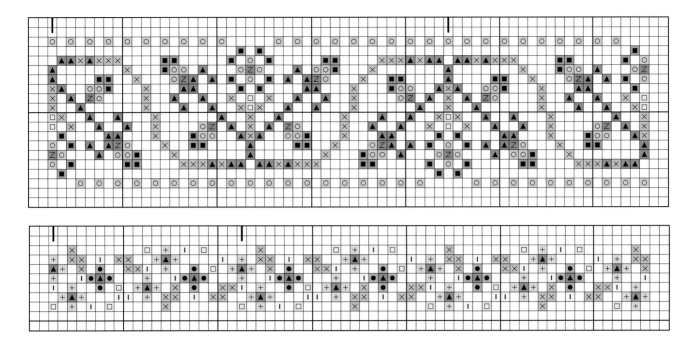

TOWEL TRIM

1 Mark the horizontal center of the band with basting. Mount it in the embroidery hoop.

2 Work the border, referring to the chart (above) and the color key on page 106. Use two strands for cross stitch, and work each stitch over one thread block.

3 Working from the center out, stitch as many repeats as needed. When the work is complete, take it out of the hoop and press lightly.

4 At each end of the band, press ⅜ in. (1 cm) to the wrong side. Pin the trim across the towel, then slip-stitch it in place using the white sewing thread.

Little flowers in shades of pink and yellow create a dainty narrow border.

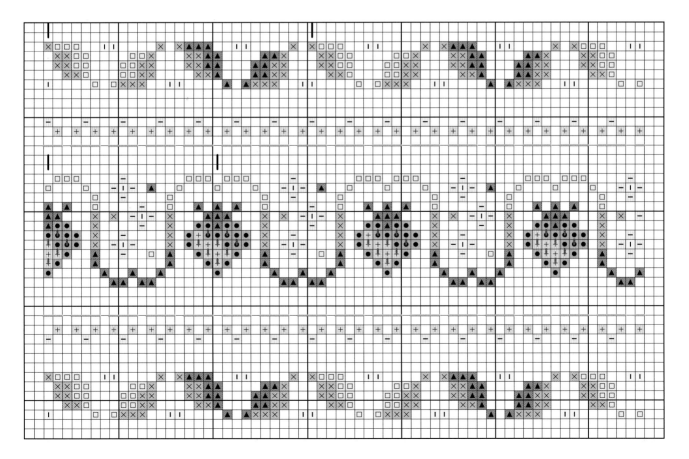

LINEN BANDS

For a personal gift, try stitching a decorative pattern onto a natural linen band to upgrade a simple flat cosmetic bag, or to create an unusual wrapping for soap.

YOU WILL NEED

❀ Embroidery materials as listed on page 106

❀ 2-in. (5-cm) and 3¼-in. (8-cm) wide 26-count evenweave linen band with scalloped edges, the required length plus ¾ in. (2 cm)

❀ Matching sewing thread or coordinating ribbon

1 Fold the linen band in half lengthwise and baste along the foldline to mark the horizontal center. Work the border, referring to the appropriate chart (below) and the color key on page 106.

2 Use two strands of floss for cross stitch and one strand for backstitch. Working each stitch over two linen threads, stitch as many repeats as needed, following the black repeat lines on the appropriate chart.

3 When the work is complete, take it out of the hoop and press it lightly. Press in ⅜ in. (1 cm) at each end. Slip-stitch it across the front of the bag, or wrap it around a bar of soap and tie it in place with ribbon.

A trellis in shades of green frames tiny lemon and lavender flowers.

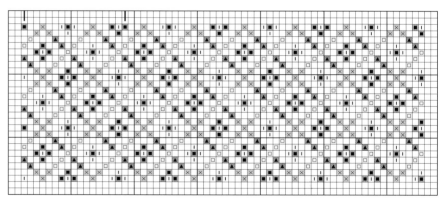

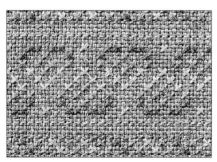

Hearts in soft shades of pink and rose look pretty on a natural linen background.

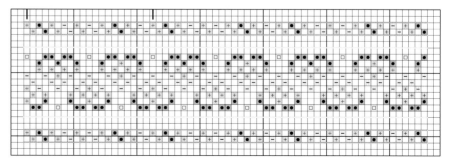

VALENTINES

PHOTO FRAME AND BOX

An extravagant design with pink hearts is used to decorate
a frame for a favorite photo and a satin trinkets box.

YOU WILL NEED

For both items:

❋ DMC stranded floss as listed
in the color key

❋ Tapestry needle, size 26

❋ Thread for basting

❋ Embroidery hoop (see
page 12)

For the frame:

❋ 16-count white aida, the size
of the finished frame plus 2 in.
(5 cm) all around

❋ Materials for making a frame
as listed on page 299

❋ Graph paper and pencil

For the box:

❋ Box with a padded lid for
embroidery (design is
adaptable for different sizes
and shapes of box)

❋ 16-count white aida, the size
of the box lid plus 2 in. (5 cm)
all around

❋ Double-stick tape

COLOR KEY

COLORS		SKEINS
◎	760 Old rose	1
−	761 Light rose	1
+	819 Palest ice pink	1
◼	3712 Coral pink	1
✕	3713 Baby pink	1
Backstitch		
◥	3685 Wine red	1

This pretty frame makes a suitably romantic present for the occasion. A loving word or a name can be backstitched over the hearts, using letters from the chart on page 116. Instructions for making the frame are on pages 299–300 (here the padding has been omitted although you could pad the frame if you wish).

MAKING THE FRAME

1 On the graph paper, copy the letters for the chosen name from the chart on page 116. Overcast the edges of the aida to prevent fraying. Baste two rectangles in the center of the aida to mark the outer and inner edges of the frame. Mount the fabric in the embroidery hoop.

2 Refer to the chart (below) and the color key (opposite) to cross-stitch the design. Use one strand of floss and stitch over one thread block. Start at the top left-hand corner of the outer basted rectangle, and fill the area between the basted rectangles, repeating the design as required at the right-hand and lower edge.

3 When all the cross stitch is complete, backstitch the lettering, using two strands of floss. Take the finished piece out of the hoop and press lightly on the wrong side. Make the frame as described on pages 299–300.

Cross stitch worked on alternating blocks forms a gingham effect.

The elaborate scrolled letters are worked in backstitch over the cross-stitched hearts.

WORKING THE BOX LID

1 Overcast the edges of the aida to prevent fraying. Baste a rectangle in the center of the aida to mark the outer edge of the padded box lid insert. Mount it in the embroidery hoop.

2 Referring to the chart (above) and the color key (opposite), cross-stitch the design using one strand of floss. Work each stitch over one thread block, and start at the top left-hand corner of the basted rectangle. Repeat the design widthwise and lengthwise if necessary to fill the lid area.

3 When the work is complete, remove it from the hoop and press lightly on the wrong side. Trim the edges ⅝ in. (1.5 cm) outside the stitching. Remove the padded insert and cover it neatly, securing the fabric edges on the underside with double-stick tape. Replace the pad in the lid.

HEART PLACE SET

Designed for a romantic dinner, this charming place set features scattered hearts and a subtle coordinating pearl cotton edging. The place mat, like the padded heart frame shown on page 112, features the word "amour"; but this time the letters are worked in stem stitch rather than backstitch to create a heavier line.

The place mat and the napkin are worked on gleaming white Hardanger fabric. The finished mat measures about 16½ x 12 in. (42 x 30 cm) and the napkin is 12 in. (30 cm) square.

The larger heart, which overlaps a small one, is worked in old rose, with highlights stitched in baby pink.

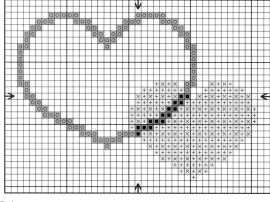

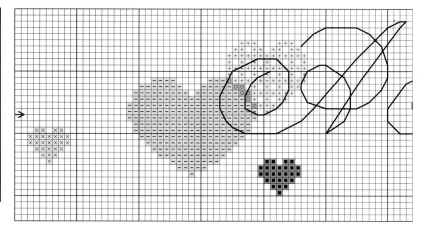

114

The lettering on the Hardanger place mat is worked in stem stitch.

THE PLACE MAT

1 Mark the center of the horizontal part of the design (right-hand arrow) with a line of basting 4¼ in. (11 cm) above the bottom edge of the fabric. Mark the center of the vertical part with basting, the same distance from the right-hand edge. Overcast the raw edges, and mount the fabric in the embroidery hoop.

2 Cross-stitch the design from the center out, referring to the chart (below) and the color key (opposite). Use one strand of floss and work each stitch over one pair of fabric threads. When the cross stitch is complete, stem-stitch the letters using two strands of floss and work each stitch over two pairs of fabric threads.

3 Take the finished piece out of the hoop and press it lightly on the wrong side. Press ⅜ in. (1 cm) then 1¼ in. (3 cm) to the wrong side all around, mitering the corners, as described on pages 277–278. Baste in place, close to the inner edge. Set the machine to a medium-width zigzag. Lay the pearl cotton on the right side of the mat, just outside basting, and stitch in place, holding thread taut, securing hem at same time; overlap thread ends neatly for about ½ in. (1 cm).

THE NAPKIN

Overcast the fabric edges to prevent fraying. Baste lines to mark the horizontal and vertical centers of the design 3½ in. (9 cm) in from two adjacent edges. Mount the work in the hoop.

Work the design as in step **2** (left), but omit the lettering. Remove the fabric from the hoop and press lightly on the wrong side. Follow step **3** (below left) to make the hem, but press ⅜ in. (1 cm) then ⅝ in. (1.5 cm) to the wrong side.

The napkin has a large heart outline overlapping a smaller heart.

VALENTINE

A single initial worked over hearts makes a very special valentine. Select the letter from the chart (below right), and draw it on the hearts chart (below).

YOU WILL NEED

❋ A blank greeting card designed for embroidery

❋ A square of 16-count white aida

❋ DMC stranded floss as listed in the color key on page 114 (except 3713 baby pink)

❋ Tapestry needle, size 26

❋ Thread for basting

❋ Double-stick tape

---

1 Overcast the edges of the aida fabric to prevent fraying. Mark the center of the aida with two lines of basting.

2 Referring to the chart (below) and the color key on page 114, work the design from the center out. Use one strand for cross stitch and two for backstitch.

3 When the embroidery is complete, remove it from the hoop and press lightly on the wrong side. Insert the stitched piece in the greeting card following the instructions given on pages 293–294.

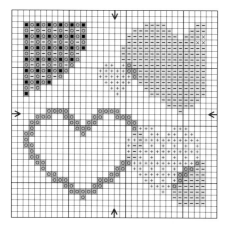

HEARTS AND CROSSES

THESE ELEGANT VELVET-BACKED STITCHING
ACCESSORIES WERE INSPIRED BY
VICTORIAN VALENTINES.

For both items:

- ❋ DMC stranded floss as listed in the color key
- ❋ Tapestry needle, size 26
- ❋ Embroidery hoop (see page 12)
- ❋ Sewing needle and thread for basting and hand-stitching
- ❋ Sewing machine

For the wallet:

- ❋ 28-count cream evenweave fabric, 18 x 15 in. (46 x 38 cm)
- ❋ 14¼ x 11½ in. (36 x 29 cm) of dark lilac velvet
- ❋ 1 yd. (1 m) of ⅜-in. (1-cm) wide velvet ribbon

For the pincushion:

- ❋ 28-count cream evenweave fabric, 6 in. (15 cm) square
- ❋ Two 5-in. (12.5-cm) squares of crimson velvet
- ❋ Batting
- ❋ ⅝ yd. (50 cm) fine cord

COLOR KEY

COLORS	SKEINS
Cross stitch	
◤ 553 Dark lilac	1
⊟ 554 Pale lilac	1
■ 601 Dark pink	1
U 603 Medium pink	1
+ 605 Pale pink	1
H 993 Pale aqua	1
◉ 3814 Dark aqua	1
Straight stitch and backstitch	
◣ 553 Dark lilac	
◤ 554 Pale lilac	
◣ 601 Dark pink	
◣ 603 Medium pink	
◣ 993 Pale aqua	
◣ 3814 Dark aqua	
Interweaving threads	
◣ 553 Dark lilac	
◣ 601 Dark pink	
Drawn threads	
▦ Remove two threads	

EMBROIDERY SET

The embroidery wallet and matching pincushion feature dainty drawnthread borders to reveal the rich velvet beneath, and interwoven threads for added textural interest.

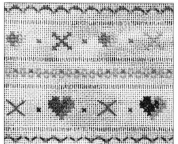

On the second and sixth borders below the top, interweaving threads link the cross stitches. Working from the right side, slip the threads behind the crosses.

MAKING THE WALLET

1. Baste a 13½ x 10¾ in. (34 x 27 cm) rectangle, in the center of the evenweave. Overcast edges and mount fabric in hoop.

2. Working from the top left corner of the chart (opposite), work the design parallel to the long edges, ⅜ in. (1 cm) in from the basting all around; repeat as required. One square on the chart represents two fabric threads. Use two strands of floss throughout. Cross-stitch and backstitch over two threads; straight-stitch over the number of threads indicated on the chart.

3 Work the section of chart given, turn it upside down, and work the section between the arrows again, omitting the band between the red lines. On the second and sixth borders down, work the cross stitches first, then add the interweaving threads.

4 When the stitching is complete, pull out a row of two threads, indicated by the beige squares on the chart, gently lifting each in turn with the tapestry needle. Press the work from the wrong side.

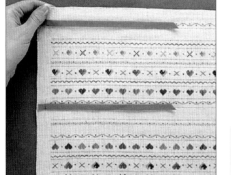

5 Trim the fabric ³⁄₈ in. (1 cm) outside the basting. Cut the ribbon into four pieces. Baste two pieces to each side edge, 1¹⁄₂ in. (4 cm) and 6 in. (15 cm) down from the top. ▲

6 Placing right sides together, stitch the velvet to the linen, taking a ³⁄₈ in. (1 cm) seam allowance and leaving a gap to turn through. Trim the corners and turn right side out. Slip-stitch the opening closed, and press the work lightly.

7 Fold up 4 in. (10 cm) along the lower edge to make the pocket. Slip-stitch the side edges together, and machine-stitch down the pocket 3¹⁄₄ in. (8.5 cm) in from each side edge to subdivide it. Trim the ribbon ends diagonally.

MAKING THE PINCUSHION

1 Mark the center of the evenweave fabric. Working outward from the center, pull out pairs of threads to make nine 1-in. (2.5-cm) squares. Pull out pairs of outer threads to make a border. ➤

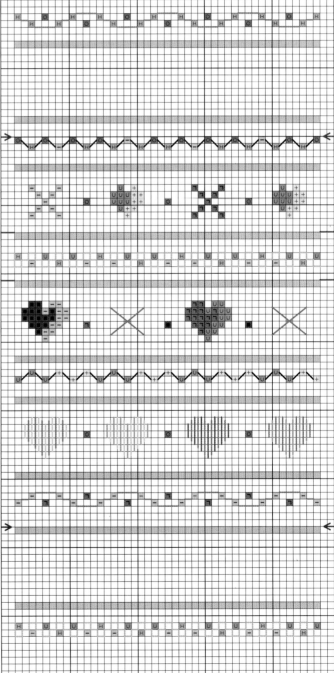

2 As in Making the Wallet, step **2** (opposite), stitch a motif at the center of each square. Trim to 5-in. (12.5-cm) square. Baste a velvet square, right side up, behind it. Make the pincushion as in step **6** (left), adding batting. Sew on cord.

119

HEART NEEDLECASE

The needlecase is decorated with border designs from the chart on page 119 to complete the stitchery set. The needles are stored inside the case on a felt heart with pinked edges.

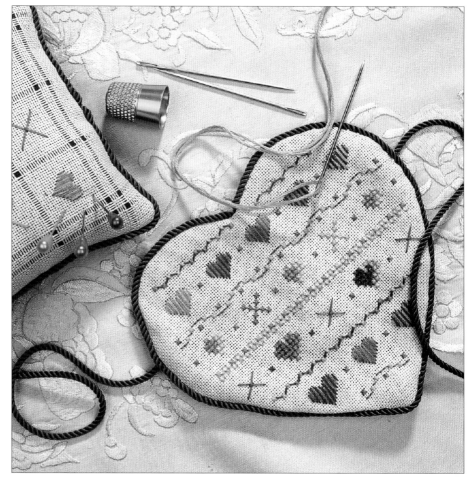

YOU WILL NEED

* 28-count cream evenweave fabric, 8 in. (20 cm) square
* DMC stranded floss as listed in the color key on page 118
* Velvet and felt, 6-in. (15-cm) square of each
* 1 3/8 yd. (1.2 m) fine cord
* Tapestry needle, size 26
* Sewing needle and thread for basting and hand-stitching
* Tracing paper and pencil
* Pinking shears
* Embroidery hoop (optional; see page 12)

1 Fold the tracing paper in half, and trace the half heart outline (below), with the fold aligned between the top indent and the bottom point. Turn over the tracing, and trace the other half of the heart. Using the tracing as a template, baste the heart outline onto the evenweave fabric.

2 Following Making the Wallet, step **2**, page 118, work the bands of your choice across the heart, 3/8 in. (1 cm) inside the basting.

3 Press the finished work, and trim it 3/8 in. (1 cm) outside the basting. Cut a heart the same size from the velvet. Then use the pinking shears to cut a felt heart, 3/4 in. (2 cm) smaller all around. Stitch the velvet and linen hearts together as in Making the Wallet, step **6** page 119.

4 Hand-stitch the felt heart to the velvet side of the needlecase, stitching through the velvet only. Snip a stitch at each side edge, and slip in the ends of 12-in. (30-cm) long cord ties. Stitch cord around the edges, catching in the ends of the ties as you work.

For the straight-stitched hearts, make the stitches over the number of threads indicated on the chart, taking care to keep the stitching tension even.

BRIGHT IDEAS

SCISSORS FOB

This embroidered, velvet-backed fob is a stylish way to identify your own embroidery scissors in a class or workshop. Choose a motif and border from the chart on page 119, and follow the instructions for the pincushion. Make a small tassel and cord from embroidery floss (see pages 313–314). Sew the tassel to one corner and the cord to the opposite corner.

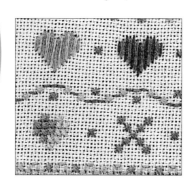

STAINED GLASS

REPEAT DESIGNS AND RADIANT
COLORS INSPIRED BY STAINED-GLASS
WINDOWS SHOW UP TO GREAT EFFECT
AGAINST BLACK FABRIC.

STORAGE BOX

A trio of bright panels based on stained glass makes a stunning cover for a practical box.

The glorious colors of the thread —ruby red, sapphire blue, jade green, and golden topaz—gleam against the black background fabric. Narrow unstitched borders outline the colored areas, imitating the leading between the glass pieces in stained-glass windows.

The stitched area of the design measures 11½ x 6¾ in. (29.5 x 17 cm). The box shown here is specially made for embroidery; but if you cannot get one like it, you could use an ordinary box, adding a layer of batting, or simply frame the design (see pages 297–298).

YOU WILL NEED

✸ Box with 17¾ x 14¼-in. (45 x 36-cm) padded lid

✸ 28-count black evenweave fabric, 24 x 20 in. (61 x 51 cm)

✸ DMC stranded floss as listed in the color key

✸ Tapestry needle, size 26

✸ Thread for basting

✸ Rectangular embroidery frame

✸ Staple gun and staples or tacks and hammer

COLOR KEY

COLORS		SKEINS
◎	321 Red	1
▲	743 Gold	1
⊟	798 Blue	1
⊠	3812 Green	1

1 Mark the center of the fabric with basting, and overcast around the raw edges to prevent fraying. Mount the fabric on the embroidery frame.

2 The chart (opposite and below) shows the lower half of the design. Cross-stitch this half first, working from the center out. Use two strands of floss and refer to the color key (opposite). Each square on the chart represents one stitch worked over two fabric threads.

3 When the lower half of the design is complete, rotate the chart 180 degrees to work the upper half of the design. Take the finished work off the frame, and press it lightly on the wrong side.

4 Take the padded top off the box lid, and center the fabric over it. Pull the edges firmly to the underside, smoothing out any wrinkles and keeping the design centered. Pleat the excess fabric neatly at the corners and tack or staple the edges to the underside. Reassemble the lid.

At the center of the side panels two red shield shapes overlap against a background of sapphire blue.

A narrow border of unstitched black fabric surrounds each colored area to imitate the leading in stained glass.

BRIGHT IDEAS

CLEVER COIN PURSE

Experiment by rotating and repeating an area of the design to create a kaleidoscope effect. The corners from the main panel on the box are repeated in a square on the front of this purse, cleverly incorporating the flap. To make a flap-style bag, see pages 291–292.

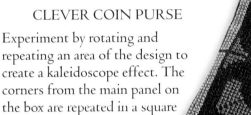

COVER STORY

Smarten up a favorite old book with a bright new cover featuring a variation on the stained-glass panel. The stitched area of the design is 7 x 4¼ in. (17.5 x 11 cm). To work out how much fabric is needed, see the instructions on pages 301–302.

YOU WILL NEED

* Hardcover book to cover
* 28-count black evenweave fabric of the required size
* DMC stranded floss as listed in the color key on page 122
* Tapestry needle, size 26
* Sewing needle and thread for basting and stitching
* Embroidery hoop (see page 12)
* Lining fabric
* Lightweight cardboard and batting
* Glue

1 Overcast the fabric edges. Measure the book's height and total width (including the spine). Baste a rectangle this size in the center of the fabric. Baste a line to mark the inner edge of the front cover, then two lines for the center of the front cover.

2 Cross-stitch the top half of the design from the center out, referring to the chart (left) and the color key on page 122. Stitch over two fabric threads using two strands of floss.

3 When the top half of the design is complete, rotate the chart 180 degrees and work the bottom half. Remove the work from the hoop and press it lightly. Make the book cover as described on pages 301–302.

CANDY BANDS

IMAGES OF COLORFULLY
WRAPPED CANDIES WILL
BRIGHTEN UP A USEFUL
STATIONERY SET.

LETTER RACK AND PENCIL HOLDER

Letters, envelopes, pencils, pens, and rulers need never be lost again with these cheerfully decorated containers.

YOU WILL NEED

- ❈ 14-count royal blue aida, 28 x 20 in. (71 x 50 cm)
- ❈ DMC stranded rayon and cotton floss as listed in the color key
- ❈ Tapestry needle, size 26
- ❈ Thread for basting
- ❈ ½ yd. (40 cm) of 36-in. (90-cm) wide contrasting fabric for lining
- ❈ Embroidery hoop (see page 12)
- ❈ Materials to make the desk set as listed on pages 303–304, except for the furnishing fabric

COLOR KEY

COLORS		SKEINS
◉	30552 Dark purple	1
▣	30553 Purple	1
⊟	30554 Lilac	1
▲	30601 Bright pink	1
△	30602 Candy pink	1
Ⓝ	30603 Light rose	1
⊞	30726 Lemon	1
⊡	30746 Palest yellow	1
◎	30913 Spearmint	1
☑	30955 Pale spearmint	1
☒	30964 Aqua	1
⊟	33820 Old gold	1

Backstitch (cotton floss)

◩	310 Black	1

In this unusual design, the candies are stitched mainly in shiny rayon thread, which catches the light to imitate cellophane and foil wrappers. Black backstitching outlines the shapes and adds details to the satin-stitched twists at the ends of the wrappers. (Stranded cotton floss can be used instead of rayon, if desired.) Both the letter rack and pencil holder are lined with a contrasting silk fabric. The stitched design is 2¼ in. (6 cm) deep and each repeat is 8¾ in. (22 cm) long.

LETTER RACK

1 Cut a 26 x 10-in. (66 x 25-cm) piece of aida and overcast the edges to prevent fraying. With the short edges at the sides, baste the horizontal center 2½ in. (6.5 cm) above the lower edge, then baste the vertical center in the usual way.

2 Work the design from the center out, referring to the chart (below right) and the color key (left). Use two strands of thread for cross stitch and one strand for backstitch. Work each stitch over one block. Satin-stitch the twisted wrapper ends using two strands of two of the shades used for the candy.

3 Repeat the design as required to fit the fabric width, finishing with a complete candy, 1 in. (2.5 cm) in from the side edges. When the work is complete, remove it from the hoop and press it gently on the wrong side.

4 Make the letter rack following the instructions on pages 303–304; center the fusing web when fusing onto the stitched fabric, use contrasting fabric for the lining and omit the stands.

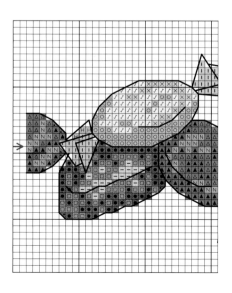

PENCIL HOLDER

Cut a 14½ x 8-in. (37 x 20-cm) piece of aida and overcast the edges to prevent fraying. With the short edges at the sides, baste the horizontal center of the design 2½ in (6.5 cm) above the lower edge; fold the fabric in half vertically and baste along the foldline to mark the vertical center.

Stitch the design and make the pencil holder as for Letter Rack, steps **2–4** (opposite).

The twisted wrapper ends are satin-stitched using two shades of the candy color. Start near the twist with the deeper shade, blending into the lighter shade toward the edge.

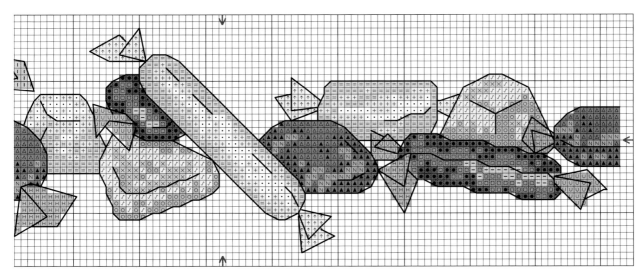

NOTEBOOK, RULER, AND CLIP

A handful of candies brightens up a notebook cover and ruler, and a single candy makes a fun trim for a paper clip. The design on the notebook is 4 x 2¾ in. (10 x 7 cm). The special ruler and clips are available through needlework stores or by mail order.

STITCHING THE RULER

1 Mark the center of the Hardanger fabric with basting and overcast the edges. Mount the fabric in the embroidery hoop. Mark the horizontal centers of the top two and the lower two candies on the chart (right).

2 Following Letter Rack, step **2** on page 126, stitch the top two candies to the right of the center line. Rotate the chart 180 degrees and work the other two candies to the left of the center line. Remove the work from the hoop and press lightly on the wrong side. Trim the fabric to fit, and insert in the ruler.

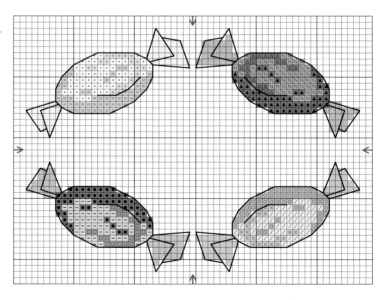

MAKING THE NOTEBOOK

1 Cut out the aida to fit the book following the instructions on page 301. Baste a rectangle to mark the area of the front cover. Overcast the edges, and mark the center of the front cover rectangle with basting.

2 With the shorter edges of the basted rectangle at either side, work the design as in Letter Rack, step **2** on page 126 but referring to the chart above. When complete, assemble the cover following the instructions on pages 301–302.

ALL THAT JAZZ

STRIKE A STYLISH CHORD WITH THESE
MUSICAL MOTIFS, WHICH ARE IDEAL
FOR TRIMMING A RANGE OF ACCESSORIES.

JAZZ IT UP

These lively musical motifs, with their muted wood and brass tones, show up best on rich, vibrant fabrics and can be used to embellish a host of ready-made items.

YOU WILL NEED

* Items to embroider
* DMC stranded floss as listed in the color key
* 14-count waste canvas, 6 in. (15 cm) square
* Crewel needle, size 9
* Sewing needle and thread for basting
* Tweezers
* Embroidery hoop (optional; see page 12)

COLOR KEY

COLORS	SKEINS
☐ Blanc	1
▦ 351 Coral	1
▦ 742 Gold	1
▦ 743 Yellow	1
☐ 745 Pale yellow	1
▦ 913 Green	1
☐ 955 Pale green	1
▦ 996 Blue	1
▦ 3830 Rust	1

Backstitch

◪ Blanc

You can achieve different effects by stitching the motifs in cool white on a rich blue background, or in warm yellows on a vibrant red background.

If you are stumped for a gift idea for a musical friend, these unusual motifs, showing a double bass, trumpet, saxophone, and notes, could help you to find the answer. The motifs can be stitched onto any ready-made item from plain cotton socks to silk shorts or scarves.

If you decide to use a silk item, take extra care handling the fabric. First, mount the fabric in an embroidery hoop. Baste on the waste canvas using a very sharp, fine needle to avoid snagging or leaving holes in the silk, and follow the instructions on pages 23–24. Water can leave marks on silk, so try to dampen the waste canvas only slightly when you are removing it.

STITCHING THE DESIGNS

1 For each motif cut the waste canvas into 3-in. (7.5-cm) squares. Fold each square in half both ways, and mark the center with basting stitches. Baste the canvas in place on the item you wish to stitch.

2 Work the design from the center out. Use three strands of floss for cross stitch and two strands for backstitch, and work over one pair of threads. When the design is complete, remove the basting stitches.

3 Dampen the canvas slightly with a cloth. Remove the waste canvas threads carefully with tweezers. Press the design with a warm iron on the wrong side.

For the double bass greeting card (page 132), you can create a realistic effect by using single strands of floss as the strings. Make single long stitches, allowing them to lie loosely against the cross stitch.

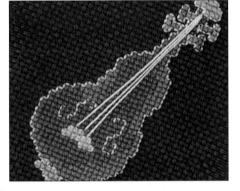

If you plan to stitch the umbrella, remember that the design should be upright when the umbrella is open.

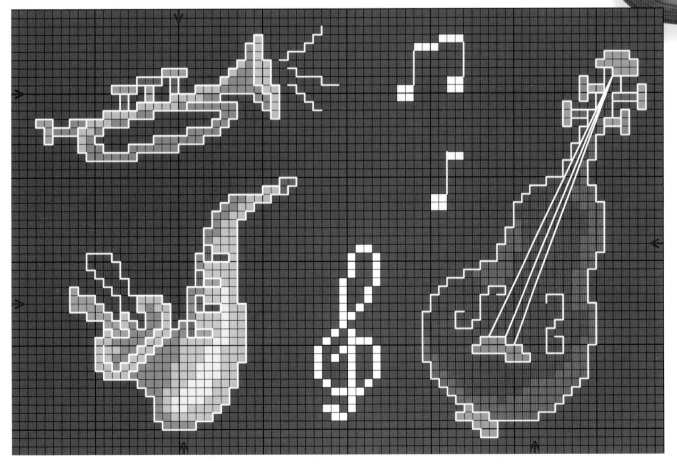

GREETING CARDS

For a greeting card that is ideal for a musically minded friend, stitch the instruments directly onto a small piece of brightly colored Hardanger. For a small motif, work the design over a single pair of Hardanger threads. For a larger motif, try working the same design over two pairs of threads—as illustrated by the saxophone (left).

Mount the embroideries directly onto interesting textured papers for an expensive-looking result—make sure that the paper is firm enough to support the embroidery. Special papers are available from stationers and art supply stores.

YOU WILL NEED

* ❀ 22-count Hardanger, 6¼ in. (16 cm) square
* ❀ DMC stranded floss as in color key on page 130
* ❀ Textured paper, approximately 8½ x 11 in. (22 x 28 cm)
* ❀ Tapestry needle, size 26
* ❀ Thread for basting
* ❀ Embroidery hoop (optional; see page 12)
* ❀ Fusible or fabric glue

1 Fold the Hardanger in half both ways and baste down the foldlines. Mount in the embroidery hoop if using one.

2 Work the design from center outward, using two strands of floss for cross stitch and one strand for backstitch.

3 Press design on wrong side. Trim embroidery into a rectangle with a ½-in. (12-mm) border all around. Remove threads round the edges with needle to make a ¼-in. (6-mm) fringe.

4 Fold paper in half and tear the paper along the fold. Fold in half again. Fix embroidery to paper with fusible or fabric glue.

BRIGHT IDEAS

JAZZY SOCKS

Brighten up plain socks with eighth notes or a treble clef. For the effect shown here, use a dark pair of socks, a square of 14-count waste canvas, a size 9 crewel needle and 5283 (silver) DMC stranded floss. Baste the canvas in place, then stitch the motif using three strands of floss over one pair of threads.

FESTIVE FUN

CHRISTMAS MOTIFS, WORKED
IN BANDS OR USED ALONE, ADD A TOUCH
OF SEASONAL SPARKLE TO GREETING CARDS
AND A CAKE.

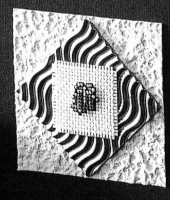

CHRISTMAS CARDS

Handmade greeting cards carry a special message. Position bands of glittering motifs behind cut-out shapes for cards with a personal touch.

YOU WILL NEED

For each card:

❊ 18-count aida in red or green, 8 x 6 in. (20 x 15 cm)

❊ DMC stranded floss, one skein of each color listed in the color key

❊ DMC Art. 278 metallic threads, one spool of each color listed in the color key

❊ DMC Art. 317 metallic thread, one skein of 5282, gold

❊ Tapestry needle, size 26

❊ Thread for basting

❊ Embroidery hoop (see page 12)

❊ Colored card stock or stiff paper, 13½ x 7 in. (34.5 x 18 cm)

❊ Tracing paper

❊ Utility knife, metal ruler, and pencil

❊ Double-stick tape

COLOR KEY

COLORS

☐ 351 Deep coral

▣ 435 Dark tan

Tweeded

⊟ 340/4012 Lilac/purple metallic

☒ 666/4015 Red/red metallic

◤ 699/4057 Dark green/green metallic

◎ 702/4052 Medium green/lime metallic

⊡ 742/5282 Tangerine/gold metallic

⊞ 744/5282 Yellow/gold metallic

Backstitch

◧ 310 Black

Choose from two cut-out shapes—with the Christmas tree, the motifs look like Christmas-tree ornaments; with the domed shape, they resemble patterns on a stained-glass window. The designs use ordinary cross stitch and "tweeded" cross stitches—these are worked with two strands of floss and a strand of metallic thread to add sparkle.

For the card blanks, most art supply stores carry a huge range of attractive papers and card stock. The cards shown here are worked on red and green aida to complement the traditional Christmas color scheme, but either design looks just as good set against crisp white aida, as you can see in the picture on page 133.

134

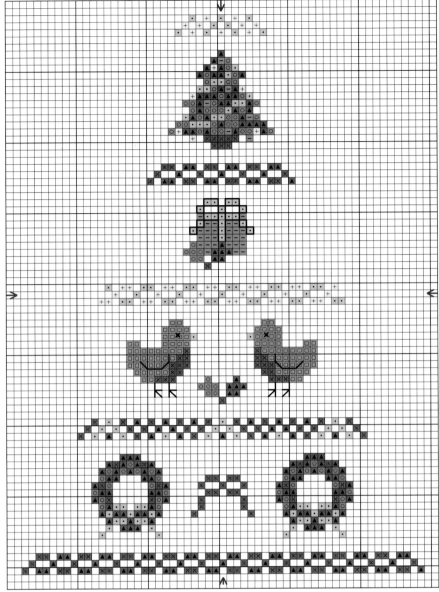

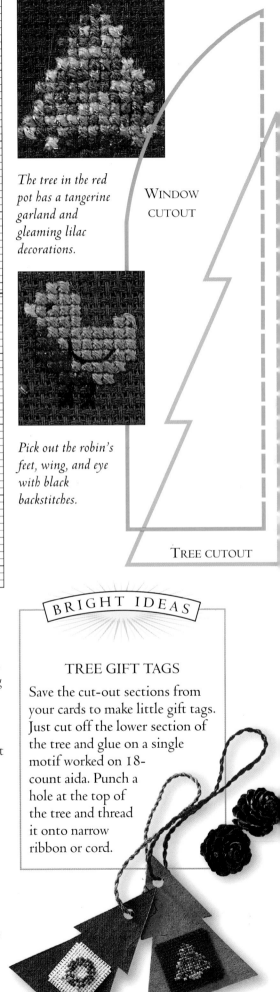

The tree in the red pot has a tangerine garland and gleaming lilac decorations.

WINDOW CUTOUT

Pick out the robin's feet, wing, and eye with black backstitches.

TREE CUTOUT

MAKING THE GREETING CARDS

1 Mark the center of the aida with basting, overcast the edges and mount it in the embroidery hoop. Refer to the color key (opposite), and either the chart above for the tree design or the chart on page 137 for the window design. Each square on the charts represents one stitch worked over one thread block.

2 Work from the center out. For the cross stitches, use two strands of embroidery floss; for the tweeded cross stitches, use two strands of floss plus one strand of metallic thread. Use one strand of black for the backstitching. When the work is complete, remove it from the hoop and press lightly from the wrong side.

3 Fold the card 4½ in. (11.5 cm) in from the short edges to make a double-fold card. Fold the tracing paper in half, and trace the appropriate template with the fold on the dashed line. Cut out, unfold, and use as a pattern to cut the opening. Position the base of the tree 1⅜ in. (3.5 cm) above the base of the card, and the window ¾ in. (2 cm) above the base of the card. For detailed instructions, see page 293.

4 Trim the aida a little larger all around than the opening, stick it in place, and complete the card. For detailed instructions, refer to page 294.

instructions, see page 293.

page 294.

BRIGHT IDEAS

TREE GIFT TAGS

Save the cut-out sections from your cards to make little gift tags. Just cut off the lower section of the tree and glue on a single motif worked on 18-count aida. Punch a hole at the top of the tree and thread it onto narrow ribbon or cord.

135

MOTIF CARDS

A single festive motif fixed to layered mats of different colored tissue and stiff paper makes a fine focal point on a handmade card. The motifs in the chart (opposite) use the same threads as the tree design on page 135.

MAKING THE CARDS

1 Select a motif from the chart (opposite or on page 135) and mark its center with arrows. Mark the center of the aida.

2 Stitch the motif from the center out, referring to Making the Greeting Cards, steps **1–2** on page 135. Each square on the charts represents one stitch worked over one thread block.

3 Trim the aida all around, six blocks outside the stitching, keeping the design centered. Fray one block of aida all around. Fold the card in half and select the papers for mounting.

4 Cut the papers to shape using sharp scissors or a utility knife and metal rule. For tissue paper mats, outline the shape with a damp paintbrush; tear along the line while it is damp.

5 Arrange all the layers of the mat, centering the larger oblong background mat toward the top of the card; arrange the smaller mats toward the top of the background mat. Use the glue to stick the mats and the stitched motif in place. ▲

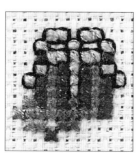

Black backstitched outlines enhance the glittering yellow giftwrap ribbon.

The Christmas holly wreath is dotted with red berries and tied with a shiny tangerine bow.

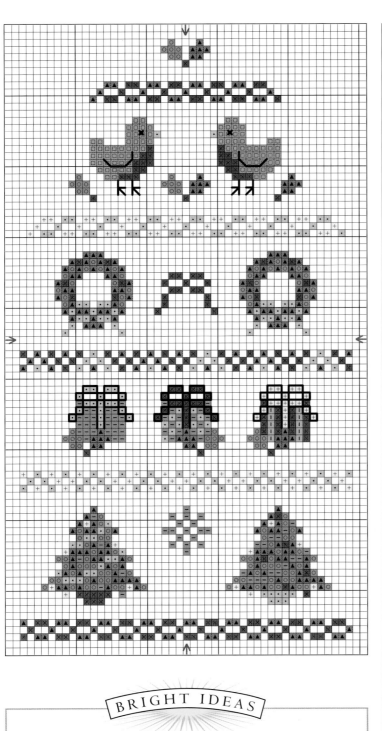

YOU WILL NEED

For each card:

❀ 18-count aida—white, red, or green—3¼ in. (8 cm) square

❀ DMC stranded floss, one skein of each color listed in the color key

❀ DMC Art. 278 metallic threads, one spool of each color listed in the color key

❀ DMC Art. 317 metallic thread, one skein of 5282, gold

❀ Tapestry needle, size 26

❀ Sewing needle and thread for basting

❀ Colored card stock, 8¼ x 6 in. (21 x 15 cm)

❀ Scraps of stiff paper and tissues

❀ Utility knife, glue, metal ruler, pencil

❀ Watercolor brush (optional)

COLOR KEY

COLORS

I	351 Deep coral
▣	435 Dark tan

Tweeded

−	340/4012 Lilac/purple metallic
⊠	666/4015 Red/red metallic
▲	699/4057 Dark green/green metallic
◉	702/4052 Medium green/lime metallic
·	742/5282 Tangerine/gold metallic
+	744/5282 Yellow/gold metallic

Backstitch

◤	310 Black

BRIGHT IDEAS

NOEL NAME LABELS

Distinctive place-setting labels add a personal touch to the Christmas table. Stitch the motifs as for the cards (opposite). Cut 3⅜ x 2¾ in. (8.5 x 7 cm) pieces of card stock or stiff paper, and fold them in half lengthwise. Glue the motif to one end of the label, and write the guest's name beside it.

CHRISTMAS CAKE BAND

A traditional English yuletide treat—a rich fruitcake covered with royal icing and wrapped in ribbon—is given extra class with a cross-stitched band.

YOU WILL NEED

* 14-count aida band, (2½ in. (6.5 cm) wide, to fit around the cake plus 1½ in. (4 cm)
* DMC stranded floss, one skein each as listed in the color key
* DMC Art. 278 metallic thread, one spool of each color listed in the color key
* DMC Art. 317 metallic thread, one skein of 5282, gold
* Tapestry needle, size 26
* Thread for basting

COLOR KEY

COLORS

☐ 435 Dark tan

Tweeded

⊟ 340/4012 Lilac/purple metallic

☒ 666/4015 Red/red metallic

▲ 699/4057 Dark green/green metallic

◯ 702/4052 Medium green/lime metallic

• 742/5282 Tangerine/gold metallic

+ 744/5282 Yellow/gold metallic

Backstitch

◥ 310 Black

1 Mark the center of the aida band with basting. Referring to the chart (below) and the color key (right), work the design from the center outward. Each square on the chart represents one stitch worked over one thread block.

3 When the work is complete, press it lightly from the wrong side. Finish the ends of the band and press ¾ in. (2 cm) to the wrong side at one end. Wrap the band around the cake, lapping the pressed-in end over the other end; pin it in place.

2 Cross-stitch using two strands of floss; for the tweeded cross stitches use two strands of floss plus one of metallic. Use one strand of black for the backstitching. Repeat the design as many times as required.

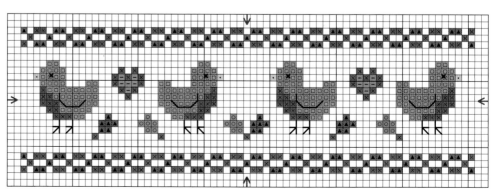

138

CHRISTMAS MOTIFS

TRADITIONAL DESIGNS
STITCHED IN RICH, GLOWING
COLORS LOOK GREAT
ON DECORATIONS TO HANG
FROM A TREE, IVY BRANCHES
OR A MANTELPIECE.

HEARTS AND STOCKINGS

These felt Christmas decorations are quick and easy to make with cross-stitched designs on aida patches—and they will last for years.

YOU WILL NEED

- 14-count green and red aida, 4-in. (10 cm) square for each motif
- DMC stranded floss as listed in the color key
- Felt squares in red and green
- Metallic gold sewing thread
- Ribbon, red and green, 9 in. (23 cm) of ⅛-in. (3-mm) wide for each item
- Polyester stuffing for hearts
- Tapestry needle, size 26
- Sewing needle and thread for basting
- Sharp scissors
- Pinking shears

COLOR KEY

COLORS	SKEINS
− Blanc	1
321 Red	1
415 Gray	1
• 699 Dark green	1
T 701 Medium green	1
Z 703 Spring green	1
▲ 740 Bright tangerine	1
U 741 Tangerine	1
743 Yellow	1
816 Wine	1
O 3705 Strawberry	1
Backstitch	
∇ 310 Black	1

The colorful old-style festive motifs are worked on little aida patches and stitched to the hearts and stockings with gleaming gold sewing thread. The felt shapes are cut with pinking shears to give zigzag edges, and are so easy to make that children could stitch their own. There are six designs to choose from—three charts are given opposite, and there are three more on pages 142–143.

The hearts are 3½ in. (9 cm) high, and the stockings are 4¾ in. (12 cm); the templates are given on page 141. One 8½-in. (22-cm) felt square makes two items.

MAKING THE HEARTS

1 Mark the center of the aida with basting. Stitch your chosen motif from the center outward, referring to the color key (left) and the appropriate chart (opposite or on pages 142–143).

2 Use three strands of floss for the cross stitch and one strand for the backstitch. One square on each chart represents one stitch worked over one thread block.

3 When the motif is complete, press the work lightly from the wrong side. Trim the aida three blocks outside the stitching to make a square or rectangular patch.

4 Using the red template (opposite), cut out two felt hearts with the pinking shears; for a green aida patch use red felt, for a red one use green felt.

5 Pin the aida patch to the center of one heart. Using gold metallic thread, stitch all around with running stitches worked two blocks in from the raw edges. Fray the edges of the patch over one thread block. ▲

6 Fold the ribbon into a loop, and sandwich the raw ends between the two hearts at the top indent; pin to hold. Using the metallic gold thread, begin stitching the hearts together with running stitches worked ¼ in. (5 mm) in from the edge; catch in the ribbon ends as you stitch. When the stitching is nearly complete, fill the heart with stuffing, then finish the stitching. ▲

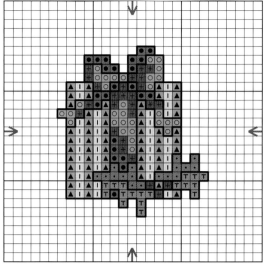

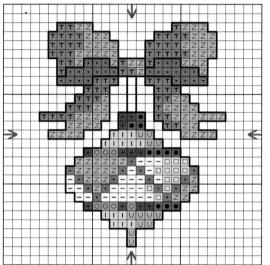

MAKING THE STOCKINGS

Stitch your chosen motif, and trim the aida, following Making the Hearts, steps **1–3** (opposite).

Using the blue template here, cut out two felt stockings with the pinking shears. Make the stocking as for the hearts, steps **5–6** (opposite), but position the loop at the top on the back edge, leave the top edge open, and omit the stuffing.

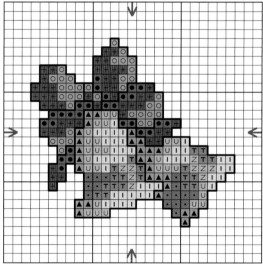

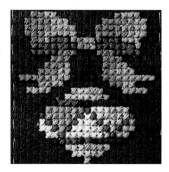

The glass ball is suspended from a bow stitched in three shades of green. Darker shades of floss at the right-hand edge of the ball give it a rounded effect.

141

WHITE AND GOLD SACHETS

Aida patches interwoven with glittering gold threads add a celebratory note to festive motifs. The patches are stitched on enticing little sachets, perfect for Christmas surprises.

The designs shown here use the same threads as the hearts and stockings on pages 140–141, so if you are making those, there is no need to buy any extra skeins. The sachets measure 6 x 3½ in. (15 x 9 cm). To fill the sachets, see page 144.

MAKING THE SACHETS

1 Stitch your chosen design in the center of the aida square, referring to Making the Hearts, steps 1–2 on page 140. When the work is complete, press it lightly from the wrong side. Trim the aida four thread blocks outside the stitching to make either a square or rectangular patch.

2 Place the sachet fabric right side up with the short edges at the top and bottom. Place the top edge of the stitched motif on the fabric, 3½ in. (9 cm) down from the short top edge and centered across the width; pin. ▲

3 Using the metallic gold machine thread, machine stitch the patch in place all around, three squares in from the raw edge. Repeat, stitching next to the first row of stitching.

4 Using a pin or needle, fray the outer two thread blocks on each edge of the patch.

5 Fold the fabric in half widthwise, right sides together, so that the short edges are even. Zigzag stitch the long edges together using the gold metallic machine thread.

6 Turn the sachet right side out and zigzag stitch around the top edge, using the gold metallic machine thread.

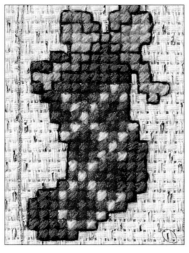

The stocking has a dark green toe, heel, and top, and a festive yellow bow. The leg is stitched in a classic diamond pattern.

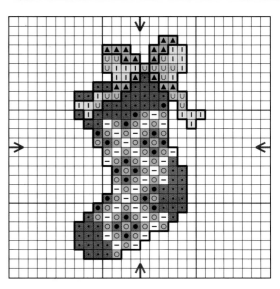

142

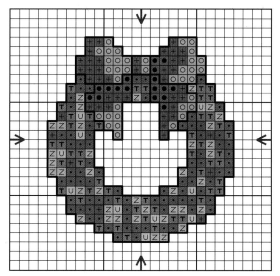

YOU WILL NEED

For each sachet:

* 14-count white and gold aida, one 4 in. (10 cm) square
* DMC stranded floss as listed in the color key on page 140
* Metallic gold machine thread
* Tapestry needle, size 26
* Thread for basting
* Sharp scissors
* Fabric for the sachet, 12½ x 4 in. (32 x 10 cm)
* Ribbon or cord for bow, 20 in. (50 cm)
* Ribbon for loop, 8 in. (20 cm) of ⅛-in. (3-mm) wide
* Sewing machine

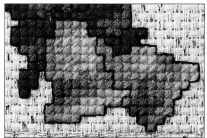

The bells are stitched in yellow and two shades of tangerine to give a rich golden color. Backstitching, worked in a single strand of black, outlines the bells and the bow trim.

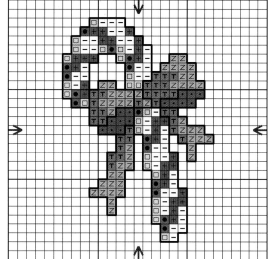

FILLING THE SACHETS

Fill the sachets with Christmas candies or fragrant cinnamon sticks. A single sachet makes a splendid wrapping for a small gift or trinket.

1 Half-fill the sachets with the chosen gifts—it is important not to overfill them, or they will look bulky and shapeless.

2 Fold the narrow ribbon in half, and knot the ends together to make a loop. Thread the ribbon for the bow through the loop and pin the ribbons to the back of the sachet. ▲

3 Secure the ribbons with a couple of stitches at the back, taking care to stitch through the back only, and remove the pin. Tie the ribbon around the neck and fasten it in a bow. Trim the ends of the ribbon at an angle. ▲

BRIGHT IDEAS

CHRISTMAS EXTRAS

For an extra-festive touch, stitch Christmas motifs directly onto glittering aida hearts and stockings. Using the templates on page 141, baste two hearts or stockings onto 14-count white and gold aida. Stitch your favorite motif in the center of one of the shapes. Cut out the shapes with pinking shears, and stitch them together with gold metallic thread, adding a ribbon loop and stuffing if desired.

SNOWMEN

DRESSED IN COLORFUL HATS AND
SCARVES, THESE APPEALING
SNOWMEN WILL ENLIVEN YOUR
CHRISTMAS STOCKINGS AND CARDS.

145

SNOWMAN STOCKING

A smiling snowman pulling a fir tree brings Christmas cheer to a jolly jester stocking.

The snowman is worked on navy Hardanger to form the stocking front, which is trimmed with a red toe cap and a jester border at the top. The stocking back and lining are also made from red fabric. The snowman motif is 5 1/2 in. (14 cm) high, and the stocking is 15 in. (38 cm) from top to bottom.

COLOR KEY

COLORS		SKEINS
•	Blanc	1
■	310 Black	1
▬	434 Golden brown	1
●	498 Wine red	1
▣	666 Bright red	1
▲	699 Dark green	1
◉	701 Medium green	1
❘	742 Orange	1
＋	744 Yellow	1
✕	762 Pale gray	1

Backstitch

◹	310 Black
◹	666 Bright red
◹	701 Medium green
◻	744 Yellow

The fir tree is stitched in two shades of green with black backstitching to outline the shapes of the branches.

STITCHING THE STOCKING

1 Mark the center of the Hardanger with basting, and overcast or zigzag stitch the edges to prevent fraying. Mount the prepared Hardanger in an embroidery hoop.

2 Work the design from the center out, referring to the chart (opposite top) and the color key (left). Use four strands of floss for cross stitch and two strands for backstitch. Work each stitch over three pairs of fabric threads.

3 When the work is complete, remove it from the hoop and press lightly on the wrong side. Trace the stocking template given here. Use a photocopier to enlarge it to twice its size, then cut out the enlargement to make a pattern.

4 Use the pattern to cut out the complete stocking front from the Hardanger, with the snowman centered across the width and its top edge 5 1/4 in. (13 cm) below the top of the pattern.

5 From the red fabric: cut out three complete stocking shapes, two top border pieces, and one toe cap piece; 5/8 in. (1.5 cm) seam allowances are included on all these pieces.

6 Press 5/8 in. (1.5 cm) to the wrong side along the top edge of the toe cap. Baste the toe cap to the toe of the Hardanger piece with the right sides uppermost and the raw edges matching. Stitch it in place along the pressed edge.

7 Place the two red top borders together with right sides facing, and stitch along the pointed edge. Trim and clip the seam, then turn the border right side out and press it. Place the border over the Hardanger piece with the right sides uppermost and top and side edges even. Baste along the sides and the top edge.

The stocking snowman is worked using four strands of floss for the cross stitch.

8 Stitch the Hardanger piece and one red piece together with right sides facing, leaving the top edge open. Stitch the other two red pieces right sides together, leaving the top edge open and a gap on one side edge for turning through.

9 Place the lining inside the Hardanger stocking with right sides together, and stitch around the top edge. Turn right side out through the gap in the lining and hand-stitch the opening. Tuck the lining inside the stocking, press. Sew a double loop of ribbon to the back seam, and sew a bell to each point on the top border.

147

SNOWMEN GREETINGS

YOU WILL NEED

* 18-count navy, bright red, or deep green aida: 6¾ x 6 in. (17 x 15 cm) for each card
* DMC stranded floss as listed in the color key on page 146
* Tapestry needle, size 26
* Thread for basting
* Embroidery hoop (see page 12)
* Greeting card blank or folio
* Double-stick tape
* Cord and tassel trim (optional)

Send Christmas greetings to your family and friends with a jolly snowman card or gift folio. The patches for the three snowmen vary slightly in size, but they are each about 3 ½ x 3 in. (9 x 7.5 cm).

1 Overcast the edges of the aida. Mark the center with basting, and mount the fabric in the hoop.

2 Work your chosen design from the center out, referring to the appropriate chart (below or on page 147), and the color key on page 146. Use two strands of floss for the cross stitch and one for the backstitch. Work each stitch over one thread block.

3 Take the completed work out of the hoop and press it lightly on the wrong side. Stem-stitch a border all around, positioning it five blocks outside the stitching; use two strands of white floss, and work each stitch over two thread blocks.

4 Trim the aida three blocks outside the border, and fray the edges back to the border. Stick the design onto the card or folio with the double-stick tape. Add a cord and tassel trim if desired.

The snowmen are stitched in white with pale gray in the shadow areas to make them look rounded. Black backstitch outlines all the details and forms the lamp holder.

Chapter 4
For Babies and Children

TOY CLOWNS

CUDDLY TOY CLOWNS IN NURSERY
PASTELS ADD PLAYFUL NOTES TO
ACCESSORIES FOR A BABY.

151

BLANKET AND BAG

These appealing clowns embellish a soft blanket and a useful drawstring bag for baby things.

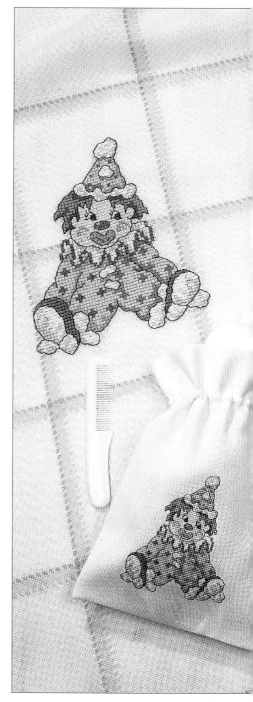

The clown sitting in the center of the blanket is worked in a large size to make a bold, attention-grabbing image. Smaller clowns juggle in the corners—arrange them so that they seem to aim their batons at each other. The sitting clown is 7½ x 6¼ in. (19 x 16 cm), and the juggling clowns are about 5 x 3¼ in. (12.5 x 8 cm). The clown sitting in the center of the little drawstring bag is worked on a smaller scale and measures about 4¼ x 3½ in. (11 x 9 cm).

The finished blanket is 39½ x 34½ in. (100 x 88 cm), including the 2¾-in. (7-cm) self fringe, and the bag is 10 x 6¼ in. (25 x 16 cm).

STITCHING THE BLANKET

1 On the grid-patterned fabric, baste a six- by five-square oblong; leave at least one full row of squares all around the basting. Use basting to mark the centers of the corner squares inside the oblong. Then mark the center of the oblong with 10-in. (25-cm) long vertical and horizontal lines of basting.

2 Mount the central area of the fabric in the hoop with the long edges of the oblong at the sides. Work the sitting clown from the center out, referring to the chart (opposite top) and key (left). Use three strands for cross stitch and two for backstitch, and work each stitch over two fabric threads.

3 In the same way, work one juggling clown in each corner square, referring to the appropriate charts (opposite and on page 154), and the pictures here and on page 151. When the work is complete, take it out of the hoop and press it gently.

4 Make a 2¾-in. (7-cm) basic fringe all around the basted oblong, trimming the fabric as necessary, as shown on page 315.

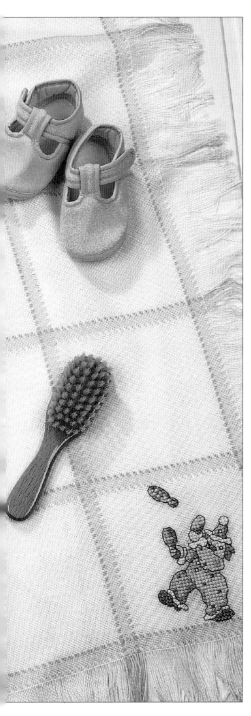

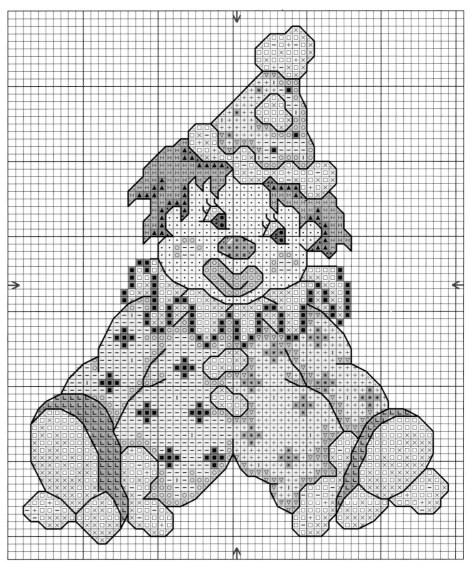

STITCHING THE BAG

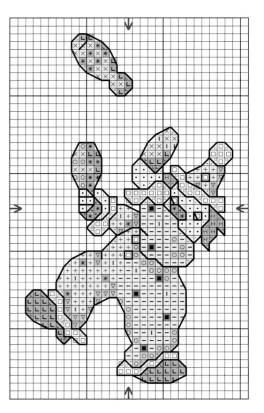

1 Mark the vertical center of one piece of fabric, then mark the horizontal center of the design 3¾ in. (9.5 cm) above the lower edge. Overcast the edges of the fabric, and mount it in the hoop.

2 Work the sitting clown from the center out, referring to the chart (above). Use two strands for cross stitch and one for backstitch. Work each stitch over two fabric threads.

3 Take the finished piece out of the hoop and press it gently. Referring to the instructions on page 284, make the embroidery into a bag with a headed casing; use the other fabric piece for the back and the cord for the drawstring.

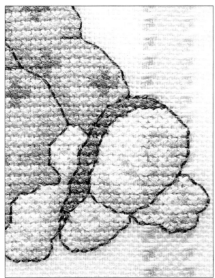

As you stitch over the grid bands, treat each one as two fabric threads.

PLAY BLOCKS

1 Mark the centers of the evenweave fabric squares with basting, and overcast the edges. With the fabric stretched in the hoop, stitch a juggling clown on each piece. Refer to the charts (below and on page 153) and Stitching the Bag, steps **2–3** on page 153. Press gently.

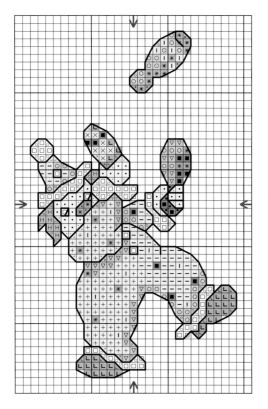

2 Trim the stitched clown pieces to 4¾ in. (12 cm) square with the clowns centered. From each fabric remnant, cut two 4¾-in. (12-cm) squares. Fuse interfacing to the wrong side of all six fabric squares.

3 Stitch the coordinating fabric squares together to form a loop: take ⅜-in. (1-cm) seams, and begin and finish stitching ⅜ in. (1 cm) from the ends of each seam. Press the seams open.

4 Pin, then stitch a clown square to one edge of the coordinating squares, matching the corners and raw edges. Repeat to stitch the other clown square to the other end, but leave one edge open. Trim the seam allowances at the corners to reduce bulk. Turn right side out, fill with stuffing, and slip-stitch the opening.

BRIGHT IDEAS

CLOWN CARD

Welcome a newborn baby to the world with a cute juggling clown card. Stitch the clown on sky blue or pink evenweave fabric as for the play blocks (left), and mount it in a double-fold card with an oval opening. For details see pages 293–294.

FLEXIBLE FRAMES

THESE CHARMING PICTURE FRAMES HAVE
REMOVABLE, STAND-OUT MOTIFS INSPIRED
BY CHILDREN'S FAVORITE TOYS.

CHECKERED FRAME

The basic frame can be decorated with as many motifs as you wish, or you can leave it plain.

The chart for the frame shows one half of the design. Rotate the chart 180 degrees to stitch the second half. The finished frame measures approximately 7¼ x 5 in. (18.5 x 13 cm) with a 5 x 2¾-in. (13 x 7-cm) opening.

STITCHING THE FRAME

1 Cut an 8¼ x 6-in. (21 x 15-cm) piece of canvas; mark the vertical/horizontal center. From here, count out to the center of one inner edge of the chart (below), and begin working the patterned area, following the color key (left) and using two strands of floss.

2 After working the patterned area, stitch the inner and outer borders. When the design is complete, trim the plastic canvas, leaving one row of unworked holes around the inner and outer edges of the stitching.

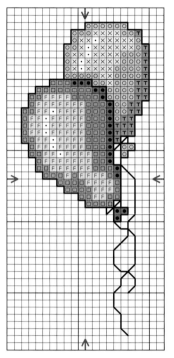

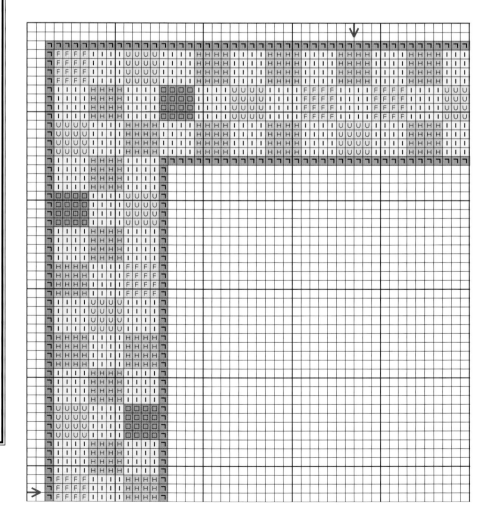

STITCHING THE MOTIFS

1 Cut the plastic canvas to required size for the motif: rag doll, 4 x 3½ in. (10 x 9 cm); each flower, 2 x 1½ in. (5 x 4 cm); and the balloons, 4 x 2 in. (10 x 5 cm).

2 Mark the center of the canvas. Work from the center outward, referring to the appropriate chart and the color key (opposite). Use two strands of floss for cross stitch and one for backstitch. When motif is finished, trim edges, leaving one row of unworked holes outside the stitching.

When you are cutting out the balloons, leave the plastic canvas intact between the strings on the tails, so that they don't become too fragile.

157

TRELLIS FRAME

COLOR KEY

For the toy motifs:

COLORS		SKEINS
⊡	Blanc	1
◼	310 Black	1
T	350 Rust red	1
O	352 Coral	1
N	414 Dark gray	1
S	415 Light gray	1
Z	435 Tan	1
⅂	701 Dark green	1
H	703 Medium green	1
U	725 Bright yellow	1
I	727 Pale yellow	1
◖	796 Royal blue	1
▣	798 French blue	1
F	809 Medium blue	1
–	948 Peachy cream	1

Backstitch

◣	310 Black

The trellis frame is decorated with a diamond trellis pattern and has toy soldier, train, and kite motifs. The frame could be left plain or decorated with any combination of motifs—including those from the checkered frame on pages 156–157.

For the frame and motifs on the charts (below and opposite), you will need the materials listed on page 156, and the stranded embroidery floss in the color keys (left and below).

For the trellis frame:

COLORS		SKEINS
⊡	Blanc	1
U	725 Bright yellow	1
I	727 Pale yellow	1
▣	798 French blue	1
F	809 Medium blue	1

STITCHING THE FRAME

Cut an 8¼ x 6-in. (21 x 15-cm) piece of plastic canvas and mark the vertical and horizontal center. Count out from the center to the center of one inner edge of the frame. Begin working the patterned area, referring to the chart (below) and the color key (left). Use two strands of floss. The chart shows one half of the design; rotate it 180 degrees to work the other half.

STITCHING THE MOTIFS

Cut the plastic canvas to the required size: soldier, 6¼ x 2¼ in. (16 x 6 cm); train, 4 x 2¼ in. (10 x 6 cm); and kite, 4 x 2 in. (10 x 5 cm). Stitch the motifs in the same way as the motifs on pages 156–157.

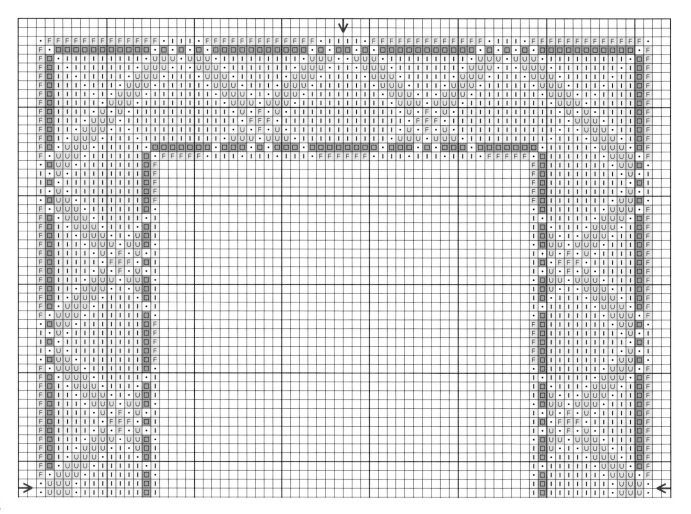

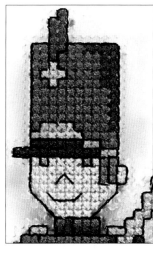

The toy soldier stands
smartly to attention,
supporting the barrel of his
rifle over his left shoulder.
Fill in the cross-stitch areas
first, then add the backstitch
outlines and facial details in
one strand of black.

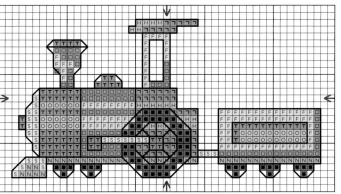

Streaks of paler
green, blue, and
red along the sides
of the locomotive
suggest the gleaming
bodywork of a brand-
new toy train.

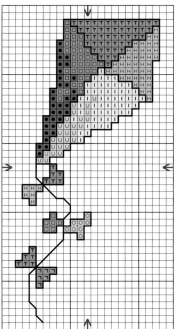

159

MAKING THE FRAME

Follow the steps below to mount the stitched frames and motifs onto foam board, and to make a stand for the frame. The foam board gives the plastic canvas extra body and allows the toys to stand proud of the frame, giving them a three-dimensional look. Foam board is a lightweight material formed from two layers of stiff paper with a layer of polystyrene between. It is sold in art supply stores.

1 From the foam board: cut a 7¼ x 5-in. (18.5 x 12.5-cm) mount with a 5¼ x 3-in. (13.5 x 7.5-cm) opening; for the backing, cut a rectangle the same size; for the stand, trace the template (right) and use it to cut a stand.

2 Butt the short top edges of the mat and backing together and join with masking tape to make a hinge. Use double-stick tape on the side edges to join the front and back of the frame.

3 Cut the stand along the dashed line through one layer of paper and the polystyrene filling, and trim this from the flap to leave just one layer of paper. Fold back the flap and, using double-stick tape, stick it to the center of the backing card with the sloping edge at the base. ▲

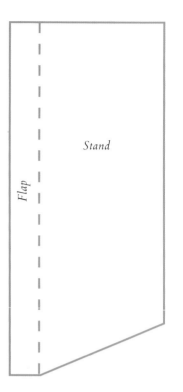

Stand

Flap

ADDING THE MOTIFS

Using double-stick tape, attach blocks of foam board to the wrong side of the motifs. Stick double-stick tape to the other side of the foam board, and attach the motifs to the frames.

Cross stitch the doll's hair in tan floss and work her hair ribbon in royal blue. Lines of backstitching in black suggest her part and the locks of hair falling over her forehead.

LEARNING TO COUNT

FAMILIES OF FRIENDLY FARMYARD ANIMALS ARE
FUN FOR CHILDREN TO COUNT IN THIS
COLORFUL CLOTH BOOK.

CLOTH BOOK

Work some animal magic on the pages of this cute, washable counting book.

This practical cloth book is worked on five separate pieces of fabric. The largest design forms the outside front and back cover, and the other pages—numbers two through five—are worked on smaller pieces of fabric.

The pages are stitched together back to back and then folded in half to make the book shape. Green running stitches worked between the cross stitch and the overcasting holds the two layers together. The book measures 6¾ x 5½ in. (17 x 14 cm).

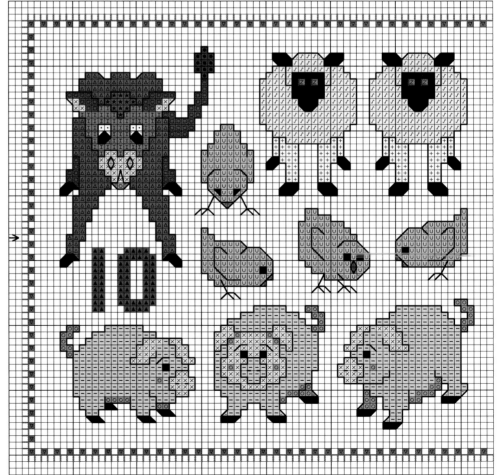

STITCHING THE PAGES

1 If you wish to change the wording, work out the new wording on the graph paper, referring to the alphabet chart on pages 164–165. Use the charts given here as a guide to space and position the letters.

2 Mark the center of each aida piece with basting. Overcast the edges, and mount the fabric in the embroidery hoop.

3 Cross-stitch each design from the center out, referring to the color key (opposite) and the appropriate chart. Use two strands of floss for cross stitch and three strands for curly cross stitch. Work each stitch over one thread block.

4 Work the design for the cover (below) on the larger piece of aida and the other designs on the smaller pieces. The smaller designs will look off-center when stitched, as extra fabric is allowed at one edge.

5 When the cross stitch is complete, backstitch using two strands, with the following exceptions: use one strand for the black backstitching and three strands of 963 (creamy pink) for the large sheep's mouth on the chart on page 165; use four strands of white to highlight the large hen's eyes on the chart on page 166. Do not backstitch the green border.

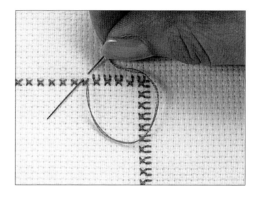

6 When the design is complete, use two strands of 701 (green) to overcast the edges just outside the green cross-stitched border; extend the stitching across the horizontal break in the top and bottom borders, as indicated on the chart (below). ▲

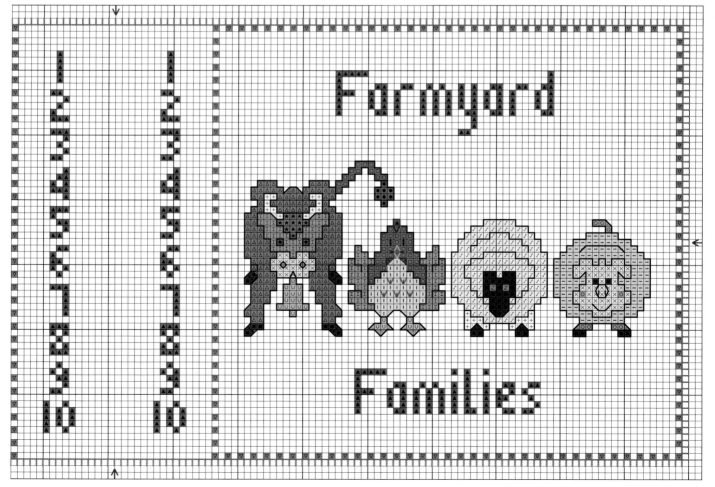

JOINING UP

1 Lay the cover wrong side up. Place page 2 (2 cows) wrong side down on the left of the cover, and page 5 (5 hens) wrong side down on the right; match the green cross-stitched borders. You may need to trim the inner edges of pages 2 and 5 so that they don't overlap.

2 Using two strands of 701 (green) join the pages with running stitch. Work over one thread block through the holes between the border and the overcasting, extending the stitching across the horizontal break in the top and bottom borders. Work with a stabbing motion.

3 Still using 701 (green) stitch back again through the same holes to create an unbroken row of stitching.

4 Place pages 3 and 4 together with wrong sides facing and borders matching. Join them following steps 2–3 (above) but stitch around only the three edges with the border.

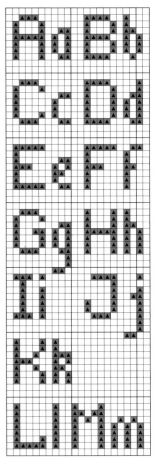

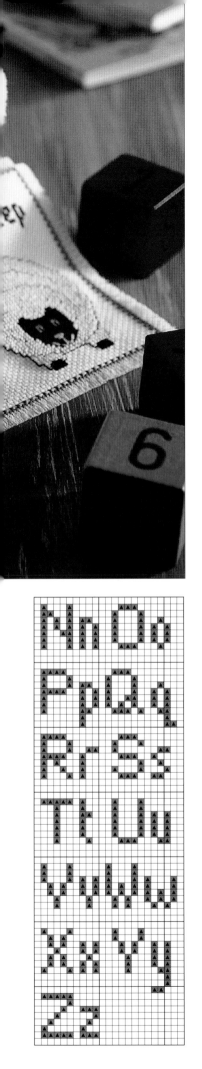

FINISHING

1 Trim each set of pages three blocks outside the border stitching, and fringe the edges.

2 Fold the book cover in half down the center, and press the fold. Slip the center pages inside, and trim the inner edges if necessary.

3 Pin the pages together. Then machine-stitch through all the layers, 1 in. (2.5 cm) from the folded edge.

The golden yellow chicks have beaks worked in dark tan fractional (three-quarter) cross stitches with black backstitched outlines.

PIG CARD

For the pig card you will need a double-fold card with a circular opening about 2¾ in. (7 cm) in diameter, a 4-in. (10-cm) square of 18-count aida, and appropriate colors of stranded embroidery floss as listed in the color key on page 162.

Mark the center of the large pig on the chart on page 165. Stitch it, referring to Stitching the Pages, steps **3** and **5** on page 163. Press the work on the wrong side with a warm iron. Mount the pig in the card, referring to page 294.

TEDDY PARADE

CUDDLY TEDDIES
ENHANCE A TOWEL,
WASHCLOTH, AND
BATHROBE. THE THEME
CONTINUES WITH A TEDDY
CARD TO STITCH.

TEDDIES ON TERRY CLOTH

Bathtime will become a high spot of the day
with these lovable teddy motifs and border
trims on bathrobe, towel, and washcloth.

The super-soft towel has a large teddy sporting a smart yellow and green checked bow tie and matching foot pads. The small teddy motif on the washcloth has bow tie and foot pads worked in two shades of green. Both motifs are worked over waste canvas, which is removed with tweezers when the stitching is complete. The large teddy is 3 ½ x 3 ¼ in. (9 x 8 cm), and the small teddy is 2 x 1 ½ in. (5 x 4 cm). The terry-cloth robe with aida borders around the hood and cuffs is specially made for cross-stitch designs. If you cannot find one of this type, use an ordinary bathrobe with a hood, and sew on separate aida bands as described on page 231.

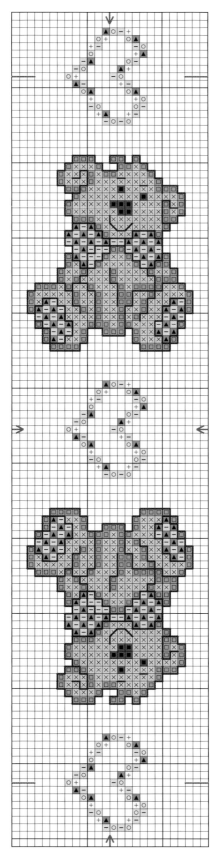

STITCHING THE TOWEL

1 Cut a 4¾-in. (12-cm) square of waste canvas and mark the center with basting. Baste the canvas in the desired position on the towel and mount the work in the hoop.

2 Work the large teddy motif from the center outward, referring to the chart (below) and the color key (left). One square on the chart represents one stitch. Use three strands of floss for the cross stitch and one for the backstitch. Work each stitch over one pair of threads.

3 When the stitching is complete, dampen the canvas and remove the canvas threads with tweezers. For detailed instructions in using waste canvas, see pages 23–24.

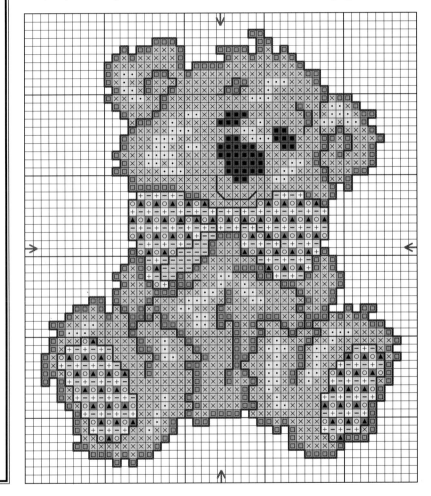

STITCHING THE WASHCLOTH

Cut a 3¼-in. (8-cm) square of waste canvas, and mark the center with basting. Baste the canvas diagonally near a corner of the washcloth. Refer to the chart on page 170, and stitch referring to Stitching the Towel, steps **2–3** (above).

STITCHING THE ROBE BORDERS

1 Mark the center of the aida borders on the hood and sleeves (or separate bands) with basting. Begin stitching the border design on the hood; work from the center outward, and refer to the chart (opposite) and the color key (above). Use two strands for cross stitch, one for backstitch.

2 Work each stitch over one thread block. Repeat the motifs as indicated by the red lines, working as many repeats as required to fill the aida bands on the hood and sleeves, or the separate aida bands.

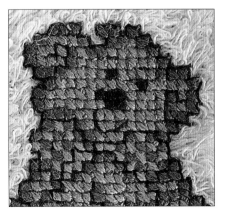

On the small teddy, bright and soft green stitches alternate to form the checked bow tie. Backstitch the mouth and the outlines with a single strand of brown floss.

TARTAN TEDDY CARD

YOU WILL NEED

- ✱ 14-count white aida, 4 in. (10 cm) square
- ✱ DMC stranded floss as listed in the color key
- ✱ Tapestry needle, size 26
- ✱ Double-fold card with a 2¼-in. (6-cm) opening
- ✱ Double-stick tape
- ✱ Sewing needle and thread for basting

COLOR KEY

COLORS	SKEINS
■ 300 Brown	1
□ 435 Tan	1
⊠ 437 Dark sand	1
▲ 911 Bright green	1
– 954 Soft green	1

Backstitch

◣ 300 Brown

BRIGHT IDEAS

TEDDY PAJAMAS

Stitch a large teddy on tartan pajamas in the same way as the one on the towel. Just select a suitable plain area on the pajamas and baste the waste canvas in place. The finished motif measures 3½ x 3¼ in. (9 x 8 cm).

1 Mark the center of the aida with basting. Cross-stitch the design from the center out, following the chart (right) and referring to the color key (above). Use two strands of floss for cross stitch and one for backstitch. Work each stitch over one thread block.

2 Work the main dark sand areas first, then add the tan stitching and the brown facial details. Finally, stitch the bow tie and foot pads in bright green and soft green. When complete, backstitch the outlines using one strand of brown floss.

3 Press the work on the wrong side. Center it behind the opening and stick it in place with double-stick tape. Fold the backing flap over the back of the fabric and stick it in place.

COUNTING SHEEP

IMAGES OF BROWSING AND FROLICKING WOOLLY
SHEEP ARE APPROPRIATE FOR THE BEDROOM—FUN
FOR CHILDREN AND FOR ADULTS, TOO.

The sheep's wool is stitched in two shades of pearl gray and white with curly backstitched spirals.

BED LINEN SET

Counting sheep at bedtime is fun with this coordinating sheet and pillowcase.

Stitched over waste canvas, two sheep motifs line up to make a border along the edge of the sheet. The cross stitch is worked with three strands of floss, though to cover very dark fabrics you may need to use four strands—if you are not sure, work a test area first.

A jumping sheep, without the fence, decorates a corner of the pillow sham. To position the motif on a plain pillowcase, measure from one corner. On a pillow sham, measure from the inner corner of the flange.

The standing sheep is 4 x 2¾ in. (10 x 7 cm); the jumping sheep with the fence is about 4 in. (10 cm) square.

STITCHING THE SHEET

1 Mark the center of the waste canvas pieces. Center one small piece at the top of the sheet, on the right side, with its center 1½ in. (4 cm) above the hem stitching. Baste it in place.

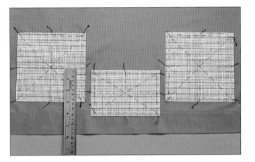

2 On each side, baste a large piece, then a small piece of waste canvas. Space them out so the centers are 6 in. (15 cm) apart; position the small pieces at the same level as the center piece and the larger pieces with their centers 4 in. (10 cm) above the hem stitching. ▲

3 With the work mounted in the hoop, stitch the standing sheep on the small pieces of canvas. Position them so that the feet point toward the hem—when the sheet is turned down, the design will be the right way up.

4 Work from the center out, referring to the standing sheep chart on page 174 and the color key (opposite). Use three strands of floss for cross stitch and two for backstitch; work each stitch over one pair of canvas threads.

5 In the same way, stitch the leaping sheep and their fences on the large pieces of canvas, referring to the chart (below). When the work is complete, dampen the waste canvas and remove the threads with tweezers. Press the work lightly from the wrong side.

The head is stitched in pearl gray with light pewter shadows. Dark pewter backstitches outline the details.

STITCHING THE PILLOWCASE

1 Mark the center of the waste canvas with basting. Baste it diagonally across one top corner of the pillowcase, positioned so that the center is about 8 in. (20 cm) in from the corner.

2 Mark the center of the sheep on the chart (above). Referring to your marked center, stitch the sheep only, following Stitching the Sheet, steps **4–5** (above).

BLANKET AND CUSHION

Snuggle up with this waffle fabric blanket and cushion, decorated with large sheep. The sheep are stitched from the same charts as the smaller ones on the bed linen (see page 173 and below), but they are worked in thicker pearl cottons and with large stitches on waffle fabric for a bold effect. The squares of the fabric are used as a stitch guide, so the size of the sheep depends upon the size and dimensions of the waffle squares. On this fabric, there are about five squares to 1 in. (2.5 cm). The sheep measure about 8 x 5½ in. (20 x 14 cm). The finished blanket is 79 x 59 in. (200 x 150 cm) and the cushion cover measures about 16½ in. (42 cm) square.

MAKING THE BLANKET

1 Mark the center of the blanket fabric with basting and mount it in the embroidery hoop. Begin working the design from the center out, referring to the standing sheep chart (below) and the color key (left).

2 Use pearl cotton for the cross stitch, and work each stitch over one square of the waffle fabric. When the cross stitch is complete, work the backstitch using two strands of the floss, again worked over one waffle square.

3 When you have finished working the sheep design, remove the work from the embroidery hoop. Press the work lightly from the wrong side with a warm iron, taking care not to crush the stitching.

4 Press ⅜ in. (1 cm) then ⅝ in. (1.5 cm) to the wrong side all around the blanket, forming miters at the corners. For detailed instructions see page 280. Baste, then machine-stitch the hem in place.

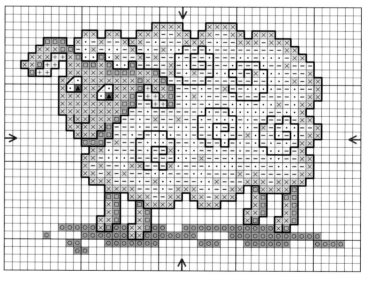

MAKING THE CUSHION COVER

1 Cut an 18-in. (46-cm) square from one end of the fabric for the cover front. Cut the remaining fabric in half widthwise to make two pieces for the cover back. Mark the center of the front piece with basting and overcast the edges to prevent fraying.

2 Mark the center of the sheep on the chart on page 173. Mount the fabric in the hoop. Referring to the newly marked center and the color key (above left), begin working the design from the center out, following Making the Blanket, step **2** (above).

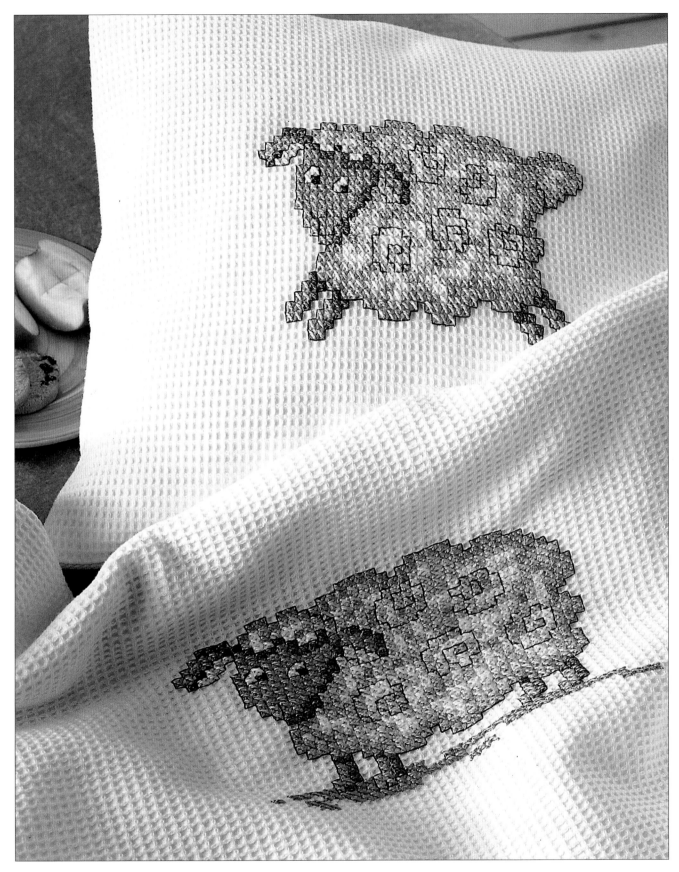

3 Remove the work from the hoop and press it lightly on the wrong side. On the cut edges of each back piece, press in and stitch a double ⅝-in. (1.5-cm) hem. Assemble the cushion cover with a simple overlapped back, referring to the instructions on page 307.

The waffle fabric, with its bubble-like surface, adds extra texture to the sheep's cross-stitched wool, which is further enhanced by the sheen of the pearl cottons.

175

SHEEP PIN

This little lamb, cross-stitched on vinyl canvas, makes a cute brooch. The lamb is cut out after stitching. When finished, it measures 2¼ in. (6 cm) from ear to tail and is about 1½ in. (4 cm) tall.

YOU WILL NEED

* 14-count vinyl canvas, 3 x 2 in. (8 x 5 cm)
* DMC stranded floss as listed in the color key
* Sewing needle, white thread, and thread for basting
* Jewelry pin
* Tapestry needle, size 26
* Permanent marker

COLOR KEY

COLORS		SKEINS
·	Blanc	1
▲	413 Dark pewter	1
✕	415 Pearl gray	1
Backstitch		
◹	413 Dark pewter	

1 Mark the center of the vinyl canvas with the permanent marker. Referring to the chart (right) and the color key (above), begin working the design from the center out.

2 Use two strands of floss for the cross stitch and one for the backstitch; work each stitch over one canvas block. Work the cross stitch first, then the backstitch.

3 When the work is complete, trim it to one row of holes outside the stitching. Sew the pin to the wrong side.

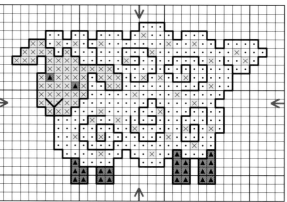

TELLING THE TIME

A CLOCK WALL HANGING
AND A STITCHED CLOCK
FACE MAKE IT FUN TO
TELL THE TIME—AND THE
SUN MOTIF BRIGHTENS UP
POCKETS AND A COAT HOOK.

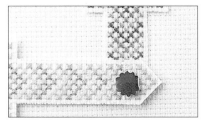

The hands swivel on a paper fastener so they can be moved to set the time wherever you like.

SET-THE-TIME CLOCK

This colorful wall hanging with its big clock face and four pockets will help any child to learn to tell the time.

MAKING THE WALL HANGING

1 From the aida: cut a 14-in. (35-cm) square for the clock face and five 8-in. (20-cm) squares: four for the pocket panels and one for the hands.

2 Mount the fabric in the hoop. Stitch the clock face, pocket panels, and hands from the center out, referring to the appropriate charts (on pages 179, 180, and 181) and the color key (left). Each square on the chart represents one stitch worked over one thread block. Use three strands of floss for cross stitch and two for backstitch.

3 Press the completed pieces on the wrong side. Trim the clock face to 10¼ in. (26 cm) square, and pocket panels to 5⅛ in. (13 cm) square.

4 Center the interfacing on the wrong side of the clock face. Fold the edges of the aida to the back; baste in place.

5 From the contrasting fabric: cut a backing panel to same size as main fabric, three 8 x 6-in. (20 x 15-cm) rectangles for the tabs, a 14¼ x 6¼-in. (36 x 16-cm) rectangle for the lower border, and four 6-in. (15-cm) squares for the pockets.

6 Press in ⅝ in. (1.5 cm) around each pocket panel. Center the panels on the pockets and topstitch in place. Zigzag-stitch (or blanket-stitch) along the top edge of each pocket; press under ⅝ in. (1.5 cm) around each edge.

7 Stitch the clock face to the main fabric 2½ in. (6.5 cm) down from the top and in from the sides. Stitch the top pockets 1½ in. (4 cm) below the clock face and 2 in. (5 cm) in from the sides. Stitch the lower pockets ¾ in. (2 cm) below the top ones. Make the tabs and baste them to the right side of the top edge with raw edges even; see pages 311–312.

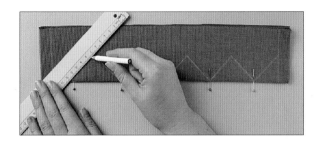

8 Placing right sides together, fold lower border in half lengthwise. Mark five 1¾-in. (4.5-cm) deep V shapes with the points on the fold; allow ⅝-in. (1.5-cm) seams at each side. Stitch along marked line and side edges. Trim ⅜ in. (1 cm) below stitching. Turn right side out and press. Baste to lower edge of main panel as for tabs. ▲

9 Lay out the main fabric, right side up. Position the backing panel, right side down, on top, sandwiching the tabs and lower border between the two pieces. Stitch all around the edges, leaving an opening in one side to turn through. Turn the wall hanging right side out and press it. Slip-stitch the opening closed. Cover the buttons following instructions on package, and complete the tabs as shown in Pointed Tab Heading, step 7 (see page 312).

10 Glue the card stock to the wrong side of the stitched hands. Using utility knife and ruler, cut out the hands one thread block outside the stitching. Attach a grommet to the inner end of each hand, three blocks in on the little hand, and seven blocks in on the big hand. Attach the hands through the center of the clock with a paper fastener.

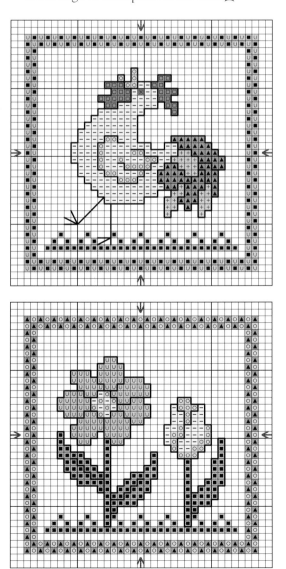

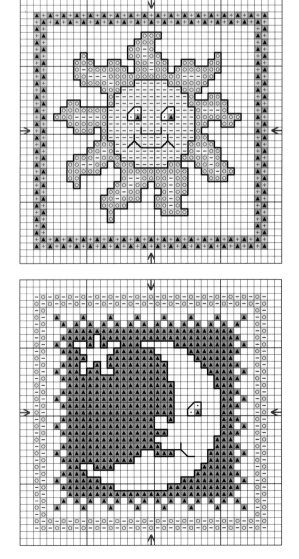

CLOCK FACE AND PICTURES

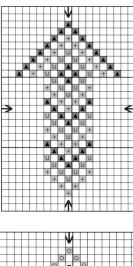

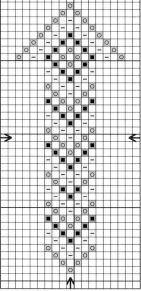

STITCHING THE CLOCK FACE

1 Mark the center of the aida with basting and mount it in the hoop. Work from the center out, referring to the chart (opposite) and the color key (on page 178). One square on the chart represents one thread block. Use two strands for cross stitch and one for backstitch.

2 Carefully count out from the center to find the position of 12; stitch this number first. Next stitch the 3, 6, and 9, then the rest of the numbers. To complete the clock face, stitch the corner borders. Stitch the sun motif in the same way, following the chart on page 179.

3 Gently press the completed pieces from the wrong side with a warm iron. Iron the interfacing to the wrong side of each piece over the back of the stitching, first cutting the clock interfacing to fit six blocks outside the stitching.

4 Trim the clock face eight blocks outside the corner borders and fray two blocks around the edge. Trim the sun motif one block outside the stitching. Remove the clock hands, make a small hole at the center of the aida, and glue the panel to the clock. Replace the hands, then glue the sun motif in place.

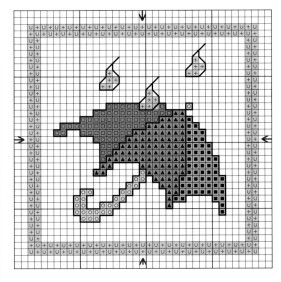
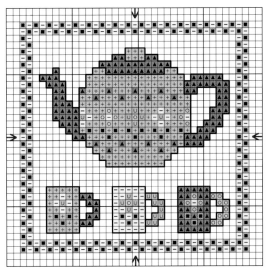

MAKING THE PICTURES

Work the pictures in the same way as step **I** (opposite) but refer to the appropriate chart (above). When work is complete, remove it from the hoop and press lightly on the wrong side. Take the pictures to a professional to be framed or follow the instructions on pages 297–298.

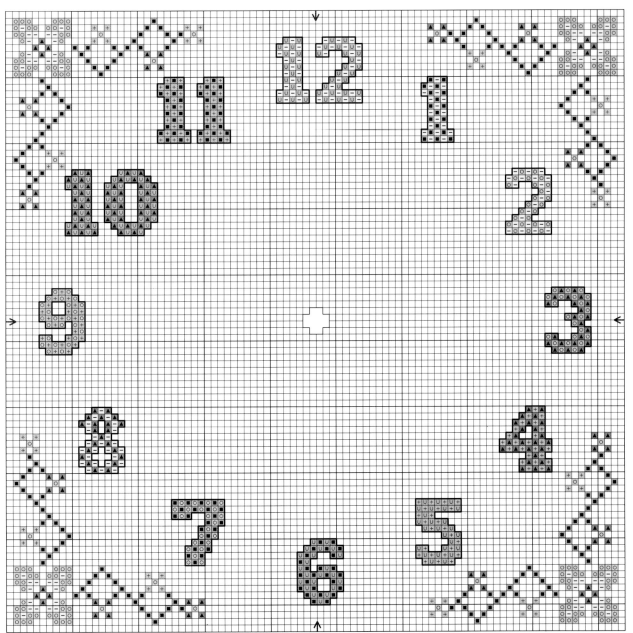

COAT HOOKS

This name panel with its smiling sun motif will delight any child. The fabric amount given is long enough for a six- to eight-letter name; for longer names add ¾ in. (2 cm) for each extra letter.

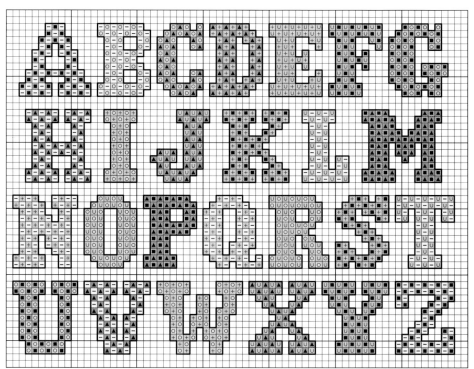

1 Using the letters from the chart, draw the name, square by square, on the graph paper. Allow one empty square between each letter. Establish the vertical center of the name, then move it 1 in. (2.5 cm) to the left to allow for the sun motif. Mark the horizontal center.

2 Mark the center of the aida with basting, and mount it in the embroidery hoop. Work the name from the marked center out, referring to your paper plan, the chart (below), and the color key (page 178). Each square on the chart represents one thread block. Use two strands for cross stitch and one for backstitch.

3 Count out sixteen squares to the left of the first letter of the name; this is the center of the sun. Work the sun, referring to the chart (page 179), the color key (page 178), and the stitching instructions (above). Remove from the hoop and press on the wrong side. Apply interfacing to the wrong side. Cut out one block outside the sun and three blocks outside the name. Stick in place with the tape.

YOU WILL NEED

* 14-count pale yellow aida, 11 x 6 in. (27 x 15 cm)
* DMC stranded floss as listed in the color key on page 178
* Tapestry needle, size 26
* Thread for basting
* Graph paper and pencil
* Iron-on interfacing
* Embroidery hoop (see page 12)
* Wooden coat-hook rail
* Double-stick tape

The shining sun has a smiling face outlined in black backstitch. The sun's rays are stitched in pale tangerine and yellow.

YOUNG GARDENERS

PERKY GARDEN BADGES AND MOTIFS LOOK GREAT ON STURDY WORKWEAR FOR BUDDING GARDENERS.

GARDEN CLOTHES MOTIFS

Encourage a child's passion for gardening with these fun motifs—potted sunflowers, a pail and trowel, and a watering can.

YOU WILL NEED

For all items:

* ❋ Child's garment
* ❋ DMC stranded floss as listed in the color key
* ❋ Crewel needle, size 6
* ❋ Thread for basting
* ❋ Embroidery hoop (see page 12)
* ❋ Pins
* ❋ Tweezers

For the potted sunflowers:

* ❋ 10-count waste canvas, 5 x 4 in. (13 x 10 cm)

For the pail and trowel:

* ❋ 10-count waste canvas, 4½ x 4 in. (11 x 10 cm)

For the watering-can patch:

* ❋ 12-count waste canvas, 5 x 4 in. (13 x 10 cm)
* ❋ Gingham fabric, 5 in. (13 cm) square

COLOR KEY

COLORS	SKEINS
◆ 300 Brown	1
＋ 402 Peach	1
∩ 414 Medium gray	1
✕ 415 Light gray	1
▲ 699 Emerald green	1
▣ 702 Grass green	1
▬ 704 Lime green	1
Ⅰ 742 Orange	1
• 744 Yellow	1
↑ 762 Pale silver	1
◎ 3776 Ginger	1

Backstitch

◣ 300 Brown	
◣ 890 Dark green	1

It's easy to stitch these jolly motifs directly onto children's workwear using waste canvas. When the cross-stitch design is complete, the waste canvas threads are removed, leaving just the motif on the garment. On very tough fabrics and areas that are awkward to get at, such as pants knees, it is easier to work the motif on a colorful patch, and then stitch the patch to the garment (as was done for the watering-can patch, above). For more details on using waste canvas, see pages 23–24.

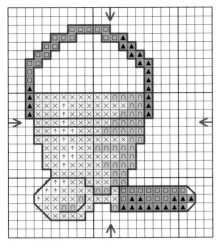

Work the pail and trowel motif in the same way as the potted sunflowers.

POTTED SUNFLOWERS, PAIL, AND TROWEL

1 Mark the center of the waste canvas and baste it squarely to the garment at the desired position, (see page 23).

2 Work the motif from the center outward, referring to the color key (opposite) and the appropriate chart (above or right). Cross-stitch with four strands of floss and work each stitch over one pair of threads.

3 Backstitch with two strands. When the design is complete, dampen the waste canvas and remove it with tweezers.

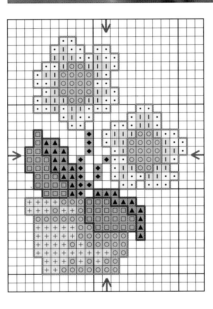

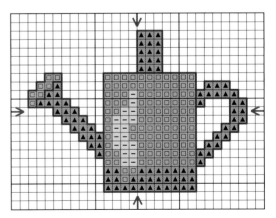

WATERING-CAN PATCH

1 Mark the center of the waste canvas and baste it diagonally to the center of the gingham fabric. Stitch the watering-can motif as for Potted Sunflowers, steps **2–3** (above), but use three strands for the cross stitch and two for the backstitch. Remove the waste canvas.

2 Press ⅜ in (1 cm) to the wrong side all around, following the lines of the gingham. Pin the patch diagonally to the garment at the desired position.

3 Using six strands of 702 (grass green), stitch the patch close to the edges all around with running stitches. Use the gingham squares as a guide to keep the stitches even.

185

YOU WILL NEED

For all items:

❋ DMC stranded floss as listed in the color key on page 184, except 414, 415, and 762

❋ Permanent marker

❋ Sharp scissors

❋ Sewing needle and thread

❋ Jewelry pin finding or small safety pin (optional)

For the sunflower:

❋ 7-count green plastic canvas, 5 x 3 in. (13 x 8 cm)

❋ Tapestry needle, size 22

For the snail:

❋ 7-count green plastic canvas, 4½ x 3 in. (12 x 8 cm)

❋ Tapestry needle, size 22

For the watering can:

❋ 14-count plastic canvas, 3 in. (8 cm) square

❋ Tapestry needle, size 26

Work the watering-can badge as for the sunflower and snail badges, but use two strands for cross stitch and one for backstitch.

SUNFLOWER AND SNAIL BADGES

Stitched on plastic canvas with a brooch or safety pin on the back, these designs make jaunty badges. For very young children, it is safer to stitch the badges onto the garment. For more information on using plastic canvas, see page 21.

1 Mark the center of the plastic canvas with the permanent marker. Use eight strands for cross stitch and four for backstitch. Refer to the color key on page 184 and the appropriate chart. Make each stitch over one canvas mesh.

2 When finished, trim the plastic canvas to shape, leaving one row of unworked holes all around.

3 If you wish, sew a jewelry pin finding or safety pin onto the back; or secure the badge to the garment with a few stitches.

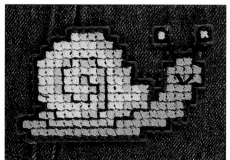

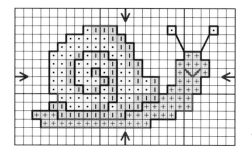

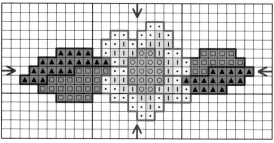

MARY'S GARDEN

THE NURSERY RHYME
CHARACTER MARY AND
HER PRETTY FLOWERS
IN A ROW MAKE CUTE
MOTIFS FOR
LITTLE CLOTHES.

MARY'S DRESS SET

Mary tends her flower garden in this charming scene for a dress or bag.

The whole scene from the chart (opposite below) can be used to decorate the front of a child's shoulder bag; the stitching is worked directly onto evenweave linen, in this case a rich blue. The design is about 5½ x 4¼ in. (14 x 10.5 cm), the bag 6 x 5½ in. (15 x 14 cm).

Parts of the design can be worked on garments using waste canvas to create coordinating outfits. The section with Mary carefully watering her flowers fits neatly onto the front bodice of a dress, while single flower heads look sweet around the sleeves of a plain white T-shirt.

YOU WILL NEED

For all items:

❋ DMC stranded floss as listed in the color key

❋ Thread for basting

❋ Embroidery hoop (see page 12)

❋ Pencil

For the dress and T-shirt:

❋ 14-count waste canvas, 6 x 5 in. (15 x 12.5 cm) for the dress, and six 1½-in. (4-cm) squares for the T-shirt

❋ Crewel needle, size 6

❋ Tweezers

For the bag:

❋ 31-count blue evenweave linen, 16 x 9½ in. (40 x 24 cm)

❋ Tapestry needle, size 26

❋ Firm iron-on interfacing, 16 x 9½ in. (40 x 24 cm)

❋ Sewing needle and thread to match the linen

❋ 1 yd. (1 m) of cord trim

STITCHING THE DRESS AND T-SHIRT

1 Decide which part of the design you wish to stitch, and mark the center of this area on the chart (opposite). The red arrows show the vertical center of Mary.

2 Mount the fabric in the embroidery hoop. Mark the center of the waste canvas with basting and baste it to the chosen area on the garment.

3 Work the design from the center out, referring to the chart and the color key (opposite). Use two strands of floss for cross stitch and French knots and one strand for backstitch, and work each stitch over two canvas threads.

4 When complete, remove the hoop, dampen the waste canvas, and remove the threads. Press lightly.

MAKING THE BAG

1 Overcast the edges of the linen to prevent fraying. Fold it in half widthwise; press lightly. Baste a rectangle 6 x 5½ in. (15 x 14 cm) on one half, placing one shorter side on the fold and centering it across the width. This area will form the front of the bag. Mark the center of the rectangle with basting. Mount the linen in the hoop.

2 Stitch the complete design as in Stitching the Dress and T-shirt, step **3** (opposite), but work each stitch over two fabric threads. When the work is complete, take it out of the embroidery hoop and press lightly on the wrong side.

3 Fuse the interfacing to the wrong side of the linen. Fold the linen in half with right sides together along the lower edge of the basted rectangle. Stitch up the sides of the rectangle, continuing to the top edge of the linen. Trim and finish the seams.

4 Turn the bag right side out. Finish the top edge, press 2 in. (5 cm) to the wrong side, and slip-stitch in place.

5 Knot the cord trim 2 in. (5 cm) from each end, then unravel the ends below the knots to make tassels. Stitch the knots firmly to the outside of the bag at the top to form the shoulder strap.

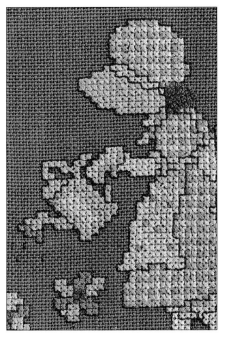

Mary's gingham bonnet and dress are worked in three shades of yellow, and ginger French knots form her curls.

COLOR KEY

COLORS	SKEINS
T 209 Lavender	1
S 211 Pale lavender	1
▲ 335 Rose pink	1
− 504 Pale sea green	1
Z 703 Spring green	1
◎ 742 Pale tangerine	1
+ 744 Buttercup	1
I 776 Ice pink	1
∕ 819 Palest pink	1
● 844 Black pearl	1
□ 3770 Warm cream	1
· 3823 Pale lemon	1

Backstitch

◥ 701 Christmas green	1
◤ 844 Black pearl	

French knots

⊠ 3776 Ginger	1

Mary's Flowers

The flowers from Mary's garden are worked as separate motifs on the front of a casual skirt. The long-stemmed sunflower from the chart below blooms on the front of a dark jacket.

The flowers on the skirt are 1½–2½ in. (4–6.5 cm) high, and the long-stemmed sunflower is about 4 in. (10 cm) high.

YOU WILL NEED

- 10-count waste canvas: 6 x 3 in. (15 x 8 cm) for the top and four 4 x 3-in. (10 x 8-cm) pieces for the skirt
- DMC stranded floss as listed in the color key on page 189
- Crewel needle, size 6
- Thread for basting
- Embroidery hoop (see page 12)
- Tweezers
- Pencil

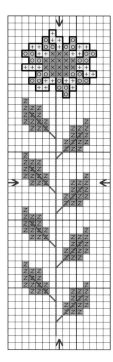

STITCHING THE SKIRT

Mark the center of the individual flower motifs on the chart on page 189. Mark the center of the waste canvas pieces, and baste them onto the skirt front above the hem.

Work a flower over each piece of waste canvas as for Stitching the Dress and T-shirt, steps **2–4**, on page 188.

WORKING THE TOP

Work the sunflower on the chosen area on the top; refer to Stitching the Dress and T-shirt, steps **2–4**, page 188, but follow the chart (left).

The sunflower petals are outlined in backstitch using black pearl cotton, while Christmas green backstitching forms the stems.

190

RAG DOLL

WITH HER AUTHENTIC
NATIVE AMERICAN OUTFIT,
THIS RAG DOLL MAKES A
DELIGHTFUL TOY.

MAKING AND DRESSING THE DOLL

Once you have made the doll, there is a complete mini wardrobe to make for her, with a patterned dress, moccasins, headband, belt, and strings of beads.

YOU WILL NEED

- ❀ 28-count cream linen-and-cotton evenweave: two 10-in. (25-cm) squares for the body
- ❀ 28-count blue or wine red linen-and-cotton evenweave: two 10-in. (25-cm) squares for each dress
- ❀ DMC stranded floss as listed in the color key
- ❀ Tapestry needle, size 26
- ❀ Sewing needle and thread for basting and hand-stitching
- ❀ Beading needle
- ❀ Embroidery hoop (see page 12)
- ❀ Lightweight iron-on interfacing: two 10-in. (25-cm) squares
- ❀ Polyester stuffing
- ❀ Selection of small beads
- ❀ Leather lace for belt
- ❀ Miniature feather
- ❀ Sewing machine

The doll is made from Zweigart Quaker cloth, but you could use a similar evenweave fabric. Her features, hair, underwear, and moccasins are stitched onto the body pieces; her braids are made from a whole skein of black floss and are sewn into the seams.

The dress seams are finished with blanket stitch, and the sleeves and hems are frayed to create an authentic look. Complete your doll's wardrobe by making her beaded necklaces, a headband, and a leather tie belt. The doll is about 6½ in. (17 cm) tall.

The rag doll's nose, eyelids, eyelashes, and eyebrows are backstitched using one strand of floss. Her mouth is backstitched using two strands, and her bangs with four strands.

COLOR KEY

COLORS		SKEINS
◼	310 Black	2
▦	321 Red	2
T	433 Brown	2
I	436 Tan	2
+	744 Yellow	1
✕	761 Pink	1
—	996 Turquoise	1
Backstitch		
◣	310 Black	
◥	321 Red	
◹	841 Coffee	1

THE BODY

1 Overcast the edges of the two cream fabric squares to prevent them from fraying. Mark the center of each square with two lines of basting. Mount one square in the embroidery hoop.

2 Work the doll front from the center out, referring to the chart (right), the color key (above), and steps **3–4** (below). Use two strands of floss for cross stitch. One square on the chart represents one stitch worked over two fabric threads.

3 Cross-stitch the undershirt and pants first. Then, counting down carefully, cross-stitch the moccasins. Outline the edges of the moccasins in backstitch, using one strand of black floss.

4 Next, count up carefully to work the face. Cross-stitch the cheeks and eyes, then complete the features in backstitch, referring to the chart and key for colors. Use one strand for the nose, eyelids, eyelashes, and eyebrows; two strands for the mouth, and four strands for the hair.

5 Using matching sewing thread in the sewing needle, backstitch along the outlines of the arms, legs, neck, and face, as indicated by the green lines on the chart. Take the finished work out of the hoop and press it lightly from the wrong side. Remove basting.

6 Mount the other cream fabric square in the embroidery hoop. Stitch the back of the doll in the same way as the front, but refer to the chart on page 194. Remove the work from the hoop and press as before. Remove the basting.

The hair on the doll's head is backstitched on the fabric using four strands of black floss. The braids are made separately and inserted into the seam when the back and front sections are joined.

ASSEMBLING THE DOLL

1 Lay out the complete skein of black embroidery floss, and slide off the paper labels. Cut through the loops at each end to make two bunches of threads.

2 Firmly tie the top of each bunch with black floss, then braid it for about 2 in. (5 cm). Use 996 (turquoise) and 321 (red) to bind the bunch tightly just below the braid, then bind it with 744 (yellow) near the bottom of the threads. Trim the ends of the ties and neaten the ends of the braids.

3 Lay the stitched doll front and stitched doll back right side down. Fuse the lightweight interfacing to the wrong side of each piece. Neatly cut out each doll piece, 3/8 in. (1 cm) outside the backstitched outline.

4 Using a warm iron, press 3/8 in. (1 cm) to the wrong side all around each piece, carefully easing the curves. Snip into the seam allowances where necessary so that they lie flat and smooth.

The undershirt and pants are stitched directly on the body. The lower edge of each garment is finished with a cross-stitched fringe to imitate soft buckskin.

5 Place the two doll sections together with wrong sides facing. Using matching sewing thread, begin overcasting the edges together. Make sure the stitches are small and neat. Start at the inside legs, then work up the outside legs, gently filling them with stuffing as you go. Continue up the sides of the body, down the underarms, and up the outer arms, gently adding more stuffing.

6 Finally stitch around the neck and the head; insert the ends of the braids into the seam just below the backstitched hair on the front head, stitching them firmly in place. Insert the last bit of stuffing in the head, taking care to shape the neck before completing the stitching.

MAKING THE CLOTHES

1 Use either the blue or red evenweave. Overcast the edges of each square to prevent them from fraying, and mark the centers with basting. Mount one square in the hoop. Cross-stitch the dress from the center out, referring to the chart (below) and the color key on page 193. Use two strands of floss, and work each stitch over two fabric threads.

2 When the cross stitch is complete, use matching sewing thread and the sewing needle to backstitch along the outline of the dress front, as indicated by the green lines on the chart.

3 When the work is complete, remove it from the hoop and press lightly on the wrong side. Trim the work ⅜ in. (1 cm) outside the backstitching. Repeat these three steps to make another dress piece.

4 Pin the two pieces together with right sides facing. Following the backstitched outline and using matching thread, stitch along the sides and sleeves. Leave 2¼ in. (6 cm) open at the neck, and finish level with the edge of the cross stitching at the ends of the sleeves and the hem edge.

5 Clip into the seam allowances at the underarms, then finish the seam allowances with zigzag stitch, or overcast them by hand. Turn the dress right side out.

6 On the right side, work blanket stitch along the two side seams using two strands of 436 (Tan) floss. In the same way, work blanket stitch along the top of the dress, working across the two shoulders and around the opening for the neck.

Blanket stitching along the side seams and across the top of the dress gives it an authentic finish.

7 To finish, fray back the edges of the sleeves and hem up to the cross stitching; use the tapestry needle to tease out the threads.

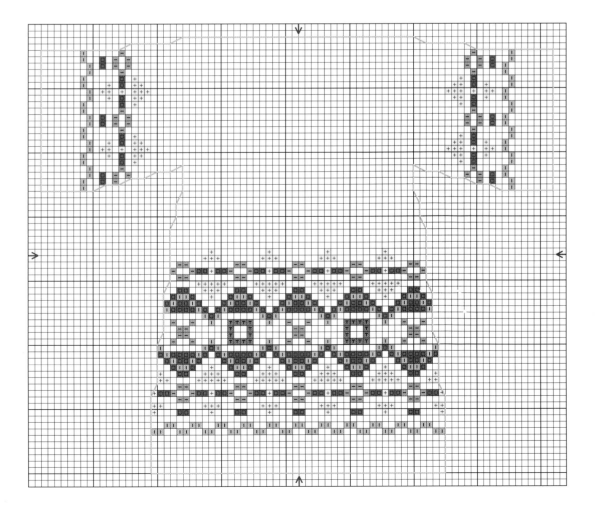

MAKING A HEADBAND

Cut three 16-in. (40-cm) lengths of stranded embroidery floss; each length should consist of all six strands. Use one color or a selection of coordinating colors. Use the lengths to make a twisted cord trim, as shown on page 314. Wrap the cord around the doll's head and pull the knotted end through the loop at the other end. Stick the feather in the back of her hair.

MAKING NECKLACES

Choose beads that coordinate with the dresses, and arrange them in an attractive design. Using the beading needle, thread the beads onto one strand of embroidery floss to make a necklace about 5 ½–7 in. (14–18 cm) long. Knot the thread ends together firmly and trim them.

MAKING THE BELT

Tie the leather lace around the doll's waist and make a knot in the center. Trim the ends at a slant.

Fray the edges of the sleeves and hem up to the cross stitch.

196

JUNGLE FEVER

THE TEEMING LIFE OF THE WORLD'S TROPICAL
JUNGLES, WITH THEIR EXOTIC MAMMALS AND REPTILES,
INSPIRED THESE CUTE CROSS-STITCH FIGURES.

JUNGLE MOBILE

Fierce tigers, creepy snakes, and an acrobatic orangutan, worked on plastic canvas, make lifelike images for this jungle mobile.

Cross-stitch designs are usually worked from the center outward, but for the mobile you can use the plastic canvas more economically by starting the motifs at the edges, following the layout in Making the Mobile, step **1** (opposite). The stitched animals are backed with felt, and assembled into the mobile. (If you cannot find a ring, make one from metal or plastic wire, fastening the ends with electrical tape.) The thread quantities given are enough for all of the projects.

YOU WILL NEED

- ❋ 10-count plastic canvas, 14 x 11 in. (35 x 28 cm)
- ❋ DMC stranded floss as listed in the color key
- ❋ Tapestry needle, size 24
- ❋ Sharp scissors
- ❋ Fine marker
- ❋ Green and orange felt
- ❋ White glue
- ❋ Ring from an old lampshade, approx. 12 in. (30 cm) in diameter
- ❋ Green bias binding
- ❋ Jute string and artificial ivy

COLOR KEY

	COLORS	SKEINS
N	Blanc	1
▣	301 Mahogany	1
■	310 Black	3
−	402 Pale ginger	2
I	415 Pearl gray	1
U	436 Medium tan	1
S	471 Pale avocado	1
X	472 Spring green	1
T	562 Dusty green	1
F	725 Pale old gold yellow	1
+	738 Tan beige	1
·	761 Pink	1
▲	904 Dark apple	2
⊙	906 Apple	3
✳	976 Caramel	2

Backstitch

◥ 310 Black

Black backstitches highlight the snake's fangs and forked tongue.

MAKING THE MOBILE

1 Referring to the chart (right), work two tigers, one orangutan, and two snakes on the plastic canvas; arrange them as shown below with at least two squares between each motif. One square on the chart represents one stitch worked over one canvas mesh. Use four strands of floss for cross stitch and two for backstitch. ▼

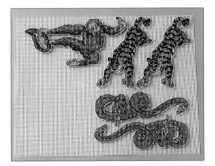

2 Start with the top right-hand black cross stitch at the tip of the tiger's tail; position it three holes in from one short edge of the plastic canvas, and four holes down from the adjacent long edge. When the first tiger is complete, work the second tiger, starting with the paw nearest to the first tiger's paw. Continue in this way to stitch the remaining animals.

3 Trim each animal one canvas mesh outside the stitching. Use them as patterns to draw their shapes on yellow or green felt with the fine marker. Cut out the shapes just inside the drawn lines. Glue them to the backs of the animals with the white glue.

4 Bind the ring with the green bias binding, sticking down the ends with the white glue. Coil the ivy around the ring.

5 Cut six 12–36 in. (30–90 cm) lengths of string, and knot each one at intervals. Tie them onto the ring, spacing them out evenly.

6 Tie the animals onto the strings. If you like, add more knotted lengths of string. Hang the mobile from a ceiling light fixture, using knotted string, tied to the center of the mobile.

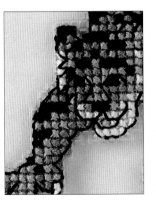

The tiger's realistic stripes are worked in black cross stitches against his pale ginger and caramel-colored fur. His tongue and inner ear are depicted in pink floss.

JUNGLE BOOKENDS

An orangutan and a grinning crocodile stand guard on a pair of bookends; the stitched motifs are mounted on blocks of foam board so that they stand out. You can use scraps of foam board left over from other projects, but if you don't have any, thick corrugated cardboard works just as well.

YOU WILL NEED

❋ Pair of bookends

❋ 10-count plastic canvas, 8½ x 4½ in. (22 x 11 cm) for the orangutan, 7 x 6 in. (18 x 15 cm) for the crocodile

❋ Embroidery materials and equipment listed on page 198

❋ Permanent black marker

❋ Green or yellow felt

❋ Scraps of foam board

❋ Utility knife and metal ruler

❋ White glue

❋ Double-stick tape

1 Mark the center of each piece of plastic canvas using the permanent black marker, then stitch each design from the center out, referring to Making the Mobile, step 1 on page 199. Cut out the stitched animals and back them with felt, referring to step 3 on page 199.

2 With the utility knife and metal ruler, cut eight 1 x ⅝-in. (2.5 x 1.5-cm) pieces of foam board. Use the double-stick tape to stick them together in pairs to make blocks, then stick two blocks to the back of each animal's body area. ➤

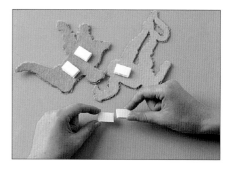

3 Stick the animals onto the bookends with the double-stick tape, adjusting the positions of the foam board blocks if necessary.

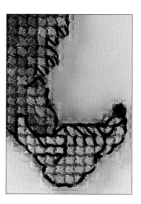

Perfectly in character, the orangutan clutches a banana in his hand. Black backstitches delineate his long fingers.

⟨ BRIGHT IDEAS ⟩

PILLOW CROC

The Jungle Fever animals add fun to fabric furnishings, such as this pillowcase. For the crocodile, baste a 10-in. (25-cm) square of 10-count waste canvas onto the pillowcase, and work the design using a size 6 crewel needle. For details on using waste canvas, see pages 23–24.

TRAVEL ZONE

THESE DESIGNS FOR PATCHES
AND A PICTURE FRAME FEATURE
TRAVEL BY ROAD AND AIR, AND
EVEN INTO OUTER SPACE.

COLOR KEY

COLORS	SKEINS
⊡ Blanc	2
▧ 310 Black	2
△ 317 Dark gray	1
I 318 Medium gray	1
– 444 Bright yellow	1
✕ 445 Pale lemon	1
▨ 666 Bright red	1
☑ 701 Green	1
⋂ 703 Lime green	1
I 762 Light gray	1
T 798 Blue	1
+ 800 Pale sky blue	1
■ 816 Dark red	2
■ 820 Midnight blue	1
U 970 Orange	1

Backstitch

| ◥ Blanc |
| ◥ 310 Black |
| ◥ 666 Bright red |
| ◥ 970 Orange |

TRAVEL PATCHES

Delight youngsters with these patches for clothes, bags, and bedroom, featuring modes of travel by road and air, plus a rocket and a flying saucer.

CAR NAMEPLATE

1 On graph paper, draw two parallel lines seven squares apart to show height of letters. Copy the letters of the name from the chart (opposite) onto the graph paper, leaving one square between each letter. Then mark one space and 21 squares for the car.

2 Mark the center of the whole design on the graph paper. Mark the center of the green aida.

3 Following your graph-paper chart for the name and the printed chart for the car, stitch the design using three strands of floss for cross stitch and two for backstitch. Work over one thread block.

4 Trim aida to size, then fringe one block all around. Fuse interfacing to wrong side. Stick in place with double-stick tape, or stitch.

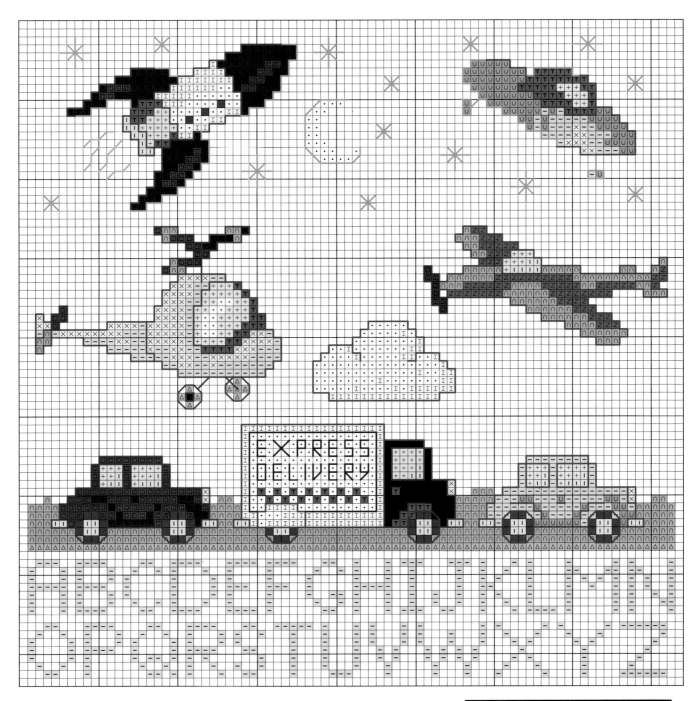

TRUCK AND CAR PATCH

Mark the center of the delivery truck and car motif on the chart (above), then mark the center of the red aida. Stitch the design using three strands of floss for the cross stitch, and two strands for the backstitch. Work over one thread block. When the stitching is complete, press in ³⁄₈ in. (1 cm) all around. Backstitch in place two blocks from the edges, using three strands of blue floss.

ROCKET PATCH

A red, white, and blue rocket gives a little pizzazz to a denim jacket. The patch is worked separately and then sewn on.

Mark the center of the rocket on the chart, then mark the center of the blue aida with basting. Stitch the design using six strands of floss for cross stitch and three strands for backstitch. All the stitches are worked over four thread blocks (two vertical and two horizontal). Add a few stars as shown (right). Press in ³⁄₈ in. (1 cm) all around. Backstitch in place as for the truck and car patch.

After completing the rocket, scatter a few stars above and below. Vary the angles and give one or two of them extra-long points for a spangly effect.

SPACE-AGE FRAME

A professional framer can cut you a mat of the size needed for this frame; or you can cut one yourself from mat board.

1 Work from the chart (below), starting in the top right-hand quarter of the aida. Refer to the color key on page 202 and work over one thread block, using three strands of floss for cross stitch and two for backstitch.

2 Rotate the chart 90 degrees to work the next quarter of the design. Repeat twice more. Press the work on the wrong side.

3 Cover back edges and front of mat with double-stick tape. Attach batting to one side and trim around opening. Center aida on batting, and secure excess at the back.

4 Trim fabric in center, and secure excess at the back. Stitch cord trim in place. Center picture behind the opening and stick a piece of card stock over the back.

BRIGHT IDEAS

BOOT CLIP

Separate motifs make fun decorations for items such as the bookends pictured on page 201, or this boot clip. Stitch a motif onto a 6 x 5-in. (15 x 13-cm) piece of 10-count plastic canvas, then cut around it, leaving one square of canvas all around. Glue it to a painted wooden clothespin. For the bookends, use the cloud with the helicopter and airplane.

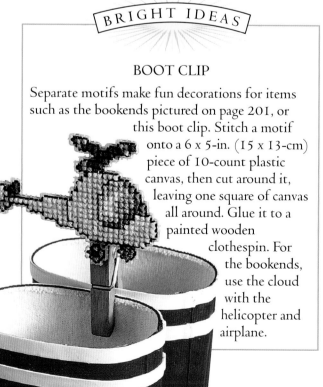

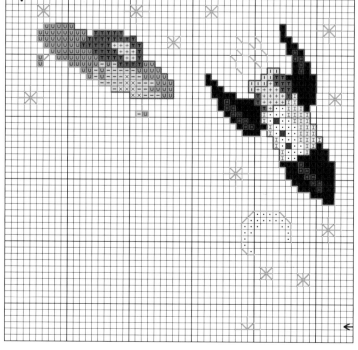

ANIMAL FUN

THREE FAVORITE ANIMALS WITH LOTS OF CHILD APPEAL MAKE FUN STORAGE-BOX LABELS AND A PATCH POCKET.

ANIMAL PATCHES

An inquisitive lion with a magnificent mane, a cuddly panda with a shy smile, and a frog eyeing up a tasty fly decorate aida box labels.

The animals, framed by bright borders are quick to stitch on 14-count aida. The lion and panda are both 4 in. (10 cm) square, and the frog is 4 x 2¼ in. (10 x 5.5 cm).

The panda clutches its favorite food—a stick of freshly plucked bamboo.

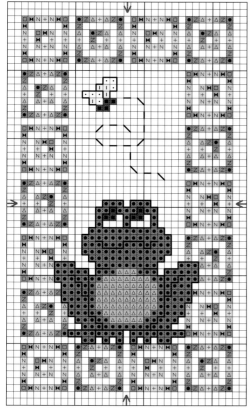

1 Overcast the raw edges of the aida to prevent fraying, and mark the center with two lines of basting. Mount the fabric in the embroidery hoop.

2 Cross-stitch the chosen animal from the center out, referring to the color key (opposite) and the appropriate chart (this page and opposite). Use two strands of floss, and work each stitch over one thread block.

3 When all the cross stitch is complete, backstitch the outlines and details using one strand of floss. For the frog design, depict the fly's flight path with running stitch and one strand of black floss.

4 Take the finished piece out of the hoop and press it gently on the wrong side, taking care not to crush the stitching.

5 Trim the work two blocks outside the stitching all around, then fray the threads for one block all around. Stick the patch onto the box with the double-stick tape. ►

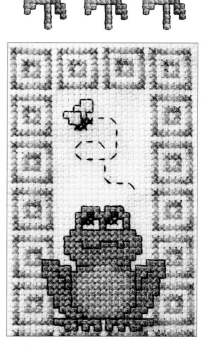

Cross-stitch the fly's wings in white, and backstitch around them in black, but leave the white of the frog's eyes unstitched.

207

POCKET LION

The lion peeping out over the top of a leafy plant decorates a useful pocket sewn onto a bathrobe. The pocket is very easy to make: simply work the design on aida in the usual way, then press in the side edges, hem the top, and stitch the pocket in place.

YOU WILL NEED

✽ 14-count white aida, 8 in. (20 cm) square

✽ DMC stranded floss as listed in the color key on page 206

✽ Tapestry needle, size 26

✽ Sewing needle and thread for basting and stitching

✽ Embroidery hoop (see page 12)

✽ Child's bathrobe

✽ Sewing machine

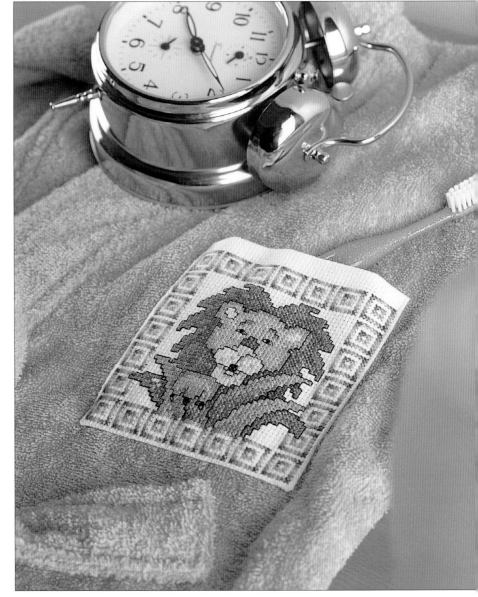

1 Overcast the raw edges of the aida to prevent fraying, and mark the center with two lines of basting. Mount it in the hoop.

2 Cross-stitch the lion design from the center out, referring to the color key on page 206 and the chart on page 207. Use two strands of floss and work each stitch over one thread block.

3 When all the cross stitch is complete, backstitch the outlines and details using one strand of floss. Take the finished piece out of the hoop and press it lightly on the wrong side.

4 Carefully trim the side and bottom edges of the aida ³⁄₈ in. (1 cm) outside the stitching. Trim the top edge ⁵⁄₈ in. (1.5 cm) above the stitching.

5 Along the side and bottom edges, press the excess fabric to the wrong side, leaving one thread block outside the stitching all around. Along the top edge, press in ¼ in. (5 mm), then ³⁄₈ in. (1 cm). Machine-stitch the top hem.

6 Pin the pocket in the desired position on the bathrobe. Machine-stitch it in place close to the side and bottom edges.

Clever shading using pale tan and ivory-beige suggests the slightly rough texture of the lion's muzzle.

Chapter 5
Around the World

BORDER STORY

NAIVE FOLK ART BANDS AND DECORATIVE
ALPHABETS PROVIDE A GREAT CHOICE OF
BORDERS FOR HOME ACCESSORIES AND TRIMS.

BATHROOM SET

Border patterns stitched in various shades of blue on white linen or aida bands provide a fresh finishing touch for your bathroom.

The variegated thread gives these border patterns a subtle finish. Each item uses motifs taken from the sampler design (opposite); the soap bag also uses letters from the alphabet sampler on page 215. The borders are stitched on fine ready-made linen bands, except the towel, which is ready-made with an aida panel.

POT BAND AND TOWEL

1 Mark the horizontal center of the house border on the chart. Baste to mark the horizontal center of the linen band or aida panel. Mount the fabric in the hoop.

2 Work the house border from the center out, referring to the key (above) and the chart (opposite). Use two strands of floss and work each stitch over two linen threads on the pot band or one thread block on the towel panel.

3 Work one stitch at a time so the thread changes color smoothly. Stitch as many houses as needed, stopping at least ¾ in. (2 cm) from the ends. Work borders above and below the houses, leaving four-thread-block gaps.

4 When the work is complete, take it out of the hoop and press it lightly. For the pot band, press in ⅜ in. (1 cm) at one end. Fix the band to the pot with the double-stick tape, lapping the pressed end over the raw end.

SHELF EDGING

1 Mark the horizontal center of the band with basting. Work the borders, referring to the chart (right) and complete one stitch at a time. Use one strand and work each stitch over one thread intersection. Leave one linen thread between each border.

2 Start 1¼ in. (3 cm) from the left edge and five threads below the top of the band. Work the square border first, then the small alphabet, working all the letters on one line. Leave a three-thread gap between each full alphabet and work a cross stitch in the gap.

SOAP BAG

1 Fold the band in half widthwise and press a crease—this marks the bottom of the soap bag; unfold. Use basting to mark the vertical center of the band, then mark the horizontal center of the design 2⅛ in. (5.5 cm) above the crease.

2 Mark the center of the "V" on the chart on page 215. Mount the band in the hoop. Work the word "SAVON" from the center out as for Shelf Edging, step **1** (above), but refer to the chart on page 215. Work one of the backstitched borders from the chart (right) five threads above and below the lettering, then backstitch another border six threads above and below.

3 When the work is complete, remove it from the hoop and press lightly. Trim the raw edges 6¼ in. (16 cm) from the foldline. Finish the raw edges with overcasting or zigzag stitch, press a ¾-in. (2 cm) casing to the wrong side, and stitch.

4 Fold the bag with the wrong sides together, then stitch the sides. Stop at the base of the casings. Thread ribbon through the casings to pull up.

3 Next work the tree and flower border, then the zigzag border. When complete, remove the work from the hoop and press it lightly on the wrong side.

4 Turn and stitch a double ⅜-in. (1-cm) hem to the wrong side at each end of the band. Fix the band to the shelf with double-stick tape.

Complete each stitch before working the next, so the color changes smoothly.

213

WALL HANGING AND TIEBACK

Blue stitching on natural linen bands is an attractive combination for home accessories. The wall hanging featured here is 13¾ in. (35 cm) long, and includes the borders from both charts.

YOU WILL NEED

❀ For the wall hanging: ⅞ yd. (80 cm) of 4¾-in. (12-cm) wide natural linen band with blue edges

❀ For the tieback: ⅝ yd. (60 cm) of 3¼-in. (8-cm) wide natural linen band with blue edges

❀ DMC stranded floss as specified below

❀ Tapestry needle, size 26

❀ Sewing needle and thread for basting

❀ Embroidery hoop (see page 12)

❀ Tassel, bead, and bell pull hanger

❀ Two brass rings

❀ Pencil

COLOR KEY

COLORS	SKEINS
☒ 798 Blue	3

The tieback letters are worked over two fabric threads.

MAKING THE WALL HANGING

1 Fold the linen band in half widthwise and press; this foldline marks the top of the wall hanging. Baste down the length of what will be the front to mark the vertical center. Mount the linen in the embroidery hoop.

2 Work the design from the vertical center out, referring to the chart (right). Start with the top row of stitching 1 in. (2.5 cm) below the foldline. Use one strand of floss and work each stitch over one fabric thread intersection.

3 When the alphabet design is complete, work the design from the chart on page 213 in the same way, positioning the top row of stitching three threads below the border at the bottom of the alphabet. Remove the work from the hoop.

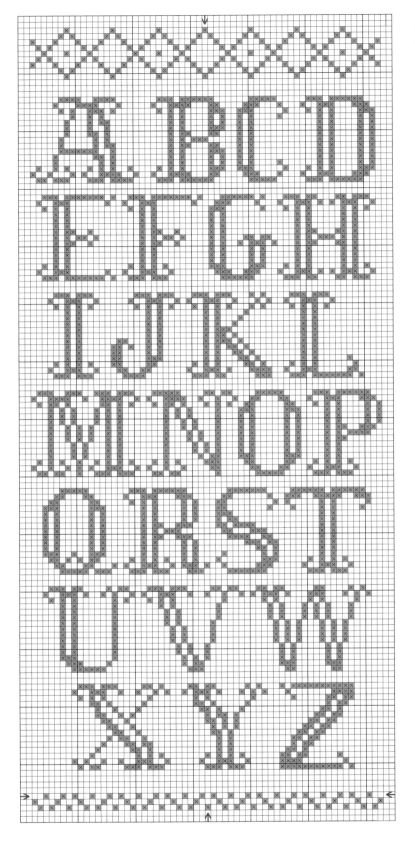

MAKING THE TIEBACK

1 On the chart (left), mark the horizontal center of the letters you wish to stitch. Decide where to position the letters on the band. Mark the center with basting. Mount the band in the embroidery hoop.

2 Work the chosen letters from the center out, referring to the chart (left). Use two strands of embroidery floss, work each stitch over two fabric threads, and leave four threads between each letter.

3 When the work is complete, remove it from the hoop and press lightly on the wrong side. Turn and stitch a double ⅜-in. (1-cm) hem at each end. Sew a ring onto each end.

The sampler is worked using one strand of floss over one fabric thread.

4 Press the work lightly on the wrong side. Fold the band along the foldline with right sides together, and trim the bottom edges into a point, allowing ⅜ in. (1 cm) for seams. Stitch around the point, clip across it to reduce bulk, turn the sampler right side out, and press.

5 Slip the bell pull hanger into the top of the sampler, and stitch the layers together along the sides. Thread the bead onto the top of the tassel, and sew the tassel to the point.

ALPHABET CUSHION

Linen bands stitched with the letters of the alphabet and woven together form the front of this ingenious cushion. The bands are woven in the same way as ribbons are woven to create decorative fabrics (see pages 25–26). You will need to stitch the letters on the vertical (warp) bands with the band held vertically in the hoop, and the letters on the horizontal (weft) bands with the band held horizontally.

YOU WILL NEED

* 5 yd. (4.7 m) of 2⅛-in. (5.5-cm) wide 26-count natural linen band

* DMC stranded floss: two skeins of 798 (blue)

* Embroidery materials as listed on page 214

* Self-adhesive labels

* Materials and equipment for weaving (see page 25)

* Fabric for cushion back, 20 x 13 in. (50 x 33 cm)

* Sewing needle and thread

* Pillow form 13½ x 11 in. (34 x 28 cm); if necessary, make one from lawn and polyester stuffing

The cushion letters are stitched at the center of squares formed by interweaving the linen bands.

1 From the linen band: cut six 15-in. (38-cm) strips and five 17¼-in. (44-cm) strips. Baste along the strips lengthwise to mark their centers. Interweave the strips using the longer bands for the horizontals (weft). Pin around the central 13½ x 11-in. (34 x 28-cm) rectangle—this area will be the front of the cushion.

2 Referring to the picture (above) label each square with the letter to be stitched on it. Mark the center of each square to be stitched with a second line of basting. ▲

3 Mark the centers of each letter on the chart on page 215. Leaving the letter labels in place, carefully separate the bands. With the linen band mounted in the hoop, work each letter from the center out, referring to the chart on page 215. Use two strands of floss and work each stitch over two fabric threads.

4 When the work is complete, remove it from the hoop and press lightly on the wrong side. Weave the bands to make a piece with a finished size of 13½ x 11 in. (34 x 28 cm) plus 1 in. (2.5 cm) all around, trimming the bands as required. Interface the cushion front as described on pages 25–26. Assemble the cushion cover with an overlapped back as shown on page 307, taking 1-in. (2.5-cm) seams.

ART DECO BORDERS

THE SHARP, GRAPHIC SHAPES, REPEATING MOTIFS, AND
STRONG COLORS OF ART DECO PATTERNS, ARE PERFECT
FOR TRANSLATING INTO CROSS-STITCH BORDERS.

ART DECO DESK SET

These border designs are typical of the Art Deco period and are ideal as edgings for books or for making a coordinating desk set.

Black cross stitch, combined with the violets and greens, gives definition to the geometric patterns of the borders.

STITCHING THE BORDERS

Cut three strips of aida: 8 x 3 in. (20 x 8 cm) for the pen holder, 15 x 4 in. (38 x 10 cm) for the book trim, and 7 x 3 in. (18 x 8 cm) for the bookmark. If your book is a different size, adjust the length of the book trim, and work fewer motifs or extra motifs, as required.

For each design, mark the center of the fabric with basting. Using three strands of floss and cross stitch, work over one block of aida following the appropriate chart (opposite). Stitch from the center of the design outward. Backstitch the outlines in two strands of floss. Press the finished pieces on the wrong side with a warm iron.

MAKING THE PEN HOLDER

With the right sides together, pin the velvet to the pen-holder embroidery. With the embroidered side uppermost, machine-stitch close to the embroidery, leaving a gap at one short end. Trim the seam allowances to ⅜ in. (1 cm). Turn the pen holder right side out. Fold the raw edges to the inside, and slip-stitch them in place.

MAKING THE BOOKMARK

1 With the embroidered side up, pin the tassel to the corners at the pointed end. Place the satin, right side down, on top; pin and baste the fabrics together. With the embroidery on top, machine-stitch close to the stitching, leaving the straight end open and pivoting the work around the needle at the point. ▼

2 Trim the seam allowances to ⅜ in. (1 cm), and clip across the point and corners. Turn the bookmark right side out, pulling the tassel down. Turn in the raw edges at the end and slip-stitch them together with matching thread.

ATTACHING THE BOOK COVER TRIM

1 Trim each long edge of the aida to leave seven thread blocks on each side of the stitching. Fold in the fabric along the two long edges, and secure them with fabric glue.

PEN HOLDER   BOOKMARK

2 Spread fabric glue over the back of the trim and glue it to the front of the book, about ½ in. (1.2 cm) in from the edge. Fold the top and bottom edges to the inside of the front cover and glue them in place. ◄

BOOK COVER TRIM

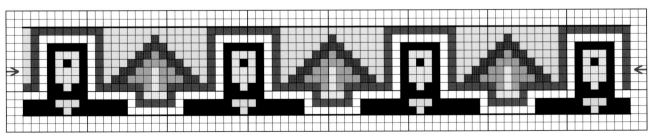

PICTURE MAT

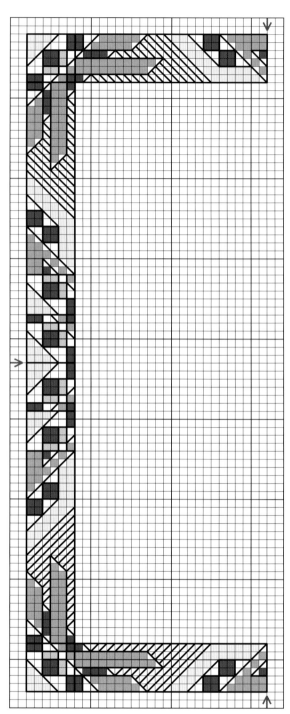

This stylish embroidery is glued over a picture mat. The mat's outer dimensions are 7½ x 5½ in. (19 x 14 cm); the opening is 6¼ x 4¼ in. (16 x 11 cm). If you can't find a mat and frame of these dimensions, you could ask a professional framer to cut the mat for you and then, when the work is finished, to make and fit the frame. Stitch half of the design following the chart (right); turn the chart around and stitch the other half of the design.

1 Mark the center of the fabric with basting and mount it in the hoop. Use three strands of floss for the cross stitch and two strands for the backstitch, and work each stitch over one thread block. Press the design on the wrong side.

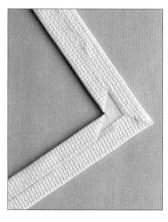

2 Trim the fabric leaving seven blocks of aida all around the embroidery. Fold it over the mat, snipping the corners so that they fold neatly. Secure the fabric with fabric glue. Place the mat, then the picture, in the frame.

CELTIC KNOTS

THE SINUOUS INTERLOCKING LINES OF CELTIC KNOTS ARE A REMINDER OF LOVERS' VOWS. IN CLASSIC GREENS AND GOLDS, THEY MAKE TRADITIONAL ORNAMENTS FOR A DRESSING TABLE.

YOU WILL NEED

For both items:

- ❋ DMC stranded floss as listed in the color key
- ❋ Embroidery hoop (see page 12)
- ❋ Tapestry needle, size 26
- ❋ Thread for basting and lacing

For the jewelry box:

- ❋ 14-count ivory aida, 7 in. (18 cm) square
- ❋ Recessed-lid card box, 6¼ x 7 in. (16 x 17.5 cm)

For the ring cushion:

- ❋ 14-count green aida, 10 in. (25 cm) square
- ❋ Gold velvet, 6¾ in. (17 cm) square
- ❋ Polyester batting

COLOR KEY

COLORS	SKEINS
◉ 699 Green	I
△ 701 Medium green	I
• 703 Pale green	I
▼ 781 Dark gold	I
○ 783 Gold	I
÷ 3821 Yellow	I
Backstitch	
╱ 699 Green	
╱ 701 Medium green	
╱ 703 Pale green	
╱ 869 Dark brown	I
╱ 895 Dark green	I

DRESSING-TABLE SET

For a handsome dressing-table set, decorate a smart, wooden jewelry box with a personalized Celtic-knot design, and embroider an elegant ring cushion with a coordinating design.

The design is mounted in the lid of a wooden card box, specially made to display embroidery.

JEWELRY BOX

1 Mark the center of the ivory aida with basting and mount it in the embroidery hoop. Cross-stitch the design on the lower half of the fabric, working from the center out and using two strands of floss. Follow the chart (opposite top) and refer to the color key (above). Then turn the chart around and work the design on the upper half of the fabric. Backstitch the outlines using one strand of dark green.

2 Work your chosen initial in the center, referring to the alphabet chart on page 215. Press from the wrong side.

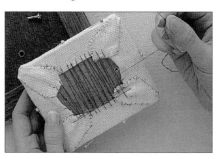

3 Remove the top of the card box and unscrew the central padded section. Center the embroidery over the pad and wrap the edges around to the back. Fold in the corners and pin to hold. Using a needle and strong thread, lace the fabric edges together, and secure the corners with overcasting stitches. Position the pad on the box lid and screw it in place from underneath. ◀

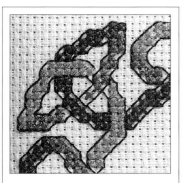

The intertwining lines are created by using different tones of one color. The backstitch outlines reinforce the intricate pattern.

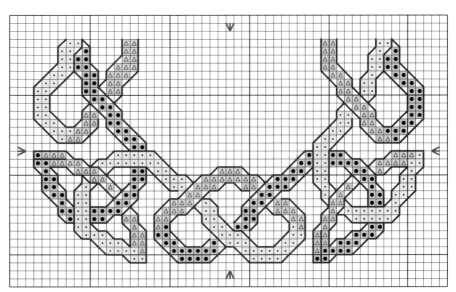

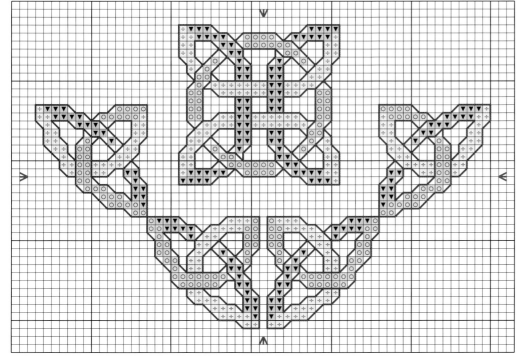

JEWELRY BOX
The chart shows half the design. Turn it around to work the other half. ▲

RING CUSHION
The central motif is complete. The rest of the chart shows half the border. Turn it around to stitch the other half. ◄

RING CUSHION

Display your jewelry on this elegant cushion, which is 6 in. (15 cm) square. To make it, use the materials and stranded floss as listed (opposite).

Mark the center of the aida with basting and mount it in a hoop. Work from the center out, using two strands of floss and follow the chart (above) to stitch the central motif and lower half of the border. Turn the chart around and stitch the top half of the border. Backstitch the outlines with two strands of brown. Trim the work to 6¾ in. (17 cm)

square. Pin the aida to the velvet with right sides facing. Stitch all around, leaving a small gap in one side. Turn right side out, fill with stuffing, and slip-stitch the gap closed.

Compact Case

A ring of Celtic knots makes an elegant motif for small items, such as a compact case. For a sumptuous effect, use rich green or gold velvet with silky coordinating braid. The cover is designed to fit a 3½-in. (8–9-cm) square compact.

COMPACT COVER

1 Work the design on aida, using two strands of floss and referring to the color key on page 222 and the chart (right), omitting the lines of backstitch. Trim the aida to measure 2¾ in. (7 cm) square, then fray the edges to make a fringe. Center work on one half of green velvet and overcast in place using all strands of pale green.

2 Fold the velvet in half widthwise, with right sides facing. Stitch the sides, taking a ⅜ in. (1 cm) seam. Along the opening edge, turn ⅜ in. (1 cm) to the wrong side and slip-stitch in place. Turn case right side out.

3 Slip-stitch the cord trim around edges of the case, tucking the ends neatly into the opening.

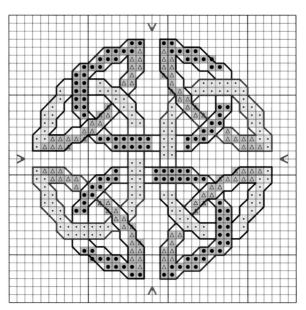

For a rich look, stitch the design on gold velvet. Baste a 4-in. (10-cm) square of waste canvas to one end of the velvet. Cross-stitch the design using two strands of 781 (dark gold). Remove the canvas (see pages 23–24), and then assemble the case. ▲

The chart combines cross-stitch symbols for the compact case and backstitch for the paperweight. ◀

BRIGHT IDEAS

PAPERWEIGHT DESIGN

For a sophisticated look that is well suited to a paperweight, work just the backstitch outlines given in the chart above. Use two shades of green on 14-count aida.

ANTIQUE BORDERS

THESE ATTRACTIVE BORDERS, WORKED IN THE
MUTED SHADES OF ANTIQUE SAMPLERS, HAVE A
TURN-OF-THE-CENTURY CHARM.

HEIRLOOM SAMPLER

The border sampler is worked in cross stitch and straight stitch. The mellow shades give the faded, aged effect of a treasured antique sampler.

1 Mark the center of the fabric with basting. Overcast the edges and mount it in the hoop or frame. Begin working the design from the center out, referring to the chart (opposite) and the color key (above).

2 Each square on the chart represents one stitch worked over two pairs of fabric threads. Work the cross stitches using two strands of floss.

3 Work the straight stitches using two strands, except for the outer border and the trellis borders, for which one strand is used. Where straight stitches are worked side by side, stitch between each pair of fabric threads.

226

4 Work the trellis borders in horizontal rows of spaced cross stitches, referring to the chart (above) and stitch detail (right). Work horizontal straight stitches in the spaces between the crosses.

5 When the stitching is complete, remove fabric from the hoop or frame and press lightly on the wrong side. Take the work to a professional framer, or frame it yourself, following the instructions on pages 297–298.

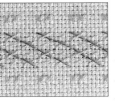

The trellis border is worked in two-tone cross stitches using metal blue and medium sea green.

SEWING SET

Delicate borders from the heirloom sampler are adapted to create charming designs for a pincushion and a scissors holder.

YOU WILL NEED

* 22-count cream Hardanger fabric, 16 x 8 in. (40 x 20 cm)
* DMC stranded floss and sewing materials as listed on page 226
* Velvet fabric, 14 x 5 in. (35 x 13 cm)
* Sewing needle and thread
* Stuffing
* ¾ yd. (60 cm) of ¼-in. (5-mm) wide ribbon

1 From one end of the Hardanger fabric, cut an 8-in. (20-cm) square for the pincushion and a 7-in. (18-cm) square for the scissors holder. Prepare the fabric and work the stitching as in Heirloom Sampler, steps **1–3** on page 226, referring to the color key on page 226 and appropriate chart (below). Press the finished designs lightly on the wrong side.

2 Make a scissors holder measuring 2¾ in. (7 cm) wide by 3 in. (8 cm) long, referring to the instructions on pages 305–306. Use the stitched fabric for the front with the design centered; use plain Hardanger fabric for the back and velvet for the lining.

3 Trim the pincushion design ⅝ in. (1.5 cm) outside the stitching. Cut velvet the same size. Stitch them together with right sides facing, taking a ⅜ in. (1 cm) seam and leaving an opening. Turn out, fill with stuffing, and slip-stitch the opening.

BRIGHT IDEAS

HEIRLOOM BAG

A velvet-lined bag makes a charming gift and keeps treasures safe and scratch-free. Choose your favorite patterns from the chart on page 227 and work them within a border to fit the bag size. Use the same fabric as for the sampler, and work the stitching in the same way. Refer to page 284 for instructions on making a drawstring bag with a headed casing.

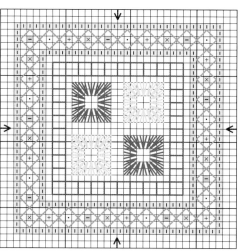

SCISSORS HOLDER

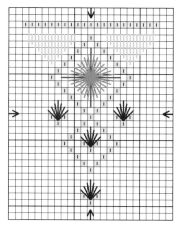

PINCUSHION

WILLIAM MORRIS BORDERS

THESE FLOWING, STYLIZED FLORAL BORDERS, WORKED
IN SOFT COLORS, WERE INSPIRED BY THE
19TH-CENTURY ENGLISH DESIGNER WILLIAM MORRIS.

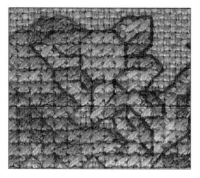

At the edges of the design, fractional (three-quarter) stitches ensure a smooth and flowing line.

TOWEL TRIMS

The colors typically used in William Morris designs are natural and subtle, like these soft blues, greens, and browns.

Designs inspired by the work of William Morris feature intricate floral patterns in mellow, natural colors. Unlike much Victorian style, they retain their popularity today, especially in England. These two towel borders use the same flowing motifs in two colorways— soft green and warm brown.

The borders look best on richly colored towels that pick up the colors used in the design.

1 Fold the band in half widthwise and press to form a crease. Baste along the foldline with contrasting sewing thread. Then mark the width and position of the design with two parallel rows of basting worked 26 threads apart and centered along the band.

2 Work the design from the center out, referring to the chart (below) and key (opposite and right) for your chosen colorway. Cross-stitch using two strands of floss over two linen threads. For the French knots, use two strands of floss.

3 Repeat the border as many times as necessary to fit across the towel, leaving at least ⅝ in. (1.5 cm) unstitched at either end for hems.

4 When the design is complete, backstitch the outlines using one strand of floss over two linen threads. Remove the basting and press the band on the wrong side with a warm iron, taking care not to crush the stitching. ▲

5 Pin the band in place on the towel, turning in the raw ends and trimming them to ⅝ in. (1.5 cm) beyond the edge of the towel. Slip-stitch the band in place using matching sewing thread. ◄

BROWN COLORWAY	
COLOR	SKEINS
Z 420 Brown	1
• 422 Pale brown	1
I 434 Golden brown	1
H 436 Camel brown	1
+ 722 Pale orange	1
▲ 738 Tan	1
T 3347 Moss green	1
U 3348 Pistachio	1
– 3828 Tawny brown	1
French knots	
O 726 Yellow	1
✕ 3078 Buttermilk	1
Backstitch	
＼ 801 Deep brown	1
＼ 869 Chestnut brown	1
＼ 975 Rich brown	1

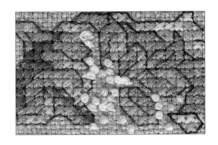

French knots in yellow and buttermilk add texture to the border design. Work the French knots using two strands of embroidery floss.

BROWN COLORWAY

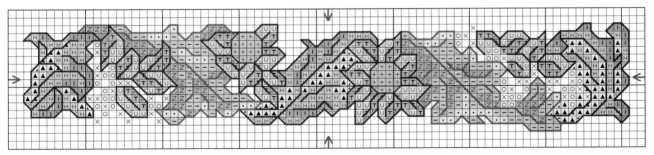

GREEN COLORWAY

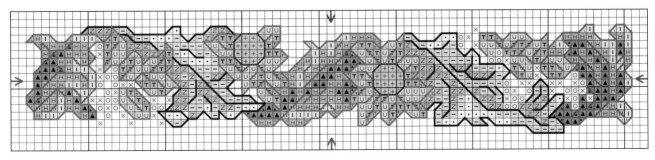

PICTURE MOUNT

Borders are easy to adapt. This lovely picture mount uses the green William Morris border four times, and it works just as well with the brown colorway. The stitched piece measures 6 in. (15 cm) square.

YOU WILL NEED
❋ 28-count oatmeal linen, 9 in. (23 cm) square
❋ DMC stranded floss as listed on page 230 or 231
❋ Tapestry needle, size 26
❋ Embroidery hoop
❋ Thread for basting
❋ Double-stick tape and masking tape

1 Mount the fabric in the hoop. Start stitching at the top left-hand corner of the linen, at least 2 in. (5 cm) in from each edge. Work the design following the chart for your chosen colorway on page 231 and the appropriate color key.

2 Cross-stitch using two strands of floss over two threads of linen. Backstitch using one strand of floss over two threads. Work the French knots with two strands of floss.

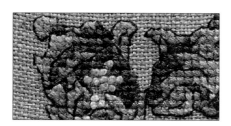

3 When you have finished working the first border, turn the linen 90 degrees and work the second border at right angles to the first. Repeat to work the remaining two sides. ▲

4 Press the completed design from the wrong side with a warm iron. Take the work to a professional framers to get a mat cut and a frame to fit.

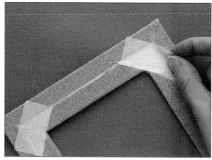

5 Cut out the center of the linen, leaving ¾ in. (2 cm) all around the stitching. Trim around the outside of the stitching in the same way.

6 Cover the mat in double-stick tape. Center the embroidery on top, and fold the excess linen to the back, snipping diagonally into the corners so that the fabric lies smoothly. Secure the fabric at the back with masking tape. ◄

CHINESE SYMBOLS

GEOMETRIC CHINESE
SYMBOLS STITCHED IN
COOL BLUES ADD A
SOPHISTICATED FINISH
TO A PLAIN BATHROBE
AND PAJAMAS.

ORIENTAL ROBE

Add a hint of the Orient to a terry-cloth bathrobe with circular Chinese characters worked in three shades of blue.

The characters are inspired by ancient symbols embroidered on antique Chinese robes to bring long life, good fortune, and joy to the wearer. There are three circular designs, and each one is worked in a different shade of blue. Seven motifs are stitched on the robe

shown here, but you may stitch as many or as few as you wish.

To stand out against the thick terry cloth, the characters need to be big and bold. They are stitched over 8-count waste canvas using four strands of floss, and they measure 3⅜ in. (8.5 cm) across.

YOU WILL NEED

* ❁ 8-count waste canvas, 5 in. (13 cm) square for each character
* ❁ DMC stranded floss as listed in the color key
* ❁ Crewel needle, size 4
* ❁ Sewing needle and thread for basting
* ❁ Embroidery hoop
* ❁ Tweezers
* ❁ Terry-cloth robe

COLOR KEY

COLORS	SKEINS
◎ 796 Dark blue	2
― 798 Medium blue	2
✕ 809 Light blue	2

STITCHING THE ROBE

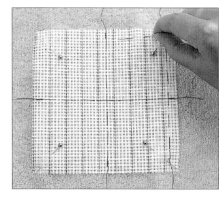

1 Mark the center of each piece of waste canvas with two lines of basting. Arrange the pieces randomly on the robe. When you are happy with the design, pin and baste the waste canvas pieces in place. ▲

2 Referring to the charts (opposite) and the color key (left), select each character in turn and cross-stitch it from the center outward using four strands of floss in the crewel needle. Work each stitch over one pair of canvas threads.

3 When all the motifs are complete, dampen the waste canvas and remove the threads with the tweezers. Press the stitching very lightly from the wrong side, using a warm iron.

Make sure that the top halves of all the cross stitches lie in the same direction.

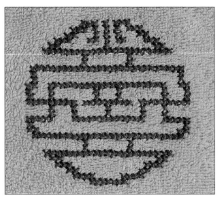

The linear designs are surrounded by broken circles of stitching.

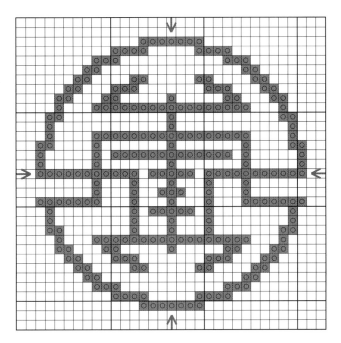

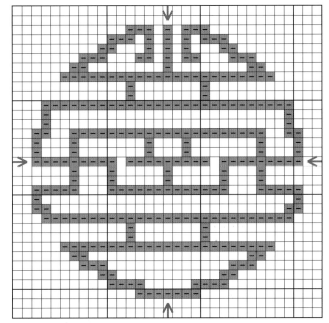

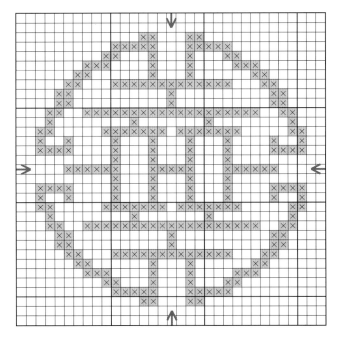

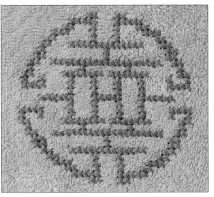

To ensure good coverage on the terry cloth, use four strands of floss throughout.

CHINESE PAJAMAS

Smaller-scale characters suit the finer fabric of the pajamas, so the designs shown here are stitched over 14-count waste canvas rather than the coarser 8-count used for the robe. For extra interest, use a variegated thread that shades from pale to dark blue. Each character measures 2 in. (5 cm) across.

YOU WILL NEED

❋ 14-count waste canvas, 4 in. (10 cm) square for each symbol

❋ Crewel needle, size 7

❋ DMC variegated stranded floss: three skeins of 121 (blue)

❋ Thread for basting

❋ Embroidery hoop

❋ Tweezers

❋ White cotton pajamas

1 Mark the center of each piece of waste canvas with basting. Arrange them on the pajamas, and baste them in place.

2 Referring to the charts on page 235, select each motif in turn and stitch it using two strands of the variegated floss. Work each stitch over one pair of canvas threads. Work from the center out, and complete each individual cross stitch before moving on to the next, so that the variegated floss color changes smoothly.

3 When the stitching is complete, dampen the waste canvas and remove the threads with the tweezers. Press the stitching lightly from the wrong side.

BRIGHT IDEAS

PAJAMA BAG

Coordinate nightwear with a smart pajama bag. Buy one ready-made or make one following the instructions on pages 283–284. Cut a 5-in. (13-cm) square of 8-count waste canvas, mark the center with basting, and baste it to the bag front. Select a motif from the charts on page 235 and stitch it as for the robe.

ANCIENT EGYPT

IMAGINE THE DYNASTIC SPLENDOR OF THE
ANCIENT EGYPTIANS WITH DESIGNS THAT REFLECT
THE COLORS AND SHAPES OF THE DESERT.

DRESSING-ROOM ACCESSORIES

Make a jewelry bag and clothes brush using designs inspired by the days of the pharaohs—scarab beetles, pyramids, and papyrus from the fertile banks of the Nile.

On a background of brilliant sky blue, these Egyptian-style designs are eye-catching. The jewelry bag is based on the flap bag shown on pages 291–292, with a bead and tassel trim for a regal finishing touch. The finished bag measures 8¼ x 4¼ in. (21 x 11 cm). For the clothes brush design, you can use a clothes brush specially made for embroidery, available from needlework stores and by mail order.

STITCHING THE JEWELRY BAG

1 Fold the linen in half lengthwise and baste down the foldline. Using two strands of floss over two linen threads, stitch the fan design, 3 in. (7.5 cm) above one short edge. Stitch the side border with the center 1 in. (2.5 cm) to the right of the fan. Work five complete pyramids. Flip the chart to stitch the left-hand border.

2 Backstitch using one strand of black over two linen threads. Handstitch the cord along the base of the fan and ⅜ in. (1 cm) below the pyramids. Trim away 2 in. (5 cm) all around the linen. Assemble the bag with a 3½-in. (9-cm) deep straight flap, as shown on pages 291–292.

STITCHING THE CLOTHES BRUSH

1 Mark the center of the linen with basting. Stitch the first half of the design from the chart, using three strands of floss and working each stitch over two fabric threads. Then turn the chart around and stitch the second half. Use two strands of black for the backstitching.

2 Take the metal backing off the brush. Center the batting, then the embroidery on top. Trim the fabrics to leave a ⅝-in. (1.5-cm) border all around the metal. Fold the edges around and stitch them securely across the metal backing. Then reassemble the brush.

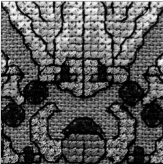

The black backstitch outlines help to define the motifs, such as this scarab beetle surrounded by a fan of papyrus. ▲

Metallic gold floss adds glittering splendor to the clothes-brush design. Metallic threads can knot and break easily, so work with lengths of no more than 10 in. (25 cm).

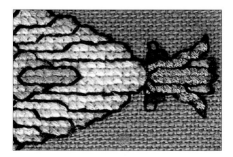

HAIR CLIP

This ancient Egyptian-style hair clip is worked on plastic canvas (see pages 21–22). You can buy hair-clip backings in notions departments.

> ### YOU WILL NEED
> * 14-count plastic canvas, 6½ x 3 in. (16 x 8 cm)
> * DMC stranded floss as listed on page 238
> * Hair-clip backing
> * Tapestry needle, size 20
> * Permanent marker
> * ½ yd. (40 cm) metallic gold cord trim
> * Sewing needle and thread

1 Mark the center of the plastic canvas with the permanent marker. Working from the center out, stitch the design, following the chart (right). Use three strands of floss and two for the backstitch. Work each stitch over one canvas mesh. Cut around the motif, leaving one square of canvas all around.

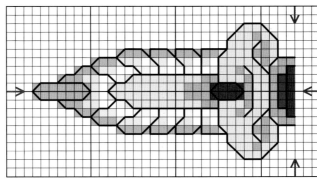

The chart shows half the design. Stitch this first, working out to one side from the center of the plastic canvas. Then turn the chart around to stitch the other half.

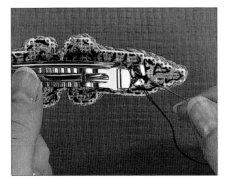

2 Using two strands of the gold floss, stitch the gold cord trim around the outside edge of the motif, so that it covers the unstitched canvas holes. Center the hair-clip backing on the back of the plastic canvas, and stitch it firmly in place. ▲

BRIGHT IDEAS

ANIMAL FORMS

The sleek silhouettes of the snake and bird of prey add an ancient Egyptian touch to silky cream lingerie. You will need 14-count waste canvas, a size 9 crewel needle, tweezers, and the stranded floss listed on page 238. For each motif, cut a 3-in. (8-cm) square of waste canvas. Mark the center and baste in place. Stitch the motif from the center out, using two strands of floss over one pair of threads. When complete, dampen the waste canvas and remove the threads with the tweezers.

GRECIAN BORDERS

THE CLEAN, SIMPLE LINES OF GRECIAN BORDER
DESIGNS ADD FRESH ACCENTS TO BATHROOM
ACCESSORIES. CHOOSE COLORS TO ACCENTUATE
THE COOL OCEAN THEME.

BORDER SAMPLER

Mix and match simple stylized borders in clear shades of aqua to make a sampler to brighten your bathroom.

This sampler features a variety of Grecian-inspired designs. Some are based on the classic key motif while others repeat geometric patterns. The square tile, the fish motifs, and the swirling waves accentuate the watery theme. Repeat sections as many times as necessary to make a bathroom sampler of your required size. To help you calculate the finished size of your design, the sections from the chart on the top right measure 6½ in. (16.5 cm) across when stitched; from the chart at middle right, 5¼ in. (13.2 cm); and those from the chart below right, 9¼ in. (23.5 cm). Allow for a space of up to ¼ in. (5 mm) between each section.

STITCHING A SAMPLER

1 Photocopy the charts (opposite). If you are making a large sampler, you will need to make several photocopies. Cut the various designs into strips, and arrange them as you like. The short vertical lines on the various designs mark the pattern repeats. Stick the strips in the correct order on a sheet of paper.

2 Mark the center of the Hardanger fabric with basting and overcast the edges to prevent them from fraying. Mount the prepared fabric in the embroidery hoop.

3 Using three strands of floss throughout, and referring to the color key (opposite), cross-stitch the sampler from the center out. Work each stitch over two pairs of threads, and leave one pair of threads between each stitch. Leave a space of four to six pairs of threads between each design. Repeat each design across the fabric to the required width, leaving 2 in. (5 cm) of fabric unstitched all around the sampler.

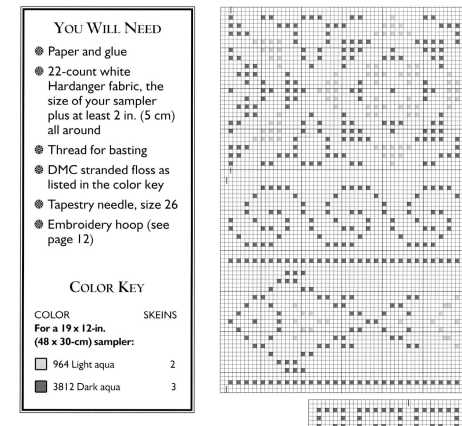

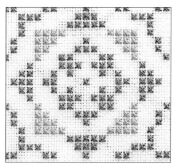

Measuring 2½ in. (6.5 cm) from top to bottom, the star border is the deepest of the border designs. Remember to leave one pair of threads between each cross stitch.

4 When the stitching is complete, remove the work from the hoop and press it on the wrong side with a warm iron over a folded towel, in order not to crush the stitching. Mount the finished piece on cardboard (see page 298), and take it to a professional for framing.

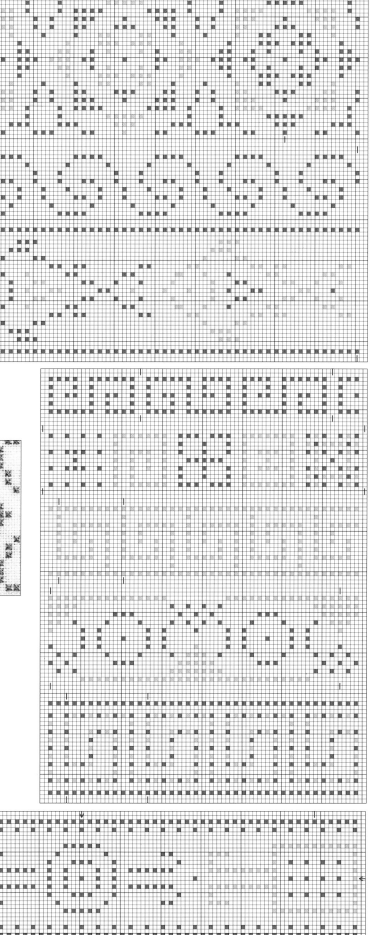

BATH MAT

Achieve a cool and clean-looking effect by using coordinating shades of aqua. The bath mat is worked in matte embroidery cotton, using half cross stitch on a large-mesh canvas. When you are stitching the corners, use the chart (below right) to help you position the fish and wave motifs correctly.

The bath mat is fully washable. To avoid distortion when it is laundered, it is important to wash the completed work and the backing fabric before you assemble the mat. The finished mat measures approximately 26 x 18 in. (66 x 46 cm).

YOU WILL NEED

* 10-count white mono canvas, 30 x 22 in. (76 x 55 cm)
* Sewing needle and thread for basting and stitching
* Masking tape
* Rectangular embroidery frame
* Large needle and button thread
* DMC matte embroidery thread as listed in the color key
* Tapestry needle, size 18
* Heavyweight white or cream cotton backing fabric, washed and ironed

COLOR KEY

COLORS	SKEINS
☐ Blanc	36
☐ 2952 Light aqua	1
■ 2134 Dark aqua	2

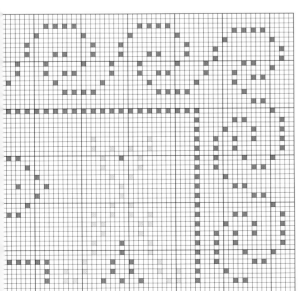

STITCHING THE BATH MAT

1 Mark the center of the canvas with basting, bind the edges with masking tape, and mount it in the rectangular embroidery frame, following the manufacturer's instructions.

2 Work the design using half cross stitch over one canvas mesh throughout. Working from the center outward, stitch the white central panel, which is 167 stitches wide and 69 stitches deep.

3 Referring to the chart, (below left), and starting at the edge of one short end of the white panel, stitch the inner single border, the fish, then the outer single border, and, finally, the waves. Flip the chart and repeat at the other short end of the inner panel. Turn the fish and wave border chart on page 243 (top right) upside down to complete the design.

4 To finish, work eight rows of white all around. Take the work out of the frame and wash it carefully in tepid water. Lay it out flat and allow it to dry thoroughly at room temperature, away from direct heat and sunlight. Press the work on the wrong side. If it is very distorted, block it to shape, referring to the instructions on pages 295–296.

5 Trim the canvas all around, 1 in. (2.5 cm) outside the stitching. Cut a piece of backing fabric the same size, and pin it to the canvas with right sides together.

6 Stitch all around with matching thread, as close as possible to the needlepoint. Leave an 8-in. (20-cm) gap in one side for turning right side out. Trim the seam allowances and clip across the corners. Turn the work right side out, and slip-stitch the gap edges together.

The wave motifs from the sampler have been subtly adapted so that they flow smoothly around the outer corners of the mat. The fish swimming along beneath the waves seem to be chasing each others' tails.

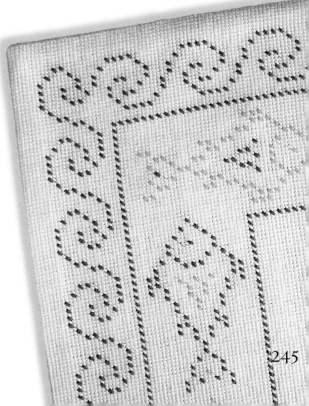

245

TOWEL AND WASHCLOTH SET

Repeat a design across aida bands to decorate a matching towel and washcloth. You could also add borders to a laundry bag, and even a bathroom curtain—it is a quick way to coordinate an entire bathroom scheme, down to the tiniest detail.

Before you start stitching, check that your chosen design fits across the band. A 2-in. (5-cm) aida band can accommodate up to 26 stitches, so if you wish to use the diamond border, for example, you will need to substitute a band at least 3 in. (7.5 cm) deep.

YOU WILL NEED

- ❋ Towel and washcloth
- ❋ Strip of 2-in. (5-cm) wide aida band to fit across towel and washcloth, plus 4 in. (10 cm)
- ❋ Tapestry needle, size 26
- ❋ DMC stranded floss as listed in the color key on page 243
- ❋ Sewing needle and thread for basting and stitching

1 Cut a strip of band long enough to fit across the towel, plus 2 in. (5 cm) for turning under. Repeat for washcloth. Fold each strip in half across the width, and mark the center with basting.

2 Cross-stitch your chosen designs from the center out, referring to the charts and color key on page 243 and following the repeats (marked in red). Use two strands of floss and work each stitch over one thread block. Leave one thread block between each stitch.

3 Press the bands on the wrong side with a warm iron. Slip-stitch them in place on the towel and washcloth, tucking in the raw ends.

The repetition of simple shapes—dark aqua rings and light and dark aqua triangles—lends the ring border an air of elegant simplicity. One thread block separates each cross stitch, giving an open effect.

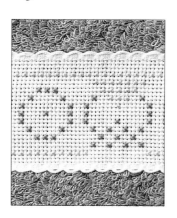

BRIGHT IDEAS

SOAP BAG

Individual motifs make quick embellishments for accessories, such as this soap bag. Work the motif on a scrap of Hardanger fabric left over from another project. Cut it out, leaving a border all around. Stitch it in place with cross stitch, ¼ in. (6 mm) in from the fabric edges. Fray the edges to create a fringe.

FRENCH-STYLE LAVENDER BAGS

THESE OLD-FASHIONED FRENCH-STYLE
BOOTS MAKE AN UNUSUAL DESIGN
FOR FRAGRANT SACHETS AND A PICTURE
FOR THE BEDROOM.

SCENTED SACHETS

Old-style, lace-up, miniature boots make unusual sachets. Fill them with lavender or fine potpourri to add a decorative and sweet-smelling touch to your closet or to a chest of drawers.

The embroidery on the boots is very simple, using cross stitch and French knots; and, if you prefer, you can use cross stitches as an alternative to the French knots.

YOU WILL NEED

To make six boots:

- ❋ 14-count cream aida, 18 x 12 in. (45 x 30 cm)
- ❋ DMC stranded floss as listed in the color key
- ❋ Six squares of coordinating fabric, 5 in. (13 cm) square
- ❋ Tapestry needle, size 26
- ❋ Embroidery hoop (see page 12)
- ❋ Sewing needle and thread for basting and stitching
- ❋ Coordinating ribbon
- ❋ Potpourri or lavender

This miniature floral pattern, worked in pink and green, is typical of old-fashioned French textile designs. The boot is worked entirely in cross stitch, using two strands of floss throughout.

STITCHING THE BOOTS

1 Divide the aida into six 6-in. (15-cm) squares. Mark the center of the aida with basting, then mount the fabric in the embroidery hoop.

2 Working from the center outward, cross-stitch using two strands of floss over one block of aida. For the French knots, use two strands of floss.

3 Once the designs are complete, remove the aida from the embroidery hoop and press it gently on the wrong side with a warm iron.

MAKING THE SACHETS

1 Place the embroidery and the backing fabric together, right sides facing, and pin. Cut around the embroidery and backing, leaving a ³⁄₈ in. (1 cm) seam allowance.

2 Stitch around the shape of the boot, as close to the embroidery as possible. Leave a 1¼ in. (3 cm) gap at the top of the boot for turning right side out.

3 Trim the seam allowances neatly, making sure that you leave two blocks of aida all around. Turn the embroidery right side out.

4 Stuff the boot with fine potpourri or lavender, making sure that it reaches the toe and heel of the boot.

5 Insert two lengths of ribbon into the opening at the top of the boot. Slip-stitch the opening edges together, securing the ribbon in place at the same time. You can either use the ribbon to hang up the boot sachet or tie it into a neat bow as a finishing touch.

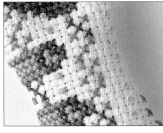

Work the lines of yellow French knots using two strands of floss.

COLOR KEY

COLORS	SKEINS
· Blanc	1
● 333 Dark violet	1
Z 340 Violet	1
N 523 Light gray-green	1
U 760 Light rose pink	1
■ 814 Dark red	1
□ 3051 Dark green	1
⌐ 3052 Medium green	1
T 3712 Dark rose pink	1
− 3713 Light pink	1

French knots

I 3822 Yellow	1

Backstitch

╲ 340 Violet	

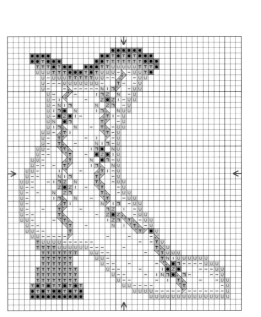

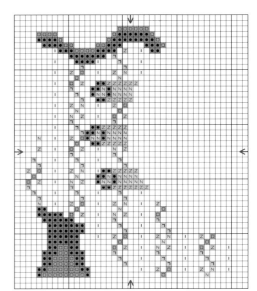

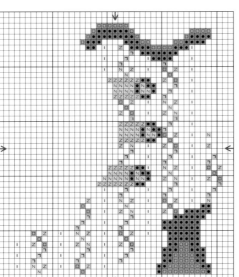

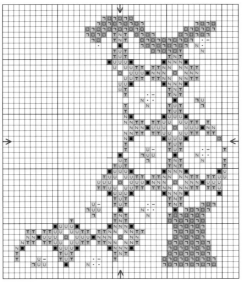

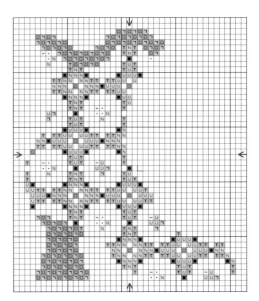

The six boot designs make up three pairs. A chart for the left boot of the pink and purple design (top) is shown on page 250 (with the picture).

249

SHOE PICTURE

The finished stitched area of this whimsical bedroom picture measures 4¾ x 4 in. (12 x 10.5 cm). You will need a 10 x 8-in. (25 x 20-cm) piece of 14-count aida and the embroidery threads and stitching equipment listed on pages 248 and 249.

STITCHING THE PICTURE

1 Stitch the shoe first, following the chart (below). Work from the center out, and use two strands of floss for the cross stitch and French knots. Make each stitch over one thread block. Refer to the key on page 249 for thread colors.

2 Stitch the border, starting at the top left-hand corner and working around following the chart. Once this is completed, work the lettering in backstitch using one strand of violet floss over one thread block.

3 When the design is complete, press it from the wrong side using a warm iron. Take the piece to a professional to have it framed or follow the instructions on pages 297–298.

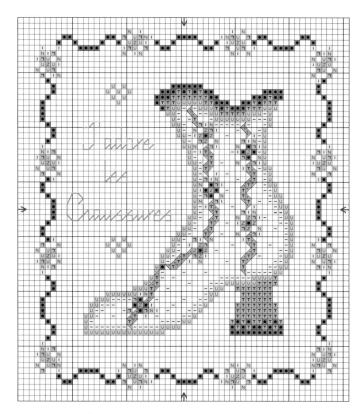

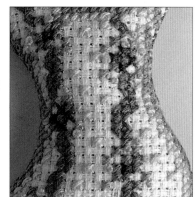

Fractional (three-quarter) stitches help to give a smooth line to the edges of the swirling ribbons, while yellow French knots add texture to the dainty posies of flowers.

Written in an elegant script, the words help to reinforce the French theme. Translated into English, the message simply reads: "I love shoes."

TABLE DRESSING

SMALL BLUEBIRDS AND SIMPLE CONIFER TREE SHAPES LINE UP IN THESE SMART SCANDINAVIAN-STYLE TABLE ACCESSORIES.

TABLE RUNNER AND MAT

Brightly plumed birds and stylized trees make excellent borders and panels for table mats.

These bluebird and conifer motifs, worked as panels at each end of the table runner, are inspired by traditional stitched sampler designs. The conifers are shaped to a point, and each stands on its own base. The birds step out smartly in their bright plumage between the rows of trees. The conifers from the main design are repeated to make a border for a coordinating mat. The completed table runner measures 30 x 12 in. (76 x 31 cm) and the finished mat measures 13 1/2 in. (34 cm) square.

The large tree is worked in diamonds of satin stitch, using a variegated thread very effectively.

TABLE RUNNER

1 Baste a 30 x 12-in. (76 x 31-cm) rectangle in the center of the table runner fabric to mark the finished size. Baste lengthwise along the center, then work two more lines of basting, 2¾ in. (7 cm) in from the short sides of the rectangle to mark the vertical center of each embroidered panel. Mount the fabric in the hoop.

2 Work the panel from the center of the design outward, using two strands of floss throughout and referring to the chart (left) and the color key. Work the cross stitch first, over two fabric threads.

3 For the satin-stitch lines, work each stitch vertically over four threads. On the large tree work the satin stitches over the number of threads indicated on the chart. Work the backstitch over two threads.

4 Take the finished piece out of the hoop and press it lightly from the wrong side. Trim the fabric ¾ in. (2 cm) outside the basted rectangle. Remove all the basting.

5 Press a ⅜ in. (1 cm) double hem to the wrong side all around the edge. Unfold the pressed edges at each corner to miter the corner, referring to the instructions on page 278. Refold the hems and slip-stitch them in place.

SQUARE MAT

1 Stitch from the center out, using three strands of floss over two fabric threads. Refer to the chart (below) and the color key (opposite). Work the first corner, placing the inner border 47 threads out from the center.

2 Turn the chart 90 degrees to work the next corner; repeat twice. Take the work out of the hoop and press it lightly from the wrong side. With the design centered, trim the mat to 13½ in. (34 cm) square.

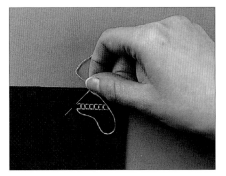

3 Using two strands of white, work four-sided stitch, ⅝ in. (1.5 cm) in from the edges, as follows: working over two threads, work straight backstitches for the right side of the stitch, the bottom, the top, and the left, so forming a cross on the wrong side. When the edging is complete, fringe back to the edging. ▲

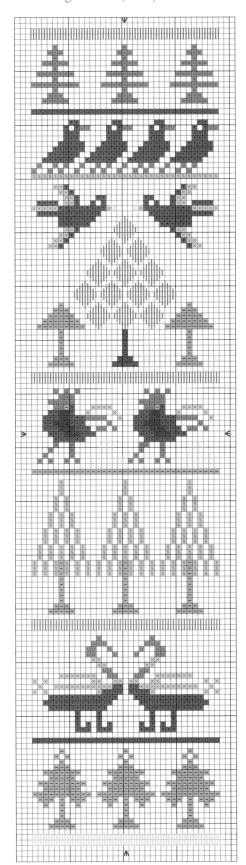

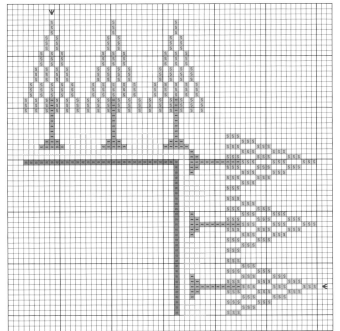

253

PLACE MAT AND NAPKIN

MAKING THE PLACE MAT

1 Baste a 16 x 12-in. (41 x 30-cm) rectangle in the center of the aida to mark the finished size. Mark the horizontal center with basting, then mark the short side edges 11 blocks in from the basted outline to indicate the top of the trees. Mount the fabric in the hoop.

2 Refer to the color key on page 252 and the tree corner chart on page 253. Use two strands of floss throughout, and work each stitch over one block of aida. Begin stitching with a tree just right of the center, placing the top of the tree level with the basted line.

3 Work ten trees at each short end of the aida, with a clump of grass between each tree. Finish each end of each border with a clump of grass and a final smaller clump, omitting the two center lines.

4 Take the work out of the hoop and press it lightly. Work the border in four-sided stitch, following Square Mat, step 3, on page 253. Use navy floss, and work seven blocks in from the basted outline. Cut to size along the basted outline and fringe the edges up to border.

MAKING THE NAPKIN

1 On the smaller piece of aida, baste a 12-in. (30-cm) square to mark the finished size of the napkin. Work the design in one corner, positioning the outer border 11 blocks in from the basted outline. Use two strands of floss and work over one block of aida, referring to the chart (right) and the color key on page 252.

2 To complete the napkin, refer to Making the Place Mat, step 4 (below left).

Work a smaller grass clump at the edges of each border on the place mat. The backstitching and the inner border finish five stitches past the clump.

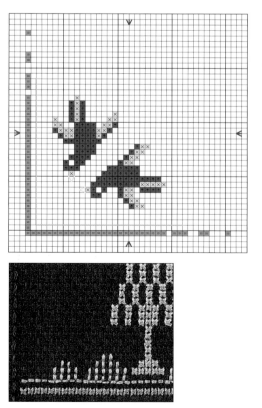

TARTAN TRIMS

ADD A TOUCH OF CLASS TO
TOWELS AND BATHROBES WITH
THESE COLORFUL DESIGNS.

BATHROBE AND TOWEL

A fluffy white bathrobe with a tartan-bordered pocket, and a single-color towel trimmed to match make a welcoming and stylish treat for guests.

The tartan borders are worked on strips of aida with special stitched borders on the long edges. The designs are worked in a mixture of single-color stitching and tweeded stitching—tweeding uses two or more colors together in the needle to create subtle color blends.

YOU WILL NEED

- ❋ Terry-cloth robe with pocket
- ❋ Towel
- ❋ 14-count antique white aida, 3¼ in. (8 cm) wide to fit across the towel and the top of the robe pocket, plus 3¼ in. (8 cm)
- ❋ DMC stranded floss as listed in the color key
- ❋ Tapestry needle, size 26
- ❋ Sewing needle and thread for basting and stitching
- ❋ Tartan ribbon, 1⅜ in. (3.5 cm) wide to fit around all edges of the towel plus 4 in. (10 cm)
- ❋ Sewing machine (optional)

MAGENTA TARTAN

COLORS		SKEINS
⊡	Blanc	1
T	909 Green	2
▬	917 Magenta	2
Tweeded cross stitch		
+	Blanc/909 Green	
S	Blanc/917 Magenta	
◢	909 Green/917 Magenta	

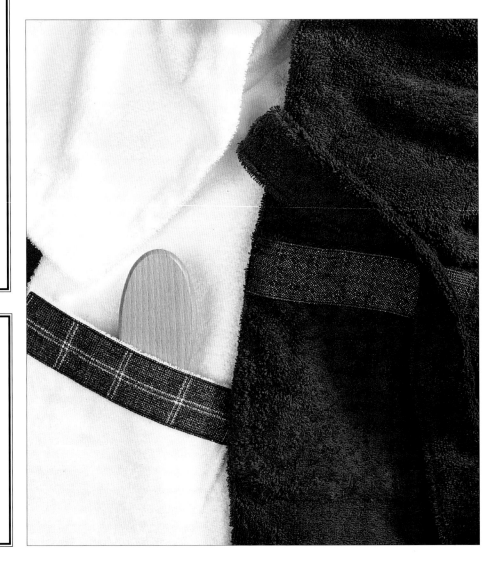

The magenta tartan has alternating checks of magenta and green with spaced double stripes of tweeded white stitching.

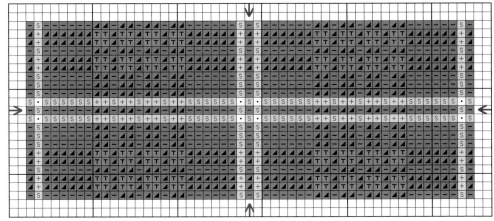

STITCHING THE POCKET TRIM

1 Mark the center of the aida strip. Cross-stitch the design from the center outward, referring to the appropriate chart and color key (opposite below and below). Use two strands of floss; for the tweeded stitches use one strand of each color. Repeat the design until it fits the pocket top.

2 Press the work lightly from the wrong side. On the long edges, fold under the excess aida, leaving one thread block showing.

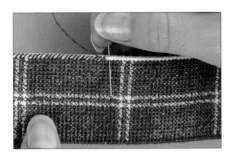

3 Using the main color, work half cross stitch along the long edges from left to right; insert the needle into folded edge and bring it out level with the stitching. ▲

4 Work back along the long edges from right to left to complete the cross stitches. Then use one strand of the main color to backstitch through both the fabric layers between the border half cross stitches and the design, as shown (above). ▲

5 Pin the strip along the top of the pocket, tucking in the raw ends. Using one strand of the main color, backstitch the strip in place along the line of the previous backstitching. Backstitch the ends in place.

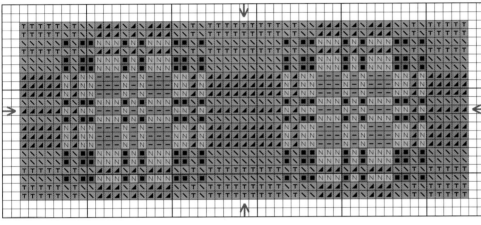

GREEN TARTAN	
COLORS	SKEINS
■ 820 Dark blue	2
T 909 Green	2
─ 917 Magenta	2
Tweeded cross stitch	
◣ 820 Dark blue/909 Green	
N 820 Dark blue/917 Magenta	
◪ 909 Green/917 Magenta	

The green tartan combines magenta with dark blue and green to make a richly colored border.

TRIMMING THE TOWEL

1 If the towel has deep hems, unpick them and trim along the foldlines. Make and sew on the tartan strip as for Stitching the Pocket Trim, steps **1** to **5** (above) but don't tuck in the short ends of the aida band; instead, trim the ends level with the edges of the towel.

2 Press a fold lengthwise in the ribbon, slightly off-center, so that one side is a little wider than the other. Sandwich the towel edges in the ribbon with the narrower part on the right side. Fold neat miters at the corners. Turn under one end of ribbon and lap it over the other, raw, end. Pin, baste, and machine stitch or backstitch the ribbon in place.

257

BABY TOWEL WRAP

A lavender plaid border gives a baby towel wrap an upscale look. Ready-made baby towels like this one—complete with aida hoods for counted thread embroidery—are sold by specialist needlecraft stores, or you can apply a separate aida band to a plain hooded towel.

If you'd rather use one of the tartan designs from pages 256–257, work the horizontal line of basting 11, rather than ten, holes above the bound edge in step **1**.

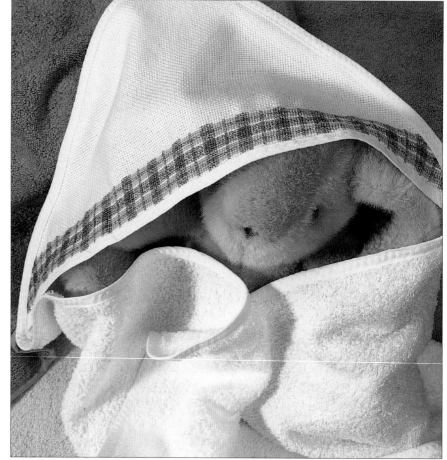

YOU WILL NEED

- ✸ Baby towel with aida corner hood or plain hooded towel
- ✸ DMC stranded floss as listed in the color key
- ✸ Tapestry needle, size 26
- ✸ Thread for basting

1 Fold the hood in half vertically and mark the fold with basting. Work a horizontal line of basting ten holes up from the bound edge. The lines of basting cross at the center of the design. The bottom of the design will be one hole above the bound edge.

2 Cross-stitch the design from the center out, referring to the chart and the color key (below), or use one of the designs from pages 256–257. Use two strands of floss; for the tweeded stitches have one strand of each color in the needle.

3 Continue stitching right across the hood and into the corner at each side, repeating the design as required; for a neat finish work right up to the bound edges at the sides. Press the work lightly from the wrong side, taking care not to crush the stitching.

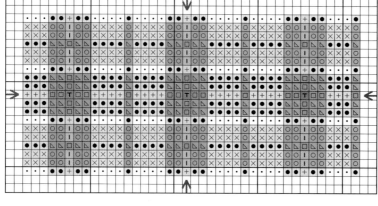

The cool lavender tartan alternates checks of pale blue and lavender with stripes of tweeded green and white.

LAVENDER TARTAN

COLORS		SKEINS
⊡	Blanc	I
◩	208 Purple	I
☒	800 Pale blue	I
▣ T	909 Green	I

Tweeded cross stitch

⊙	Blanc/208 Purple
⊞	Blanc/909 Green
◎	208 Purple/800 Pale blue
▣	208 Purple/909 Green
▯ I	800 Pale blue/909 Green

TURKISH BORDERS

RICHLY COLORED
DESIGNS FOUND ON
TILES AMONG THE
RUINED SPLENDORS
OF THE OTTOMAN
EMPIRE INSPIRED THESE
FINE BORDERS.

TURKISH BATH MAT

The turquoise border, worked in shades of clear aqua outlined in the deepest blue, is stitched on canvas to make a colorful border for a bath mat.

The border is stitched in half cross stitch using pearl cotton on stable interlock canvas. The central padded panel can be made from terry cloth or from a small towel. The finished mat measures 21 x 16 in. (53 x 41 cm).

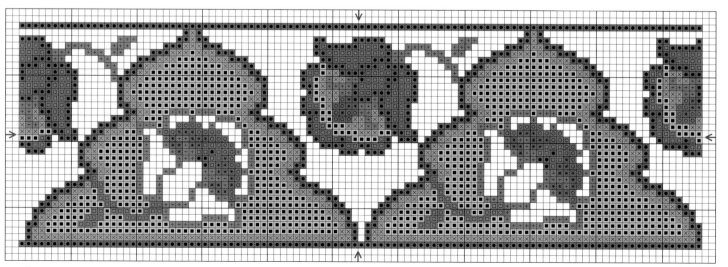

1 Bind the edges of the canvas with the masking tape, mark the center with basting and mount it on the embroidery frame.

2 Referring to the corner chart (below) and the color key (opposite), start stitching at the center of the right-hand short edge of the canvas, with the outer row of royal blue stitches 2 in. (5 cm) in from the edge of the canvas.

3 Use four strands of pearl cotton and work each half cross stitch over one canvas mesh. Work down toward the corner, then along the lower edge to complete the first corner motif.

4 Turn the chart 90 degrees counterclockwise. Work another corner motif, but this time work the motif upward to the corner and then along the top edge.

5 Referring to the border chart (opposite), work one design repeat only along each long edge, working from the right to the left. Follow the corner chart (below) to complete the two remaining corners and the other short edge.

6 Trim the canvas ⅝ in. (1.5 cm) outside the stitching. Cut the backing fabric to the same size, and trim the foam to fit the central unstitched panel.

7 Place the terry cloth on the ➤ foam, and tuck the raw edges under the foam. Hold it in place with loose basting stitches. Then hand-stitch the towel-covered foam to the central panel on the canvas.

8 Place the backing fabric and canvas right sides together and raw edges level. Baste, then stitch together all around, leaving an 8-in. (20-cm) opening at the center of one edge. Trim corners and turn the mat right side out. Tuck in raw edges and stitch the opening.

The turquoise motif is stitched in two shades of aqua with a royal blue outline. The central flower is worked in dark rose, maroon, and green.

TURKISH TILE

The blue border makes an exotically patterned frame for a mirror tile. The border is stitched in stranded floss on white aida—the white areas of the design are left unstitched. The finished frame is 12 in. (30 cm) square. The quantities of thread listed include enough to make the towel borders, too, as shown on page 264.

YOU WILL NEED

- ❋ 11-count white aida, 16 in. (40 cm) square
- ❋ DMC stranded floss as listed in the color key
- ❋ Tapestry needle, size 26
- ❋ Thread for basting
- ❋ Medium weight iron-on interfacing, 16 in. (40 cm) square
- ❋ Foam board, 12 in. (30 cm) square
- ❋ Rectangular embroidery frame or large hoop
- ❋ White glue
- ❋ Transfer fusing web
- ❋ Mirror tile, 9 in. (23 cm) square
- ❋ Utility knife

COLOR KEY

COLORS		SKEINS
◉	326 Dark rose	1
⊞	701 Green	2
⬤	796 Royal blue	6
▢	798 French blue	7
✳	814 Maroon	1
⊠	943 Aqua	5
◼	959 Pale aqua	3

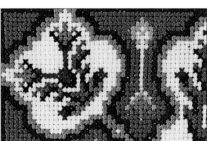

At the corners the symmetrical central motif opens to reveal two flower-like emblems surrounded by white unstitched aida.

The central part of the motif is stitched in dark rose and maroon with green leaves at the top. This is encased within a bulb-like outer layer worked in royal blue and French blue.

1 Overcast the edges of the aida and mark the center with basting. Mount the fabric in the rectangular frame or hoop.

2 Cross-stitch the design using four strands of floss over one thread block. Referring to the corner chart (below) and the color key (opposite), start with the outer row of aqua: begin at the center of one edge, about 2 in. (5 cm) in from the fabric edge.

3 Continue stitching until the first quarter of the design is complete. Turn the chart 90 degrees and work the next quarter as before. Repeat this twice more to complete the stitched frame.

4 Take the work off the frame or hoop and press it lightly on the wrong side. Fuse the interfacing to the wrong side, and trim the edges 1 in. (2.5 cm) from the stitching all around, including the opening.

5 Clip to the stitching at the inner corners. Press the excess fabric to the wrong side all around the outer edge and the opening. Secure the fabric edges with transfer fusing web, following manufacturer's instructions.

6 Trim the foam board so that it is slightly smaller than the frame. Center the mirror on top and glue it in place. Glue the frame over the board.

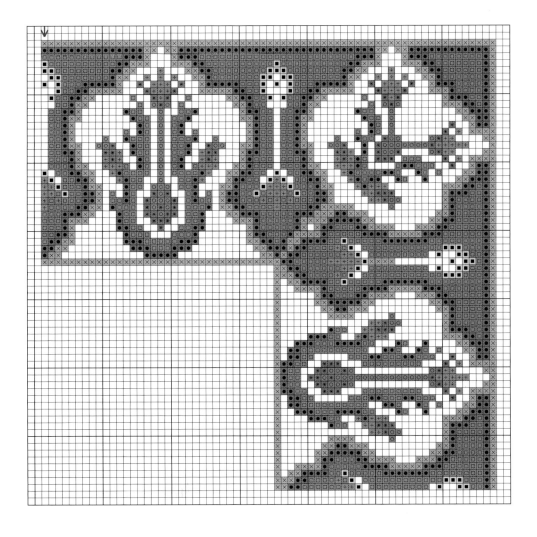

TURKISH TOWELS

These designs make coordinating trims for colored towels. They are cross-stitched on white aida, so the white areas can be left plain. The borders are 3 in. (7.5 cm) deep—you will have enough thread left over from the tile and mat to make borders for two small bath towels.

YOU WILL NEED

* 11-count white aida, 7 in. (18 cm) wide by the width of the towel plus 4 in. (10 cm)
* DMC stranded floss as listed in the color key on page 262
* Tapestry needle, size 26
* Thread for basting and stitching
* Sewing needle (optional)
* Embroidery hoop

---

1 Mark the center of the aida with basting, and overcast the edges to prevent fraying. Mount the aida in the embroidery hoop.

2 Referring to the border chart (below) or on page 260 and the color key on page 262, cross-stitch the design from the center out. Use four strands of floss and work each stitch over one thread block of the aida fabric.

3 Continue working from the center out, stitching as many repeats as required. Finish the stitching 2 in. (5 cm) from the short ends of the aida. Take the work out of the hoop and press it lightly on the wrong side.

4 Trim the work ⅝ in. (1.5 cm) outside the stitching all around, then press in the excess fabric level with the edges of the stitching. Pin the border on the towel, and stitch it in place by hand or machine.

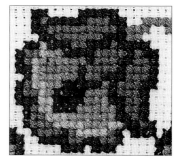

On the turquoise border, the small flower heads have outer petals stitched in two shades of blue, with aqua, green, dark rose, and maroon in the center.

264

MEXICAN BORDERS

RECREATE THE RHYTHMIC PATTERNS
OF TRADITIONAL MEXICAN TEXTILES
IN CROSS-STITCH BORDERS TO
BRIGHTEN UP PLAIN TOWELS.

TOWEL TRIMS

Ready-made evenweave fabric bands make it easy to stitch and apply these decorative borders. Choose from the three designs shown here, or stitch them all for a set.

These colorful border designs are easy enough for a beginner to make, using just cross stitch and backstitch. They are worked on special aida fabric bands with scalloped edges, so once you have worked the design, you need only press under the raw ends and slip-stitch the band in place.

Whichever design you choose from the charts (opposite), start by marking the center of the fabric band and outlining the design area with basting stitches, as shown in step **I** (below). Then follow the chart, working from the center outward. The charts are for repeat patterns, which means that you repeat the design until you have embroidered a long-enough section of the band to fit across your towel.

The quantities of embroidery floss given here are enough to complete a band to fit across a 20-in. (50-cm) wide towel. If you want to trim a larger towel, just stitch a longer band; you will need to buy extra skeins of floss.

STITCHING THE BORDERS

I Fold the band in half across the width and mark the center with basting. Then mark the width and position of the design with two parallel rows of basting, centered along the band. For instance, the Zigzag design is 18 stitches wide, so place the basting 18 thread blocks apart. ▶

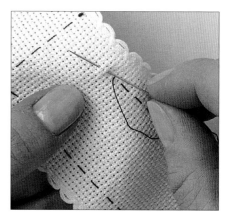

2 Work the design in cross stitch following the chart and using two strands of floss. Work the outlines in backstitch using two strands. Remove basting. Slip-stitch the band in place, turning in raw ends. ▼

Mexican borders add color across three cream towels. The fourth towel and its band were dyed and stitched in a different colorway (see page 268).

266

SCROLL DESIGN	
COLORS	SKEINS
◎ 958 Turquoise	1
U 3830 Cinnamon	2
⁄ 3371 Dark brown	1

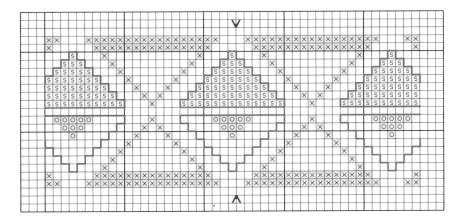

PYRAMID DESIGN A	
COLORS	SKEINS
✕ 922 Pumpkin	1
◎ 958 Turquoise	1
S 3820 Mustard	1
⁄ 3790 Soft brown	1

ZIGZAG DESIGN	
COLORS	SKEINS
◎ 958 Turquoise	1
▽ 975 Copper brown	1
S 3820 Mustard	1
⁄ 3790 Soft brown	1

Scroll stitch guide

Work a turquoise triangle in the center; then a cinnamon block on either side, and the next turquoise triangle. Continue outward, then work the borders. Finally, backstitch the outlines in dark brown.

Pyramid stitch guide

Work a mustard triangle in the center, then the turquoise triangle below. Cross-stitch the pumpkin triangles on either side. Continue outward, then backstitch the outlines in soft brown.

Zigzag stitch guide

Work a turquoise square on the central basted line, then the mustard rectangle and the brown triangle below. Continue outward in both directions. Finally, backstitch the outlines in soft brown.

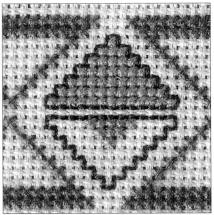

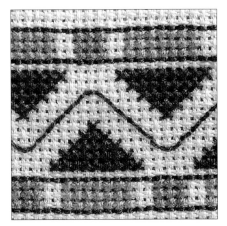

TOILETRY BAG AND TOWEL

Cross stitch borders can be used to decorate all kinds of home items, from curtains and blinds to cushions and storage bags. For an original effect, you can dye the band before stitching the design—it's a clever way to match the band to your fabric and liven up a tired color scheme. Try out this idea with a toiletry bag (right), and a matching towel (pages 266–267).

YOU WILL NEED

❁ Pale colored, pure cotton drawstring bag and towel

❁ 14-count aida band, 2 in. (5-cm) wide, to fit around bag and across towel plus 8 in. (20 cm)

❁ Pumpkin-colored washing-machine dye

❁ Tapestry needle, size 26

❁ DMC stranded floss as listed in the color key

❁ Sewing needle and thread for basting and stitching

1 Follow the manufacturer's instructions to dye the towel, bag, and aida bands. Allow them to dry, then press lightly.

2 Work the bands in the Pyramid Design B colorway. Slip-stitch the band onto the towel. For the bag, turn in one raw end of band and lay it over the other raw end at the back. Slip-stitch in place.

For a perfect match, dye the drawstring bag, aida band, and the towel the same color.

PYRAMID DESIGN B

COLORS		SKEINS
S	958 Turquoise	1
U	3820 Mustard	1
O	3830 Cinnamon	1
⁄	3371 Dark brown	1

BRIGHT IDEAS

ADDING BEADS

Choose tiny glass beads to match one of the colors in your Mexican border. Space them evenly across the band and sew them on with a fine needle and matching thread; secure the thread ends carefully.

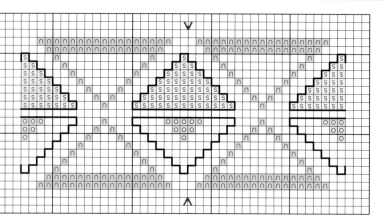

TRAVEL COMPANIONS

CHARACTERS FROM AROUND THE WORLD MAKE APPROPRIATE DECORATIONS FOR YOUR TRAVEL ACCESSORIES.

TRAVEL SET

Personalize a document folder, a bag and your luggage tags with these traditional figures.

WORKING THE DESIGNS

1 Overcast the edges of the aida. Mark the center with basting, working through the central thread blocks. Work referring to the color key and chart (opposite). Each square on the chart represents one stitch worked over one thread block.

2 Use three strands of floss for cross stitch, two for backstitch, and four for French knots, with these exceptions: use four strands to backstitch the Bavarian man's hat brim and the Canadian Mountie's buckle; use one strand for the belly dancer's veil, outlines of the Dutch girl's hair, cap, and tulip, and the Scot's tartan and stock.

BAG BADGE

Follow Working the Designs, steps 1–2 (above left) to work the chosen figure from the chart (opposite). From the chart (left), work a shield outline around the figure. Fuse the transfer web to the wrong side of the work. Cut it out in a shield shape, two blocks outside the stitching.

Fuse the badge to the bag with transfer fusing web. Sew the cord over the raw edges; leave long ends and knot them together at the base. Then tie a knot in each end and trim neatly.

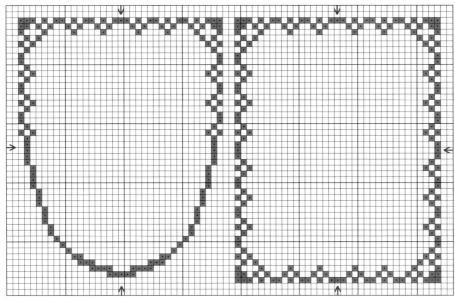

BADGE BORDER   TRAVEL RUG BORDER

LUGGAGE TAG

Stitch the chosen figure, following Working the Design, steps **1–2** (opposite). Trim to fit in the tag. Place in tag with the paper backing and squeeze the sections together.

COLOR KEY

COLORS	SKEINS
H B5200 Bright white	I
X 307 Yellow	I
■ 310 Black	I
— 353 Peach	I
Z 420 Dark hazel	I
F 437 Pale tan	I
● 561 Dark dusty green	I
U 612 Dark beige	I
▲ 666 Bright red	I
O 742 Pale tangerine	I
✕ 801 Dark brown	I
▪ 817 Deep rust	I
▽ 826 Blue	I
I 3363 Antique green	I
+ 3774 Pale cream	I
▫ 3818 Deep emerald	I
I 3820 Deep gold	I
S 3822 Pale gold	I
✳ 3826 Golden brown	I
4 5283 Metallic silver	I

Backstitch

B5200 Bright white	
307 Yellow	
310 Black	
612 Dark beige	
666 Bright red	
702 Spring green	I
742 Pale tangerine	
826 Blue	
3818 Deep emerald	
3822 Pale gold	
5283 Metallic silver	

French knots

612 Dark beige	

MAKING THE DOCUMENT FOLDER

1 Mark the vertical center of the design 7 in. (18 cm) in from short right-hand edge; mark horizontal center midway between long edges. Mount in hoop.

2 Work central figure as for Bag Badge (left). Using 561 (dark dusty green), cross-stitch four vertical lines, stitching on alternate blocks. Work the lines 3 blocks and 27 blocks from sides of shield; leave center square blank and work 41 stitches above and below the center.

3 In the same way, stitch four horizontal lines, 9 and 51 blocks above, and 8 and 50 blocks below the shield; work 26 stitches to either side of the center.

4 Work four more figures, one in each corner rectangle. Remove from hoop and press lightly on the wrong side. Cover the folder, following the instructions on pages 301–302.

TRAVEL RUG

CHARACTER CARDS

Delight a friend with a hand-embroidered greeting card. Stitch the figure as for the rug panels (right), then trim to about 3 x 1¾ in. (8 x 4.5 cm). Fray one square around the edges, then use fabric glue or double-stick tape to attach the character to the front of a plain card mount.

1 Mount the fabric in the hoop, if desired, and stitch each figure following Working the Designs, steps **1–2** on page 270. Work a rectangular red frame around each, following the chart on page 270. Remove from the embroidery hoop and press the work lightly on the wrong side.

2 Trim the aida five blocks outside the stitching. Pin, then baste the panels to the desired positions on the rug. Using white sewing thread, secure in place with running stitches around the edge of the red frame. Fray four blocks around the edges.

YOU WILL NEED

❋ 14-count white aida, 7 x 6 in. (18 x 15 cm), for each badge
❋ DMC stranded floss as listed in the color key on page 271
❋ Tapestry needle, size 24
❋ Travel rug
❋ Sewing needle and thread for basting and stitching
❋ White sewing thread
❋ Embroidery hoop (optional; see page 12)

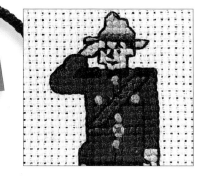

The Canadian Mountie's smart jacket is stitched in red with black epaulettes and collar. Four strands of floss are used to work the French knots for the brass buttons and to backstitch his belt buckle.

272

Chapter 6
Finishing and Making Up

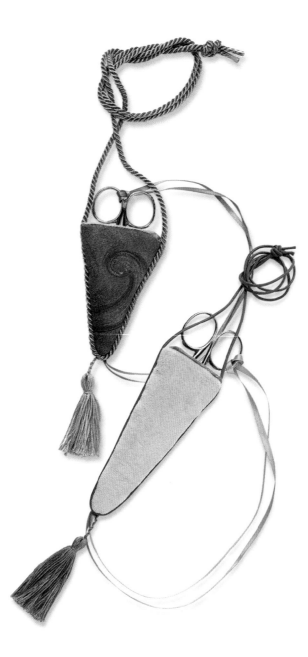

Perfect Piping

Piping—or cording, as it is also called—is the ideal way to give a tailored finish to home furnishings and garments. It is very simple to use, and you can make it in any closely woven fabric you choose, provided it is not too thick.

The most popular type of piping is simply a filler cord covered with a strip of bias-cut fabric. If you prefer, you can use ready-made bias binding—just press out the foldlines first. You can also buy ready-made ordinary piping in a range of colors from notions departments.

For a fine edging on delicate fabrics and small projects, try flat piping. For a sumptuous, more decorative look, use shirred piping. Steps on making these three kinds are given below and on the following page.

To apply any type of piping, stitch it in place on the right side of the fabric, matching up the raw edges. The steps on page 276 show how to attach piping to a cushion cover; this method is used to fix piping to any item or garment.

Types of filler cord

Twisted cotton filler cord, designed for piping, comes in several sizes. The most useful for household accessories is about 3/16–1/4 in. (4–5 mm) thick. If the item will be washed, rinse the cord in hot water for a few minutes before use. For thick piping, use rope; for a soft effect, use knitting yarn.

Standard piping

Shirred piping

Flat piping

Making standard piping

1 Place the cord or knitting yarn down the center of the wrong side of a bias strip. Fold the strip over the cord or yarn, matching the raw edges, and pin in place.

2 Using a zipper foot and stretching the strip slightly to remove any slack, machine-stitch close to the cord or yarn with matching thread.

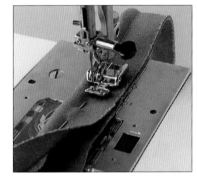

Making flat piping

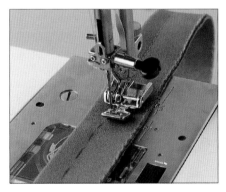

Method A Start by making standard piping, following steps **1–2** above and using knitting yarn. Then gently pull the yarn out of the strip.

Method B Fold the bias strip in half and press it. Mark the desired finished depth of the piping away from the fold. Machine-stitch along the marked line with matching thread.

Making shirred piping

1 Cut a bias strip 1½ times the length of the cord. Fold the fabric around the cord, right side out, baste and machine-stitch for about 6 in. (15 cm). Do not stitch too close to the cord, as it needs to move freely inside the fabric tube.

2 Leave the needle in the fabric, raise the presser foot, and gently pull the cord through the tubing to gather up the fabric. Then lower the foot and repeat, working 6 in. (15 cm) at a time until you reach the end of the cord.

Attaching piping to a cushion cover

Cut a piece of piping long enough to edge the cushion cover front, plus 2 in. (5 cm) extra to allow for the overlap. Stitch the piping in place as shown below. To assemble the cover, refer to the instructions on page 307. Use a zipper foot to join the front and back pieces, and stitch as close as possible to the piping stitching line.

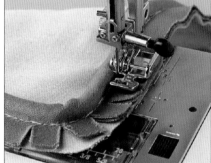

1 Matching raw edges and leaving ⅝ in. (1.5 cm) free at the start, baste piping to right side of cover front. Leave the last 2 in. (5 cm) to overlap the start.

2 Machine-stitch close to the basting, using a zipper foot. To ease the piping around corners, clip into the seam allowances to the basting.

3 Stop stitching ⅜ in. (1 cm) from the end. Leaving the needle in the fabric, cut off the end of the cord so it overlaps the first end by 1 in. (2.5 cm).

4 Unpick 1 in. (2.5 cm) of stitching from the end of the piping. Trim the cord end so it meets the other end of the cord.

5 Fold under ⅜ in. (1 cm) on the overlapping fabric end. Lap it over the other end, and finish stitching the piping in place.

Standard piping gives a neat, tailored effect.

Hems and Miters

There are various ways of hemming the edges of garments and accessories.

An item that will need to be washed often, such as a child's garment, may be topstitched by machine—an effect that is often attractive in its own right.

Two of the most popular ways of hand-stitching a hem, slip stitch and herringbone stitch, are shown below. These have the advantage of being virtually invisible from the right side. For a decorative effect, blanket stitch (see page 18) is often appropriate. If the fabric is likely to fray, use a double hem (or simply turn under the raw edge by a small amount.) Closely woven fabrics can be given a single hem and sewn in place with herringbone stitch, perhaps first finishing the raw edges with zigzag stitch.

Hems on household accessories such as table and bed linens often require the corners to be mitered. Two recommended ways of mitering a corner—single and double mitering—are illustrated below and on the next page.

Slip-stitched hem

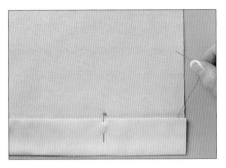

I Fold a double hem to the wrong side of the fabric and pin it in place. (Baste also, if you wish.) Thread the needle and secure the thread at the right-hand edge on the underside of the hem fold.

2 Bring the needle out at the top of the fold. Take a tiny stitch to the left into the single-thickness fabric, catching one or two threads. Slip the needle through the top of the fold for about 1/4 in. (5 mm). Continue in this way to finish the hem.

Herringbone-stitched hem

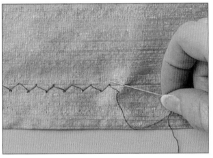

I Turn up a single or double hem; pin and baste (optional) it in place. Fasten the thread at the left-hand edge. Take a small stitch, from right to left, in the hem; then take another, very small, in the main fabric, again from right to left, diagonally up to the right. Continue in this way as shown.

Mitered single hem

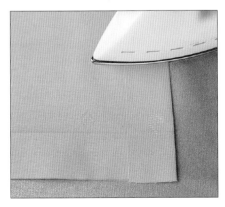

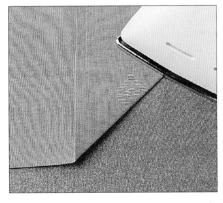

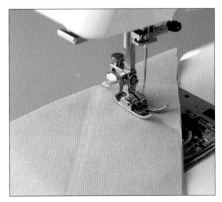

I Fold the hem to the wrong side all around and press it.

2 Unfold the hem at the corner. Fold up the corner diagonally, level with the hem fold, and press it.

3 Unfold the corner, then fold up the fabric diagonally, matching the raw edges. Stitch along the diagonal line.

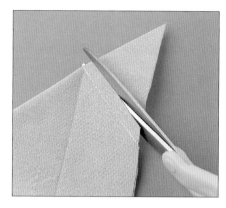

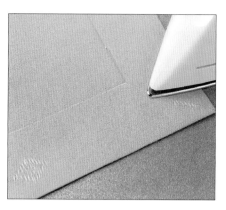

Mitered single hems lie flat and smooth, creating a neat, professional finish.

4 Trim the seam ³⁄₈ in. (1 cm) from the stitching. Press the seam allowances open.

5 Turn up the hem again, and press it in place. Finish the raw edges with zigzag stitch if desired. Stitch the hem in place.

Mitered double hem

1 Turn up a double hem all around, and press the folds carefully.

2 Unfold the double hem. Press up the corner diagonally, level with the inner foldline.

3 Press in the first hem, then fold back the top edge of the corner so that the point touches the outer corner fold; press it neatly.

4 Press in the second hem so that the edges butt together neatly at the corner. Pin to hold.

5 Slip-stitch the edges together at the corner as shown. Then stitch the hem in place using the chosen method.

After mitering the corners, secure the hem with hand stitches (top) or by machine (bottom).

Making Pillowcases

Pillowcases are are often made or bought in sets with sheets, but it is useful to have a few extra ones in complementary or contrasting colors, patterns, and styles.

The standard American pillowcase could not be easier: just cut two pieces slightly larger than the pillow, seam them around three sides, and hem the open edges, adding trimmings as desired.

The pillowcases shown here are both British styles, having a flap that tucks over the end of the pillow, holding it in place. The "housewife" pillowcase is the simpler of the two, as it is made from a single piece of fabric. French seams give it extra strength as well as a neat finish, and trimmings, such as a lace ruffle around the edges, will give it an elegant effect.

Also known as a pillow sham, the Oxford pillowcase has a mitered border, called a flange, and has a neat, tailored appearance.

The instructions given here will suit the standard American rectangular pillow.

Cutting out

Housewife pillowcase Measure the width (longer dimension) of the pillow, double it, and add on 9½ in. (24 cm); measure the depth of the pillow and add on 1½ in. (4 cm). Cut a piece of fabric to these measurements.

Oxford pillowcase

For the front: cut a rectangle of fabric the width (longer dimension) of the pillow plus 9 in. (23 cm) by the depth plus 9 in. (23 cm). For the back: cut a rectangle the width of the pillow plus 2 in. (5 cm) by the depth of the pillow plus 1¼ in. (3 cm). For the flap: cut a rectangle 8 in. (20 cm) wide by the depth of the back piece plus 1¼ in. (3 cm).

The housewife pillowcase is formed from a single length of folded fabric.

Making a housewife pillowcase

1 Press under and machine-stitch a double ⅜-in. (1-cm) hem on one short edge of the fabric rectangle. On the other short edge, press under ¼ in. (5 mm), then 1⅜ in. (3.5 cm) and machine-stitch.

2 Use the end with the narrower hem for the flap. Placing wrong sides together, fold under 6 in. (15 cm) and press. Then, with the right sides out, fold up the deeper hemmed edge to meet the pressed edge, as shown.

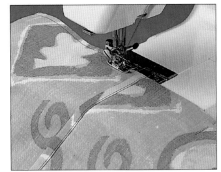

3 Stitch the raw edges, taking a ⅜-in. (1-cm) seam allowance. Trim the seam to ¼ in. (5 mm). Turn wrong side out and press flat. Stitch a ⅜-in. (1-cm) seam, enclosing the raw edges. Turn right side out and press flat.

Making an Oxford pillowcase

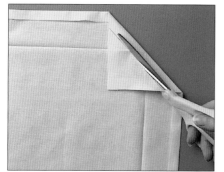

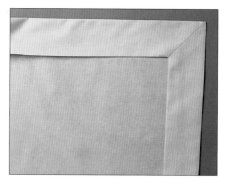

1 On the front piece, turn ⅝ in. (1.5 cm) then 2 in. (5 cm) to the wrong side all around. At each corner, unfold the 2 in. (5 cm) hem and press it diagonally, level with the inner hem fold. Trim ⅝ in. (1.5 cm) from the diagonal fold.

2 Unfold the ⅝ in. (1.5 cm) hem. Fold the fabric with right sides facing so that the fold runs diagonally across the corner. Stitch along the diagonal foldline, ⅝ in. (1.5 cm) from the trimmed edge, as shown. Stop stitching when you reach the outer fold.

3 Trim away any excess bulk on the inner seams, then turn the mitered corner right side out and press it, so that the flange lies flat and smooth. Stitch a double ⅜-in. (1-cm) hem on one long edge of the flap, and on one short edge of the back piece.

On the Oxford pillowcase, the border is created by folding the edges of the front piece to the back. At the back, the corners of the fabric are formed into neat machine-stitched miters.

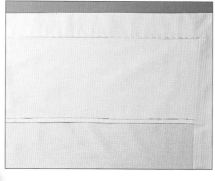

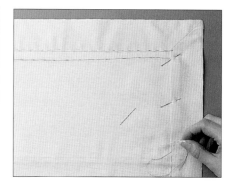

4 Lay out the front piece, wrong side up. Placing wrong sides together, slip the three raw edges of the flap under the border at one end by ⅝ in. (1.5 cm). Pin, then baste the border to the flap along the long edge of the flap.

5 Placing wrong sides together, slip the raw edges of the back piece under the border, with the hemmed end just level with the border at the flap end. Pin and baste around three sides.

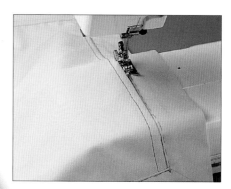

6 Working from the back of the pillowcase, machine-stitch ⅛ in. (3 mm) outside the inner edge of the border. Press the pillowcase.

Appliance Covers

From toasters and blenders to bread makers, juicers, and coffee grinders, appliances of any size or shape can be protected with a made-to-measure cover. In fact, appliance covers are an easy way to give your kitchen a quick make-over. Mix and match fabrics, and add a variety of trims—such as fabric borders and contrasting

binding—to make each cover slightly different. The steps below show how to add a border, but you can omit this if you wish.

The covers have gussets to give the necessary depth to fit, and they are fully lined and padded with batting for a soft finish. Choose closely woven, washable, medium-weight fabrics.

Cutting out

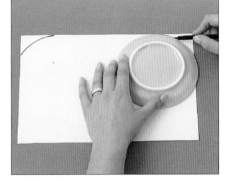

1 Measure the appliance width (**A**), depth (**B**), and height (**C**). For the front and back pattern cut a piece of paper the length of **A** plus 2¾ in. (7 cm) for seam allowances and ease by **C** plus 2¾ in. (7 cm). For the gusset pattern cut a strip of paper twice **C** plus **A** plus 8¼ in. (21 cm) by **B** plus 2¾ in. (7 cm).

2 On the front and back pattern, round off the top corners by drawing around the saucer or plate; then cut along the marked curves. From the main fabric, lining, and batting, use the patterns to cut the front and back pieces and one gusset.

Coordinate your collection of appliance covers with two or three fabrics used in a variety of ways. Choose harmonizing or contrasting colors; if you are using patterned fabrics, choose prints with small- and medium-scale motifs.

Making an appliance cover

1 Sandwich the batting front piece between the wrong sides of the fabric and lining front pieces: baste around the edges. Repeat for the back piece and the gusset.

2 If desired, cut borders to fit along each short end of the gusset, with a ¼-in. (5-mm) seam allowance at the top edge and ⅜ in. (1 cm) at the lower edge.

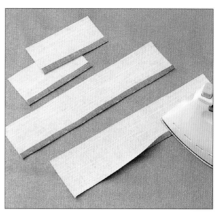

3 Repeat step **2** to cut borders to fit the lower edges of the front and back pieces. On the top edges of all the cut borders, press the seam allowances to the wrong side.

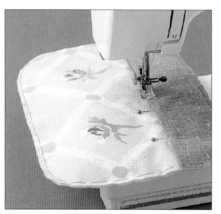

4 Position the front border, right side up, on the right side of the front cover, matching the lower raw edges. Baste in place all around, then topstitch close to the top pressed edge. Attach all the borders in the same way.

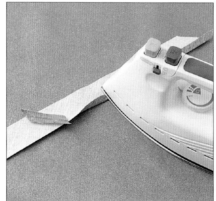

5 For binding, cut 45-degree bias strips 1¾ in. (4.5 cm) wide, totalling the required length plus extra for seams. Join strips on the straight grain; press seams open. Press under ⅜ in. (1 cm) on one long edge.

6 Stitch unpressed edge of binding to lower edge of each piece, taking ⅜-in. (1-cm) seam. Press. Turn binding to wrong side; baste, with folded edge overlapping stitching . Machine-stitch from right side over previous stitching.

7 Placing wrong sides and bound edges together, pin then baste one long edge of the gusset around the edge of the front piece; clip the curves for ease. Repeat to pin and baste the other edge of the gusset to the back piece.

8 Bind the seams as in step **6** (above), turning in the raw ends level with the bottom edge of the cover. Slip-stitch the turned-in ends of the binding.

Drawstring Bags

A drawstring bag is essentially two rectangles of fabric sewn together at the sides and the base. The top is drawn closed with cord or fabric ties. These are inserted through a hemmed casing at the top edge of the bag (below), or through a headed casing set below the top edge (see page 284), or you can thread cord through metal eyelets for a nautical look (see page 284).

Drawstring bags have endless practical and decorative potential. You can make them in any size you want. Small bags are useful for potpourri, shoes, and cosmetics, for example. Extra-large versions make great laundry and beach bags.

Choose a strong, closely woven fabric, such as chintz, sailcloth, or canvas. To work out how much fabric is required, refer to the instructions below or on the next page for the style of bag you wish to make. For the drawstring, you need enough fabric or cord to make it at least three times the bag's width.

Making a bag with a hemmed casing

A bag with a hemmed casing is both neat and practical.

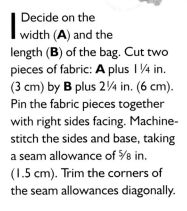

1 Decide on the width (**A**) and the length (**B**) of the bag. Cut two pieces of fabric: **A** plus 1 ¼ in. (3 cm) by **B** plus 2 ¼ in. (6 cm). Pin the fabric pieces together with right sides facing. Machine-stitch the sides and base, taking a seam allowance of ⅝ in. (1.5 cm). Trim the corners of the seam allowances diagonally.

2 Turn a ⅝-in. (1.5-cm) hem to the wrong side at the top and press. Turn a second hem of 1 ¼ in. (3 cm) and machine-stitch close to base of hem.

3 Turn the bag right side out. Unpick side seams at hem, and finish with buttonhole stitch. Thread the drawstring through the hem and knot ends.

Making a bag with a headed casing

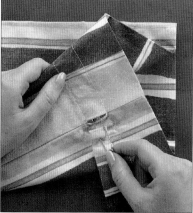

1 Cut out two fabric pieces **A** plus 1¼ in. (3 cm) by **B** plus 4 in. (10 cm). Stitch sides and base. At the top, turn a ⅝-in. (1.5-cm) hem to the wrong side and press. Then turn and press a 2¾-in. (7-cm) hem. For the casing, stitch 1½ in. (4 cm) below top and 1 in. (2.5 cm) below that.

2 Turn the bag right side out. Unpick side seams at casing, and finish edges with buttonhole stitch. Using a safety pin, thread the drawstring through the casing; knot the ends.

A casing set below the top produces a ruffled effect. Thread fabric ties or a braid in a contrasting color through the casing.

Making a fabric drawstring

Cut a strip of fabric 2¾ in. (7 cm) by at least three times the width of the bag. With right sides facing, machine-stitch together the long edges, taking a ⅝-in. (1.5-cm) seam. Trim raw edges close to stitching. Using a knitting needle, turn the drawstring right side out. Tuck in raw edges, neatly slip-stitch to close, and press.

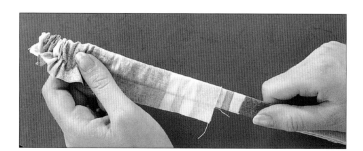

On bags with eyelets, insert an even number of eyelets to make sure that both ends of the cord leave the bag.

Making a bag with eyelets

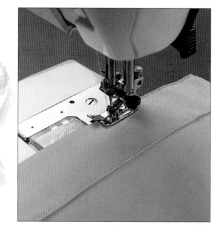

1 Cut out two fabric pieces **A** plus 1¼ in. (3 cm) by **B** plus 3¾ in. (9.5 cm). Stitch together with right sides facing along the sides and base. Turn and press a double 1½-in. (4-cm) hem along the top edge. Machine-stitch the hem close to the top and bottom edges, stitching through all three fabric layers.

2 Using chalk, mark positions for an even number of evenly spaced eyelets, placing them halfway between the two rows of hem stitching. Follow the manufacturer's instructions to insert the eyelets. Turn the bag right side out. Thread the drawstring through the eyelets and knot the ends.

Circular-Based Bags

Circular-based drawstring bags have lots of storage potential. Small ones are useful for toiletries and hosiery, while larger duffle bags are ideal for sportswear and beach gear.

The steps below show how to make a small drawstring bag, measuring 10 in. (25cm) tall. The larger duffle bag on page 286 is interlined with lightweight batting. It has a pocket and is closed with cord laced through eyelets, with a cord stay and tab.

To make a pattern for a different-sized bag, draw a circle with a diameter the desired width of your bag. Measure the circumference with a fabric tape measure. Draw a rectangle the length of the circumference by the desired height of the bag. Add ⅝ in. (1.5 cm) seam allowances all around.

Use closely woven fabrics for the main bag and the lining, matching and contrasting sewing thread, cord, pins, and paper. For the duffle bag you will also need lightweight batting and an eyelet kit.

Making a small bag

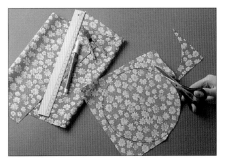

1 Use a compass to draw a 7½-in. (19-cm) diameter circle on paper; cut it out and draw around it on the fabric. Mark a 21¼ x 11-in. (54 x 28-cm) rectangle on the fabric for the side piece. Cut out both pieces.

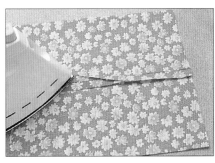

2 Fold the fabric rectangle in half widthwise, right sides facing, and pin the short side edges. Stitch, leaving a ⅝-in. (1.5-cm) gap for the casing, ¾ in. (2 cm) from the top edge. Press the seam allowances open.

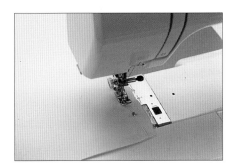

3 Placing the right sides together, pin and baste the base to the lower edge of the bag. Stitch, then remove the basting. Clip the curves with sharp scissors.

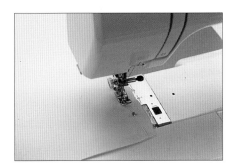

4 Make another bag in the lining fabric, following steps **1–3**, omitting the gap in the casing, and leaving a 5-in. (12.5-cm) gap in center of seam to turn through when bag is assembled. Turn the lining right side out.

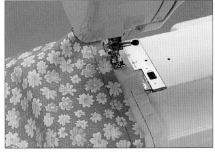

5 Slip the lining into the bag so that the right sides are together. Pin, then stitch the upper edges. Turn the bag right side out through the opening. Slip-stitch the opening closed, and press the upper edge.

6 For the casing, stitch close to the upper edge and then ¾ in. (2 cm) below. Cut a 45-in. (115-cm) length of cord, and use a safety pin to thread it through the casing. Knot the ends together and hide the knot in the casing.

Making a padded duffle bag

From fabric, lightweight batting and lining, cut an 11½-in. (29-cm) diameter circle for the base and a 34 x 19-in. (86 x 48-cm) rectangle for the sides.

From fabric only, cut a 9 x 6¾ in. (22 x 17-cm) rectangle for the pocket; a 4¼ x 3¼ in. (11 x 8-cm) rectangle for the tab; and a 6½ x 3¼-in. (16.5 x 8-cm) rectangle for the cord stay.

1 Baste the batting to the wrong side of the outer bag pieces, and machine-stitch in place.

This roomy duffle bag is 18 in. (45 cm) tall. For an extra-strong version, back the main fabric pieces with heavyweight interfacing.

2 On the top short edge of the pocket piece, press under ⅝ in. (1.5 cm) then 1¼ in. (3 cm) and stitch. Press under ⅝ in. (1.5 cm) on the other edges. Center the pocket on the right side of the outer fabric rectangle, 4 in. (10 cm) above the lower edge, then topstitch along the sides and bottom.

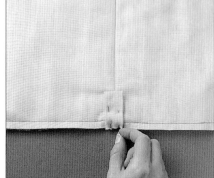

3 Join the short edges as on page 285, step 2, omitting the gap. Fold the tab piece in half lengthwise, right sides together, and stitch the long edges. Turn it right side out, then fold it in half and pin and baste it over the seam on the right side of the lower edge of the bag, as shown. Then assemble the bag, as on page 285, steps 3–5.

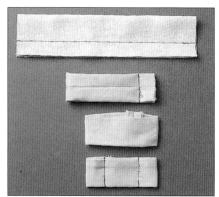

4 Fold the cord stay piece in half lengthwise, right sides together; stitch the long edges. Turn out, and stitch the short ends together. Trim the seam allowances and turn seam to inside. Fold the stay with the seam ⅝ in. (1.5 cm) from one end. Stitch across ⅝ in. (1.5 cm) from each end to make slots.

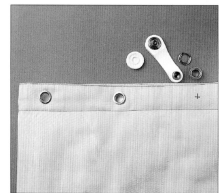

5 For the casing, stitch close to the upper edge of the bag, then 1½ in. (3.5 cm) below. Use an air-erasable pen to mark the positions for an even number of eyelets 4⅛ in. (10.5 cm) apart in the middle of the casing. Follow the manufacturer's instructions to insert the eyelets.

6 Cut 64 in. (163 cm) of cord. Thread it through the tab, the stay, and the eyelets as shown. Bind the ends together with transparent tape. Cut 1¾ x 1½ in. (4.5 x 4 cm) of fabric, and press under ⅜ in. (1 cm) on the short edges. Wrap the fabric tightly around the tape and sew firmly in place.

Box Bags

These stylish bags are very simple to make. A fabric gusset stitched between the front and back panels provides depth and creates a neat, roomy shape, ideal for storing bulky items such as toiletries.

The bags can be made in any size or shape, with or without piping. A large version will hold all your bottles and jars; a tall, narrow shape is just right for makeup brushes. For a coordinated look, make a set of three to match your bathroom, and fill them with toiletries, such as shampoo bottles, toothbrushes and tweezers, the perfect way to keep bathroom clutter out of the way.

For the best results, make your bag from closely woven, washable fabric. Use ready-made piping, or make your own, following the instructions on pages 275–276.

Cutting out

Decide on the height of the side panel (**A**) and the width (**B**). Decide how wide to make the gusset (**C**). From main fabric and lining, for the side panels, cut two pieces: **A** plus 1¼ in. (3 cm) by **B** plus 1¼ in. (3 cm). For the gusset cut one piece: twice **A** plus **B** by **C** plus 1¼ in. (3 cm). From main fabric only, cut two pieces 3¼ x 2 in. (8 x 5 cm) for the zipper tags.

For a makeup bag, make the lining from a waterproof, wipe-clean fabric for easy care. Shower curtain material, available from department stores, is ideal.

Making a box bag

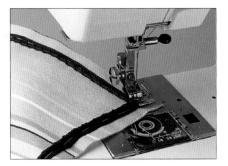

1 Press ⅝ in. (1.5 cm) to the wrong side along the top edges of the side panels: unfold. Baste the piping around the lower three edges so the basting is ⅝ in. (1.5 cm) in from the edges. Clip into the flat part of piping at the corners so that it lies flat.

2 Using either a zipper or cording foot on your sewing machine, stitch the piping in place with matching thread; start and finish the stitching at the foldline. At the corners, raise the presser foot, leaving the needle in the fabric, and pivot the work.

3 Press in ⅝ in. (1.5 cm) on the short edges of the gusset; stitch. Place the gusset on a side panel with the top edges of the gusset 1¼ in. (3 cm) below the top of the side panel. Clip at the lower corners to fit. Baste, then stitch in place with a zipper or cording foot. Stitch the other edge of the gusset to the other panel in the same way.

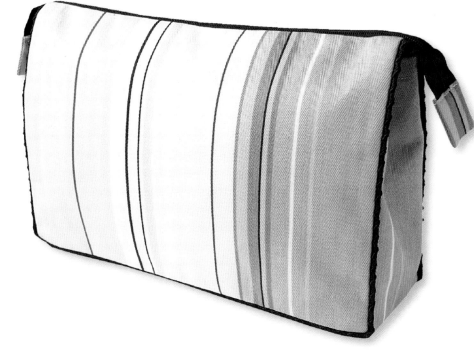

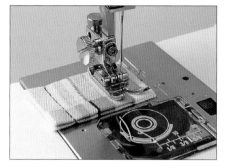

4 Press in ⅜ in. (1 cm) on the short edges of the zipper tags. Fold the tags in half, right sides together, and stitch the side edges ⅜ in. (1 cm) in. Trim the seam allowances to ¼ in. (5 mm).

5 Turn the tags right side out. Tuck each end of the zipper tape inside a tag. Machine-stitch in place, fastening off the thread ends securely.

6 With the bag inside out, center the zipper along one top edge, right sides together. Baste the zipper tape in place along the foldline. Stitch, using the zipper foot.

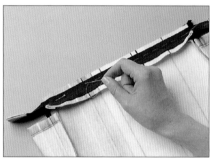

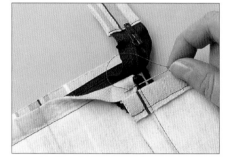

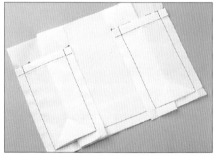

7 Baste and stitch the other zipper tape to the other top edge in the same way. Remove the basting.

8 Turn the bag right side out. At the top corners of the side panels, fold down the seam allowance and tuck the end of the piping underneath. Overcast by hand to secure.

9 Trim ¾ in. (2 cm) from one short end of the lining fabric gusset. Stitch the lining panels as in step **3** on page 287, but place the top of the gusset 1½ in. (4 cm) down from the top edges of the side panels.

The standard zipper tag size suits most box bags, including miniature versions (below). On a tall, narrow version, such as the makeup brush bag (left), longer tags suit the slimline look. For tags such as these, cut two 4¾ x 2-in. (12 x 5-cm) fabric pieces.

10 Place the lining inside the bag, with the wrong sides together. Pin the lining gussets ⅜ in. (1 cm) below the main gussets. Tuck in the raw edge of the lining to fit, then pin and slip-stitch it in place.

Beanbag

Children love big beanbags—they are great for jumping on, and they make warm, soft seats to snuggle into to watch television or for settling down with a favorite book.

The generously proportioned beanbag shown here is easy to make. It is 37 in. (94 cm) high with a built-in handle at the top and a lightweight filling, so it can be dragged or carted about by the smallest child. The outer cover has a zipper opening for easy removal when it needs washing.

For the main cover, use a tough, closely woven, washable furnishing fabric. Choose a bright solid color, or a fun print for small children. You can personalize the bag with appliqué or simple embroidery.

The inner bag is made of unbleached muslin and filled with polybeads. These are made from polystyrene, which is a non-allergenic material, and are sold by the bag in craft stores and notions departments. Two to three bags of 2 cubic ft. (0.06 cubic m) are enough to fill the beanbag shown here. Save any leftover polybeads to fill up the bag later on—the beads tend to become flattened through prolonged use.

YOU WILL NEED

* 3⅞ yd. (3.5 m) of washable furnishing fabric
* 3⅞ yd. (3.5 m) of unbleached muslin
* Scrap of medium-weight fusible interfacing
* Sewing machine
* Zipper foot
* 16 in. (40 cm) zipper
* Polybead filling
* Large sheets of paper
* Ruler and pencil

Making the pattern pieces

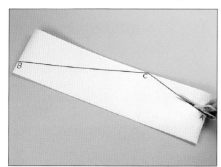

1 For the sides, cut a piece of paper 37½ x 19¾ in. (95 x 50 cm) and fold it in half lengthwise. Mark the bottom short edge 5½ in. (14 cm) from the fold (**A**); mark the top short edge 2¼ in. (6 cm) from the fold (**B**). Mark the outer edge 13 in. (33 cm) from the bottom (**C**). Join **A** and **B** to **C**. Trim away the surplus paper.

2 For the base, cut a piece of paper 22 x 19 in. (56 x 48 cm); fold it in half both ways. Lay it down with the long fold at the top and the short fold at the right. Mark the bottom edge 5½ in. (14 cm) from the fold (**D**). Draw a line from this point to the top left corner. Trim away the surplus paper.

3 For the top, cut a piece of paper 9½ x 8 in. (24 x 20 cm); fold it in half both ways. Lay it down with the folds in the same position as for the base. Mark the bottom edge 2¼ in. (6 cm) from the fold (**E**). Draw a line from this point to the top left corner. Trim away the surplus paper.

Cutting out

Unfold all three pattern pieces, and use them to cut out the main bag and muslin lining, following the instructions below. Cut each fabric piece on the straight grain, adding ⅝ in. (1.5 cm) all around for the seam allowances.
Side panels—from muslin and main fabric cut six pieces.
Top—from muslin and main fabric cut one piece.
Base lining—from muslin cut one piece.
Base main piece—from main fabric fold the base pattern in half and use this as a pattern to cut two pieces.
Handle—from main fabric and interfacing cut a 12 x 5½-in. (30 x14-cm) rectangle.

Making the beanbag

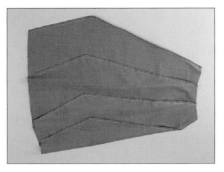

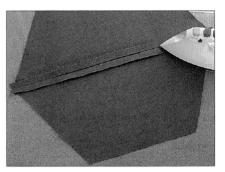

1 Placing right sides together, pin the long edges of all the side panels to form a tube shape. Stitch, beginning and ending each seam ⅝ in. (1.5 cm) in from the ends. Stitch again for strength, then finish the seam allowances and press them open.

2 Pin the long edges of the base pieces together with right sides facing; stitch 9 cm (3½ in.) in from each side edge. Baste center opening and press seam open. Center zipper face down over basting and baste in place. Using zipper foot and working from right side, stitch zipper in place. Remove basting.

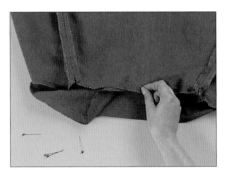

3 Placing right sides and raw edges together, pin the base to the bottom edge of the tube shape, matching the seams to the points of the base. The unstitched ends of the seams will splay out to ease the fit. Stitch twice to reinforce the seam, and then finish the edges.

4 Fuse the interfacing to the wrong side of the handle piece. Fold the piece in half lengthwise, with right sides together; stitch ⅜ in. (1 cm) from the long edges. Turn the handle right side out; press with the seam centered, then stitch close to the folds on each side.

5 Placing right sides up, center the handle across the top piece. Baste the ends in place. Open the zipper. Placing right sides together, stitch the edges of the top piece to the top edges of the side panels as in step **3**, sandwiching the handle edges. Finish the seams.

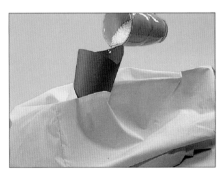

6 Make the lining in the same way as the main cover, but omit the handle and zipper and leave an 8-in. (20-cm) gap in one seam. Use a pitcher and paper funnel to pour the beads into the lining. Fill it about two-thirds full, then slip-stitch the opening closed. Insert the filled lining into the cover.

Leave the beanbag plain or add appliqué patches. These frog patches are secured with giant cross stitches.

Flap Bag

This cleverly designed bag is extremely versatile. You can make it any size you like—just adapt the specifications given in the caption below.

The bag is fully lined for a neat finish, and the seams are machine-stitched. The lining is cut in two pieces; when you join them, leave a gap in the seam to turn the bag right side out. You can secure the flap with a snap, as shown on the next page. Alternatively, use a decorative closure, such as a frog fastener, as shown left, or a button and loop.

For the best results, choose closely woven fabrics for the main piece and the lining. Cottons and linens are easy to work with, while silk and satin are more difficult to handle but give a luxurious feel.

If you want to embroider or appliqué your bag, embellish the main fabric before assembling the pieces. For a quilted bag, cut the lining to size after quilting the main piece, as quilting can "shrink" fabric.

To make a bag with a straight edge, simply omit step 1 (below). Follow the remaining steps, working with a rectangular-shaped main fabric and larger lining piece.

*Decide on the finished width (**A**), height (**B**), and depth of the flap (**C**) for your bag. From your main fabric, cut a piece: **A** plus 1¼ in. (3 cm) by twice **B** plus **C** plus 1¼ in. (3 cm).*
*From lining fabric, cut one piece: **A** plus 1¼ in. (3 cm) by **B** plus 1¼ in. (3 cm). Then cut a second, larger piece: **A** plus 1¼ in. (3 cm) by **B** plus **C** plus 1¼ in. (3 cm).*

Shaping the fabric pieces

1 For a pointed flap, fold the main fabric piece in half lengthwise. Decide how deep to make the point, and mark this measurement on the long raw edge. Draw a line from the mark to the top of the fold. Cut along the line through both layers. Repeat with the larger lining piece.

2 Trim off ⅛ in. (2–3 mm) all around both the lining pieces. This ensures that the lining will sit comfortably inside the bag without wrinkling.

Assembling the flap purse

1 Stitch the lining pieces together with right sides facing along the bottom edge. Take a ⅝-in. (1.5-cm) seam and leave a 4-in. (10-cm) gap in the center. Press the seam open.

2 Stitch the lining and main fabric together with right sides facing along the short straight edge, taking a ⅝-in. (1.5-cm) seam. Trim the seam, then turn it to the inside and press to form an edge.

3 Fold up the front edge, right sides together, to the depth B, so that the lining seam with the gap is at the base. Bring the lining from the back, enclosing the folded front edge, so right side lining lies against right side main fabric. Pin to hold.

4 Stitch through all the layers along the sides and around the pointed top, taking a ⅝-in. (1.5-cm) seam. Trim the seams and corners. Then turn the bag out through the gap in the lining seam.

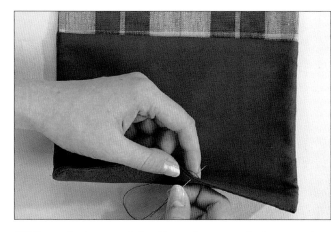

5 Press the bag carefully. Close the gap in the lining with slip stitches, using a matching thread and fastening off the ends securely.

6 Turn the bag right side out and press. Use chalk to mark the positions of the two halves of the snap on the front and the inside of the flap. Sew the snap in place.

Double-Fold Cards

Double-fold cards have an opening in the central panel for small stitched designs and pictures. When the card is folded, the picture is displayed at the front. You can buy double-fold cards in a small range of colors and sizes in needlework and craft supply stores, but it is very easy and much more economical to make your own.

The steps below and on the next page show how to make a double-fold card with either a rectangular or a round opening and a matching envelope. The card measures 6⅛ x 4¼ in. (15.5 x 11 cm). A half template for the envelope is on this page; to make a full-size template for the envelope, see the instructions on page 294.

Cutting materials

For a neat finish, use a utility knife and metal ruler to cut the basic card. If you plan to make several cards with a round opening, it is worth investing in a circle cutter, available from art and craft supply stores. You can cut round openings with a utility knife or small, sharp scissors, but it takes practice to get a professional finish.

Double-fold cards are the perfect way to display miniature stitched designs. Presented with a matching envelope, they make a thoughtful gift.

Making a card with a rectangular opening

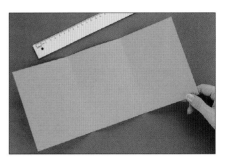

1 Cut a 13 x 5⅛-in. (33 x 15.5-cm) rectangle of paper, and lay it right side down. Fold it vertically 4¼ in. (11 cm) in from the left-hand edge. Make a parallel fold, 4¼ in. (11 cm) to the right of the first. Unfold the paper.

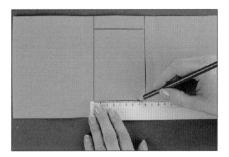

2 Mark a 3¼ x 4¼-in. (8 x 11-cm) rectangle on the central panel, positioning the long sides ⅝ in. (1.5 cm) in from the folds, the top ¾ in. (2 cm) from the top of the paper and the bottom 1 in. (2.5 cm) from the bottom.

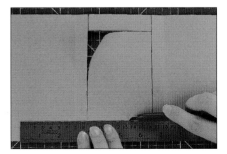

3 Place the paper rectangle on the cutting board. Using the metal ruler and the utility knife, cut out the rectangle. Gently smooth away any ragged edges with the nail file.

Making a card with a circular opening

1 Fold the paper rectangle, following step 1 (page 293). On the central panel, lightly mark a vertical line ⅝ in. (1.5 cm) in from each fold.

2 Mark a horizontal line between the two vertical lines, 1 in. (2.5 cm) from the top of the card. Then mark a second horizontal line, 3¼ in. (8 cm) below the first. Mark the center of the rectangle formed by the four lines.

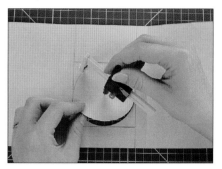

3 Set the circle cutter to 1½ in. (4 cm). With the spike of the cutter on the central mark, cut out a circle, swiveling the card as you cut. Or mark a circle with a compass and cut it out with scissors or a utility knife.

Inserting embroidery

1 **Rectangular opening** Trim picture to ¼ in. (5 mm) bigger all around than opening. Place card wrong side up with wider border at bottom. Apply double-stick tape around opening. Remove backing and center embroidery, wrong side up, on top.

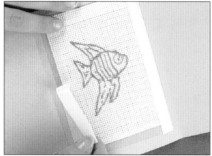

2 Apply another strip of double-stick tape close to the four outside edges of the central panel. Remove the backing strips. Fold over the left-hand panel and press it down on the tape. Write your message on the right-hand panel.

1 **Round opening** Position four 1¼ in. (3 cm) strips of double-stick tape around the opening, as shown. Then position the embroidery and complete the card as shown in steps 1–2 (left).

Making an envelope

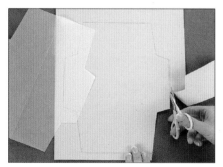

1 Fold the tracing paper. With the fold on the dotted line of the half template on page 293, trace the outline. Cut it out and unfold to make the full pattern. Draw around the pattern on paper, using a ruler for the straight lines, and cut out the shape.

2 Position the paper shape right side down with the wider, bottom flap at the right. Fold up the two side flaps and apply 2¼ in. (6 cm) of double-stick tape to each, as shown. Remove the backing strips, fold over the bottom flap, and stick it down.

3 Fold down the top flap, then open it out again. Apply 5 in. (13 cm) of double-stick tape across the flap edge, as shown. Insert the card. To seal the envelope, remove the backing strip from the tape and stick down the top flap.

Blocking Needlepoint

Even if you use a frame for needlepoint, many stitches—especially popular diagonal stitches, including half cross stitch—tend to distort the canvas, no matter how carefully you stitch. Blocking your finished work will straighten up the canvas and leave the stitching looking fresh and smooth.

Blocking is simple. Dampen the canvas, then place it on a board marked with a grid of lines. Using the grid as a guide, gently stretch the work back into shape, secure it with tacks, and leave it to dry thoroughly, which can take up to a week. As it dries, the canvas "sets" in the correct shape. A second blocking may be needed for strong vertical or horizontal designs.

Always leave the needlepoint to dry at room temperature, away from direct heat or sunlight, which can fade thread colors. Make sure the piece is bone-dry before you take it off the block, or it may become distorted again.

Block your needlepoint face down, unless the design is heavily textured; in this case, place it face up to avoid flattening the stitches.

For the blocking board, use a piece of unstained, unpainted wood at least ¾ in. (2 cm) thick and about 2 in. (5 cm) larger all around than the canvas.

YOU WILL NEED

* Plain wooden board, at least ¾ in. (2 cm) thick and 2 in. (5 cm) larger all around than the canvas
* Steel ruler
* Fine black waterproof marker
* Sheet of thick, clear plastic
* Staple gun and staples
* Water spray
* Finish nails or rustproof tacks
* Hammer
* Pincers
* Right-angled triangle (optional)

Waterproof marker

Hammer

Finish nails

Wooden board

Staple gun

Ruler

Right-angled triangle

Pincers

Making the blocking board

1 Using the waterproof marker, steel ruler, and triangle (or other flat right-angled object), mark a grid of lines on the blocking board at right angles to the edges. Position the lines about 1 in. (2.5 cm) apart. Allow to dry thoroughly.

2 Cut a piece of clear plastic about 2 in. (5 cm) larger all around than the board. Cover the board with the plastic, securing the surplus with staples on the wrong side and turning in the corners neatly.

Blocking needlepoint

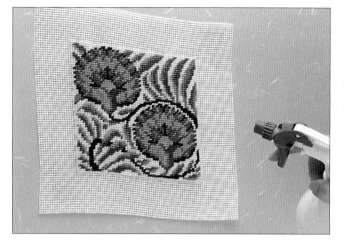

1 Trim the unworked canvas around the stitching to 2 in. (5 cm). Spray the canvas with cold, clean water to moisten it lightly. Then center the dampened canvas face down on the blocking board.

2 With the top of the stitching along one horizontal line, lightly hammer a tack into the unworked canvas at the center top. Ease the canvas downward, aligning the threads vertically. Hammer in a tack at the center bottom.

3 Hammer in a tack at the center of each remaining side of the canvas, using the grid or a right-angled triangle to ensure that the vertical canvas threads are at right angles to the horizontal threads. Hammer the tacks in lightly in case you need to adjust them later.

4 Working out from the center of each edge, insert tacks every ¾ in. (5 cm), gently stretching the canvas as you go. Check that the edges line up with the grid, and adjust if necessary. Allow to dry thoroughly. Use pincers to remove the tacks.

Half cross stitch tends to distort the canvas (below) because the diagonal stitches pull the threads out of alignment. Blocking restores the canvas to shape (right).

Framing a Design

Framed needlecraft designs often look their best with an inner frame, known as a picture mat. The mat sets off the work and stops it from touching the picture glass.

Choose a frame and mat board in colors that enhance the work and coordinate with your room scheme. A wide mat looks better than a narrow one, so if you can't decide between two frame sizes, pick the larger one. Use only acid-free mat board to prevent damage to the work.

Cutting the mat

The opening on the mount can have a straight or beveled edge. A straight edge is cut at 90 degrees to the surface with a utility or X-Acto knife and ruler. A beveled edge is cut at 45 degrees (see page 298); you will need a mat cutter —a metal ruler with a cutter which runs along a track. It is a good investment if you plan to do a lot of framing.

Matting a design

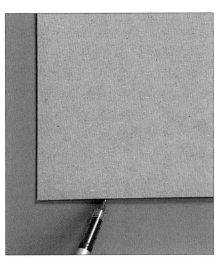

YOU WILL NEED

❋ Ready-made frame
❋ Acid-free mat board
❋ Utility or X-Acto knife
❋ Metal ruler
❋ Self-healing cutting mat
❋ Mat cutter (optional)
❋ Pencil and pins
❋ Masking tape
❋ Strong thread for lacing
❋ Sturdy needle for lacing

---

1 Check that the design fits the frame with an even border all around. Ideally, the border should be at least 2 in. (5 cm) wide, depending on the size of the design. For the best effect, the lower border should be at least ¹/₂ in. (1.2 cm) deeper than the others.

2 Remove the backing board from the frame and place it on the mat board to use as a template. Draw around it on the mat board, then cut out the mat board with a sharp utility or X-Acto knife and a metal ruler on a cutting mat.

3 Place strips of mat board around the design to decide on the crop; put the frame on top to decide how wide to make the mat. When you are satisfied, measure the width of the cropped design. Deduct this from the width of the backing board. Each side edge of the mat will be half the remainder in width. Repeat with the height of the design, but make the lower border ¹/₂ in. (1.2 cm) deeper than the upper border. Using these measurements, mark the opening position on the back of the cut mat board.

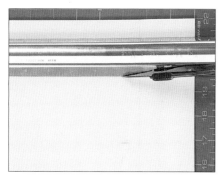

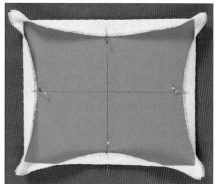

Bevel-edged mat

Straight-edged mat

4a For a straight opening edge, score along the opening lines, using the knife and metal ruler, until you cut through the board.

Mounting the embroidery

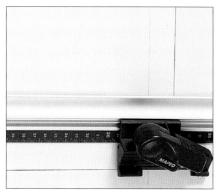

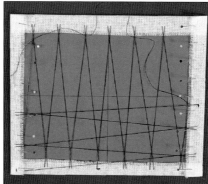

4b For a beveled edge, mark a second set of lines on the cut mat board, 1 in. (2.5 cm) inside the lines showing the position of the opening (or as instructed for your cutter). Place the mat cutter and ruler on the pencil lines, and cut along the outer lines, following the manufacturer's instructions.

1 Cut a piece of mat (or other) board larger than the opening on your mat but small enough for the edges of the fabric to wrap over onto the back. Measure and mark the center of each edge of the mat board, then join up opposite marks to form a cross. Mark the center of each edge of the design with a pin.

2 Lay the board over the back of the fabric matching the center marks. Use pins to secure the center of each edge of the fabric to the corresponding edge of the board. Remove the marker pins.

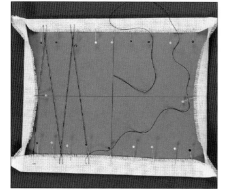

3 Pin one long edge of the fabric to the back of the board at regular intervals. Pin the opposite edge in the same way. Thread a long length of strong thread onto a sturdy needle, and lace from one side to the other, starting at the bottom left-hand corner. Keep the thread taut, and knot on additional lengths as necessary.

4 Turn the board 90 degrees and lace the short edges of the fabric in the same way. Fold in the fabric neatly at the corners to prevent bulges, and make sure it is smooth and taut on the right side. Remove the pins after working the lacing.

5 Place the design face up, and position the mat on top. Holding both securely, flip them over and tape the mounted design firmly to the back of the mat with masking tape. Place the mat and embroidery in the frame, and replace the backing board. Tape the edges of the backing board to the edges of the frame.

Padded Picture Frame

This simple but stylish frame is perfect for displaying treasured pictures. It is made from a ready-made mat, which is available from stationers and craft supply stores. Take your picture with you when you buy the mat, so you can make sure it frames the picture well. If you cannot find a mat in the size and shape you want, cut your own from mat board.

The frame is lightly padded with batting; instead of glass, the picture is protected by clear acetate, which is available from art supply stores. A sturdy stand made from fabric-covered card stock or mat board enables you to stand the frame on any flat surface. If you intend to hang the picture, you can omit the stand and sew two small rings onto the back of the frame instead. This is best done before you bond the fabric to the backing board.

For the fabric covering, use any medium-weight dressmaking or decorator fabric. If you cannot find a fabric you like, decorate solid-color fabric with fabric paint and stencils, or embroider it—in either case, embellish the fabric after cutting it out and before making the frame.

Making the frame

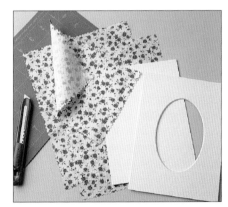

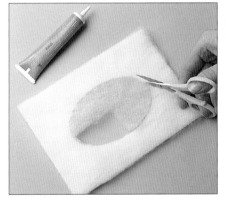

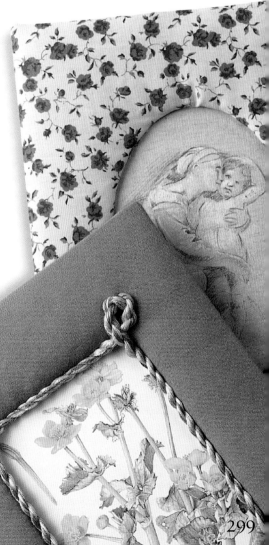

1 Use a utility knife and metal ruler to cut a piece of thick card stock or mat board $1/8$ in. (3 mm) narrower and shorter than the mat. Cut out a rectangle of fabric $5/8$ in. (1.5 cm) larger all around than the mat. On the transfer fusing web, draw a rectangle $1/8$ in. (3 mm) smaller all around and a rectangle $5/8$ in. (1.5 cm) larger all around. Fuse both rectangles to the fabric and cut out.

2 Cut a piece of batting the size of the mat, glue it to the front, and leave it to dry. Then cut into the center of the batting and trim it close to the edges of the opening.

To make a frame with a rectangular opening, follow the steps above and on the next page, but instead of snipping into the fabric at intervals all around the opening (see step 4 on page 300), cut diagonally into the corners at the opening edges.

3 Lay the mat, batting side down, on the wrong side of the fabric rectangle. Secure the fabric to the card with double-stick tape, wrapping the excess fabric over the edges and neatly mitering the corners.

4 Trim the fabric ⅝ in. (1.5 cm) from the opening. Clip into the trimmed fabric at ⅜ in. (1 cm) intervals all around the opening, then fold back the tabs and secure on the back of the mat with double-stick tape.

5 Cut away the center of the smaller bonded fabric rectangle to match the opening of the mat. Fuse this fabric frame to the back of the mat, covering the raw edges of the padded fabric piece.

6 Cover the backing board with the larger bonded fabric rectangle, sticking down the fabric excess on the back of the board and neatly mitering the corners.

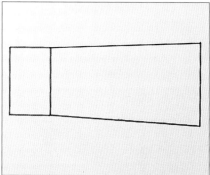

7 Draw a 1½ x 1-in. (4 x 2.5-cm) rectangle on board or card stock. Parallel to the right-hand side of the rectangle, half the height of the picture frame away, draw a 2-in. (5-cm) line, centered on the rectangle. Join this line to the right-hand corners of the rectangle.

8 Use a utility knife to cut out the stand, then score along the line across it to make a hinge. Use the stand as a template to cut out a piece of bonded fabric ⅝ in. (1.5 cm) larger all around than the stand and a piece the same size as the area below the hinge.

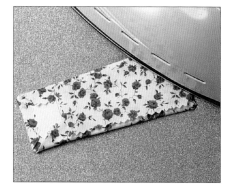

9 Fuse the larger piece of bonded fabric to the stand, fusing the excess fabric to the back and neatly mitering the corners. Then fuse the smaller piece to the back, leaving the top back uncovered.

10 Cut a rectangle of acetate ⅛ in. (3 mm) smaller all around than the mat. Apply a thin line of glue along all four edges of the back of the mat. Lay the acetate on top and gently press down. Leave to dry.

11 Center the stand on the frame back so the base extends slightly below that of the back, and glue in place. Apply glue to sides and base of back of frame front, and attach to frame back. When glue is dry, slip picture into frame through the top opening.

Fabric Book Covers

Fabric book covers are quick to assemble, and little sewing is involved.

The steps below and on the next page show how to make a fully lined wraparound cover to fit a book or notepad of any size. A layer of cardboard and some batting are sandwiched between the outer cover fabric and the lining to give the cover extra body and softness. The lining and outer cover are simply slip-stitched together. You can then stitch the wraparound flaps in place to make fitted covers, or you can leave the flaps loose.

If you plan to embroider or appliqué your book cover, do this after cutting out the outer fabric and before inserting the batting.

Materials

Fabric For the outer cover and the lining, choose closely woven, medium-weight fabrics. If making an embroidered cover using a loosely woven evenweave fabric, you may wish to back the fabric with light-weight fusible interfacing to give it more stability.

Stiffening and padding Use lightweight cardboard to stiffen the cover and medium-weight batting to plump it out.

Glue, needle, and thread Use an ordinary sewing needle and thread to stitch the cover. Glue the cardboard to the wrong side of the lining with fabric adhesive.

Making the cover

1 Measure the book's height and width (including the spine) and add 1¾ in. (4.5 cm) at each side edge for the wraps. Then add ⅛ in. (3 mm) all around for ease, plus ⅝ in. (1.5 cm) all around for the seam allowances.

2 From your main fabric, cut the outer cover piece to the dimensions you worked out in step 1. On each edge, press the ⅝-in. (1.5-cm) seam allowance to the wrong side.

3 Make a ⅝-in. (1.5-cm) deep diagonal fold at each corner. Then, to miter the corners, fold in the seam allowances over the diagonal fold. Press.

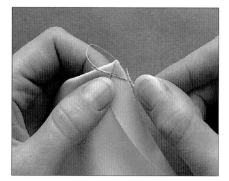

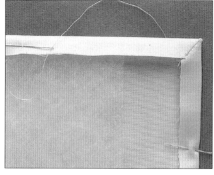

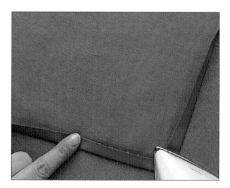

4 Slip-stitch the mitered corners closed. Use matching sewing thread and small, neat stitches.

5 Cut the batting to the book size plus ⅛ in. (3 mm) all around. Center it on the wrong side of the outer fabric. Secure the batting to the seam allowances with herringbone stitch, following the instructions given on page 277.

6 Add 4¼ in. (11 cm) to the book width and ¾ in. (2 cm) to the height. Cut the lining fabric to this size. Press a ⅜-in. (1-cm) seam allowance to the wrong side on each edge of the lining.

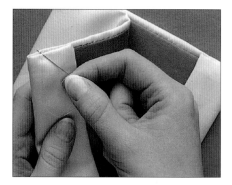

7 Cut the cardboard to the book size. Center it on the wrong side of the lining, and glue the top and bottom seam allowance to the cardboard with fabric adhesive.

8 Placing wrong sides together, pin the lining to the outer fabric. Slip-stitch the lining to the outer fabric all around.

9 Fold the book wraps 1¼ in. (3 cm) over the lining, and slip-stitch them closed at the top and bottom.

To insert your book into the fabric cover, open out the front of the book and slip it into the left-hand fabric flap. Then slip the back cover into the right-hand flap. The cover is removable, so you can use it on other books of the same size.

Desk Set

This smart letter rack and pencil holder will help to keep a home office tidy. Both items are quick to make; the pieces are cut from mounting board, folded into shape, and secured with gummed paper tape, and covered with fabric. For extra strength and detail, both the rack and pencil holder stand on two pieces of fabric-covered board.

For the covering, use a medium-weight fabric that does not fray easily, or interface a loosely woven fabric. Unless you are confident about pattern matching, avoid boldly patterned fabrics—small random designs are easier to use. If you do choose a bold pattern, cut the pieces so the pattern matches on the cover and lining.

For a stylish finishing touch, edge the accessories with coordinating bias binding.

Making the letter rack

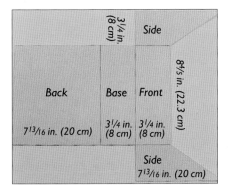

Back — 7¹³/₁₆ in. (20 cm)
Base — 3¼ in. (8 cm)
Front — 3¼ in. (8 cm)
Side — 3¼ in. (8 cm)
8⁴/₅ in. (22.3 cm)
Side — 7¹³/₁₆ in. (20 cm)

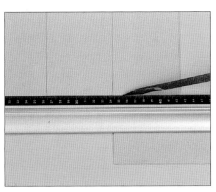

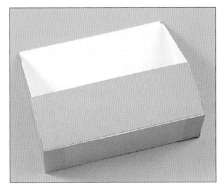

1 Lay out the mounting board, wrong side up. Use the ruler, the triangle, and the pencil to draw the shape of the box on the board, as shown above. Cut out the shape along the outer edges only, using a utility knife and metal ruler on a cutting mat.

2 Score along the lines dividing the sides from the front and along each long edge of the base, using a ruler as a guide. Do not cut right through the board. Turn over the board so that the scored side is underneath.

3 Fold up the front and back sections, then fold around the side sections to form the box shape. Cut strips of gummed tape, dampen them, and stick them along the edges to join them securely.

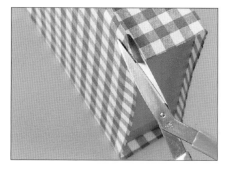

4 Mark a 25¼ x 9-in. (64 x 23-cm) rectangle on the fusing web. Fuse it to the wrong side of the fabric, then cut out the shape. With an even overlap at the top and bottom, fuse the fabric to the sides, back, and front of the rack. Trim the fabric neatly at a back corner.

5 Trim the edges of the fabric ⅝ in. (1.5 cm) beyond the top edges of the rack, then fuse them onto the inside as far as possible. Press the corners into neat miters. Glue any areas you cannot fuse. At the bottom, fuse the excess fabric to the base of the rack.

6 Mark a 24½ x 8-in. (62 x 20-cm) rectangle on the fusing web. Fuse it to the wrong side of the fabric, then cut it out. Peel off the backing paper. Spread glue on the inside of the rack, omitting the base. Stick the fabric in place, overlapping the ends at a front corner. Trim just inside the top edge.

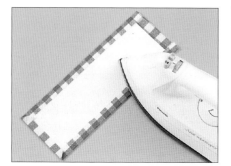

7 Cut a 8¾ x 3-in. (22.5 x 7.5-cm) piece of thin cardboard. Cut a piece of fusing web ⅝ in. (1.5 cm) larger all around. Fuse it to the fabric and cut out, then fuse it to the cardboard, fusing the excess onto the wrong side. Fit the piece into the bottom of the rack. If you wish, cover the edges of the rack by gluing on bias binding.

8 For the stand, cut 9¼ x 3¼-in. (23.5 x 9-cm) and 9¾ x 4-in. (24.5 x 10-cm) rectangles of mounting board, and cover with fabric as before. Center the smaller board on the larger one, right sides up, and glue in place. Glue the rack, centered, on top, then glue a rectangle of felt to the bottom.

Making the pencil holder

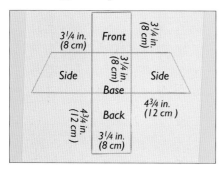

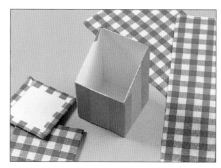

1 Lay the mounting board right side down. Use a ruler, triangle, and pencil to draw the shape of the holder on the back of the board, following the measurements given. Cut it out along the outer edges, using a utility knife and metal rule on a cutting mat.

2 Referring to steps **2–3** on page 303, score the shape, fold it into a box and secure the edges. Following steps **4–6** (above) cover the outside with a 13⅜ x 6-in. (34 x 15-cm) fabric piece and the inside with a 12⅝ x 4¾-in. (32 x 12-cm) piece.

3 Following steps **7–8** (above), use a 3-in. (7.5-cm) square of cardboard covered with fabric for the base lining. For the base stands, use 3½-in. (9-cm) and 4-in. (10-cm) squares of board covered with fabric. Finally, cover the bottom with a square of felt.

Sewing Set

This useful sewing set includes a tailormade scissor fob and a choice of two styles of needlecase. The set is simple and economical to make—the items are so small you can afford to use luxury fabrics such as silk, velvet, and satin.

The lined and padded scissor fob (below and on the next page) has a long ribbon loop to secure the scissors. The optional cord trim doubles up as a hanging cord, so that the fob can be worn around the neck. The fob can be made to fit any scissors of any size.

Instructions for making the two needlecases are given on page 306. The first has a lined and padded outer cover, and can be made from evenweave or non-evenweave fabrics. The second has a fringed outer cover, ideal for evenweave fabrics such as aida or Hardanger. Both styles of needlecase have ribbon ties and four felt inner leaves to hold the needles.

Experiment with rich fabric colors and textures, and have fun with contrasting trimmings.

A contrasting tassel sewn to the point of the fob adds extra interest.

Making a scissor fob

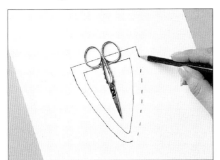

1 Make a pattern to fit between scissor bows and point, allowing ⁵/₈ in. (1.5 cm) below the point and ³/₈ in. (1 cm) either side of the bows. Add ³/₈ in. (1 cm) seam allowances all around. From main fabric, lining, and batting, cut two of each, using the paper pattern.

YOU WILL NEED
* Paper and pencil
* Scissors
* Main fabric
* Lining fabric
* Narrow ribbon
* Felt
* Lightweight batting
* Transfer fusing web (optional)
* Pinking shears
* 1 ⅛ yd. (1 m) cord trim (optional)
* Sewing needle and thread

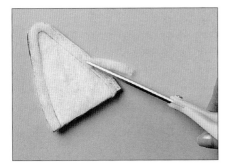

2 Place the batting on the wrong side of the main fabric pieces. Baste, then stitch all four layers together around the side edges. Trim the batting just outside the stitching.

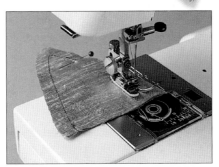

3 Pin, then stitch the two lining pieces together with right sides facing, around the side edge. Leave a 1½-in. (4-cm) opening at the center of one side edge.

4 Trim the seam allowances on the lining and the fabric pieces. Turn the lining right side out and place it inside the main fabric piece with the top raw edges level. Baste, then stitch the lining to the main fabric around the top edge.

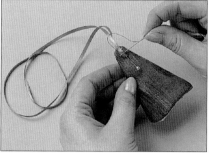

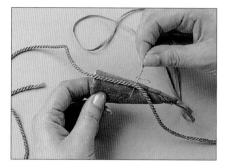

5 Turn fabric right side out through the opening in the lining. Tuck in the raw edges along the opening, and hand-stitch them together. Tuck the lining inside the main fabric.

6 Fold a ⅝ yd. (60 cm) length of ribbon in half, and tuck in the raw edges. Hand-stitch the ends to the point on the wrong side of the fob so that the ribbon loop hangs downward.

7 If you wish to add a cord trim, stitch the center section of the cord around the fob seam. Knot the ends of the cord together.

Making a padded needlecase

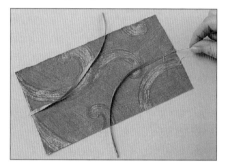

1 From main fabric, lining, and batting, cut a 8¾ in. x 4¾-in. (22 x 12-cm) rectangle. Place the main fabric piece right side up. Baste an 8-in. (20-cm) length of ribbon to the center of each short edge, so that the loose ends of the ribbons point inward.

2 Place the lining and main fabric together with right sides facing, and place the batting on the wrong side of the main fabric. Baste, then stitch together through all the layers, leaving a 2-in. (5-cm) opening at the center of one long edge. Trim the seam allowances and corners, turn right side out, and slip-stitch the opening.

3 From the felt, use pinking shears to cut one 7 x 3¼-in. (18 x 8-cm) rectangle and one 6¼ x 2¼-in. (16 x 6-cm) rectangle. Fold each piece in half widthwise and press to mark the center. Baste, then stitch the leaves to the cover along the center fold.

Making a fringed needlecase

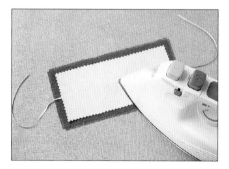

Cut the fabric 8 x 4 in. (20 x 10 cm) and fringe the edges for ¼ in. (5 mm). Cut a piece of felt ⅜ in. (1 cm) smaller all around and iron fusing web to the wrong side. Lap the ends of the ribbons under the felt, remove backing paper, and fuse the felt to the fabric. Add the leaves as for step **3** (above).

This needlecase matches the scissor fob on the previous page. The opulent outer fabric and silk lined set would bring an air of luxury to any sewing basket.

Easy Cushion Covers

The easiest type of cushion cover to make is a simple square or rectangular shape with an overlapped back opening. You can cut both the front and back pieces from fabric to make a plain cushion, as shown below, or you can use the front to display a favorite piece of embroidery, such as a cross-stitch or needlepoint panel.

Stitch small embroidered pieces onto the cushion front before assembling the cover. Larger pieces can form the whole cushion front. Instructions for both display ideas are given on the next page.

To hold the pillow form firmly in place, your cushion cover needs a generous overlap at the back. The steps below explain how to make a cover with

a 4-in. (10-cm) wide overlap, which suits cushions up to 14 in. (35 cm) square. For larger cushions, the overlap needs to be at least 6 in. (15 cm), so cut the back piece 8½ in. (21 cm) wider than the front.

To ensure that the cushion holds its shape when it is in use, always position the back overlap on a rectangular cover so that it runs widthwise (parallel to the two shorter sides).

Use fabrics that are closely woven, crease-resistant, and durable. Strong decorator fabrics made of cotton and linen blends are ideal.

Making a cover with an overlapped opening

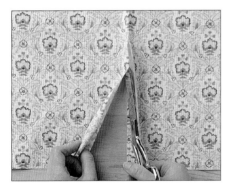

1 Cut the fabric for the front piece ⅝ in. (1.5cm) larger all around than the finished cover. Cut the fabric for the back piece 6¼ in. (16 cm) wider than the front. Cut the back piece in half widthwise.

2 Turn, press, and machine-stitch a ⅝ in. (1.5 cm) double hem along the center edge of each back piece.

3 Placing right sides together, pin the back pieces to the front. Make sure that the raw edges match all around and that the hemmed center back edges overlap by about 4 in. (10 cm).

4 Stitch around the outer edge, taking ⅝ in. (1.5 cm) seam allowances. Stitch twice across each end of overlap for strength. Trim the corners of seam allowances diagonally. Turn the cover right side out and insert the pillow form.

Making a cover with an embroidered panel and braid trim

1 Trim the canvas or fabric around the embroidery to leave an unstitched border a little narrower than the width of the braid trim.

2 Cut out the cover front as in step 1 on page 307. Center the embroidery on the right side of cover front and slip-stitch in place.

3 Machine- or hand-stitch the trim over the raw edges of embroidery. Cut out the cover back and assemble the cover as in steps 1–4 on page 307.

Making a cover with an embroidered front and cord trim

1 Block the embroidery, then trim the canvas edges to 1 in. (2.5 cm). Cut the back of the cover as in step 1 on page 307 but allow 1 in. (2.5 cm) for seams. Press and stitch a 5/8-in. (1.5-cm) double hem on center edge of each back piece.

2 Placing right sides together, pin back pieces to embroidery, overlapping hemmed edges at center. With embroidery side up, use a zipper foot to stitch all around twice, close to embroidery. Leave a 1-in. (2.5-cm) opening at the base. Trim seams to 5/8 in. (1.5 cm).

3 Clip corners carefully and turn cover right side out. Push one end of cord through opening in seam. Slip-stitch cord along seamline, all around edge. Insert other end of cord into opening and slip-stitch closed. Insert pillow form.

For cushions with an embroidered front, stitch a cord trim over the seam to conceal any canvas threads.

The neatest way to attach the braid is to cut it so that it extends to the sides of the cover.

Simple Chair Cover

A lined cover is ideal for revitalizing a worn chair or for helping an existing chair blend into a new color scheme. This one, with its roomy fit, gives a luxurious look to a room.

The cover is cut in one piece and is quick to put together. The sides meet edge-to-edge and fasten with neat cord loops and either toggles or buttons. For a more casual look, use fabric ties instead. For a smart, crisp finish, insert piping around the edge, following the instructions on pages 275–276.

The cover is fully reversible, so be sure to choose a lining that harmonizes with the surrounding decor. This gives maximum flexibility because you can then simply flip the cover lining side out when you want a change.

On most chairs, 54-in. (137-cm) wide fabric is wide enough to enable you to cut the whole cover in one piece. To work out how much fabric to buy, measure from the floor at the back of the chair, up over the chair back, across the seat, and down to the floor at the front. Add 4 in. (10 cm) for seams. Buy this amount of main fabric and lining. If you want to pipe the cover, you will need to buy extra fabric. Take $5/8$ in. (1.5 cm) seam allowances throughout.

Making a chair cover

1 For the pattern, make one long panel of paper to go over the chair from the floor at the back, up over the chair back (meeting at the sides), and down over the seat to the floor. Tape two side pieces to the seat section, and cut to fit. Temporarily tape the side edges together to check fit.

2 Mark the fastening positions on each edge of the pattern—one at the junction of the back and seat, one halfway up the back, and one halfway up each leg. Mark the button or toggle positions with circles and the loops with crosses.

3 Lay the fabrics out flat, with right sides together. Pin the pattern on top, and mark a $5/8$ in. (1.5 cm) seam allowance all around. Cut along the marked line, and transfer the fastening markings to both pieces.

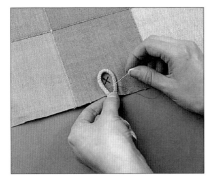

4 Cut eight 4-in. (10-cm) lengths of cord. Fold each one in half and position it on the right side of the main fabric at a loop position, with the loops facing inward. Match the cut edges to the raw fabric edge, check that the loops are big enough for the toggles or buttons, then baste them in place.

5 Lay the lining and main fabric pieces together, right sides facing, and pin all around, matching the fastening marks. Stitch, leaving an 8-in. (20-cm) gap at the center bottom of the back panel. Trim seam allowances at outer corners and clip almost up to the stitching line at the inner corners.

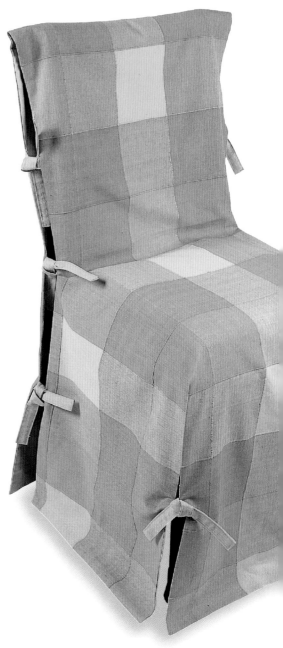

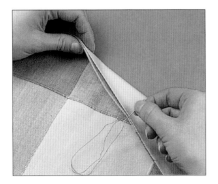

6 Turn the cover right side out, pushing the corners out with a knitting needle, and press. At the opening, turn in the seam allowances and slip-stitch the gap closed.

7 Sew toggles or buttons ¼ in. (6 mm) in from the edge opposite the loops, as marked. Place the cover on the chair, and slip the cord loops around the toggles or buttons.

Cover with fabric ties

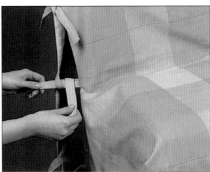

1 Follow Making a Chair Cover, steps **1–3**. Cut 16 fabric strips 9 x 2¾ in. (23 x 7 cm). On each, press in ⅜ in. (1 cm) on the long edges and one short edge. Fold in half lengthwise with wrong sides facing. Topstitch around all three turned-in sides close to edge.

2 Matching the raw edges, pin, then baste a tie across the seamline at each of the marked points. Complete the cover following steps **5–6** (above).

3 Place the cover on the chair and secure the sides together by neatly knotting each pair of ties.

Pointed Tab Heading

A pointed tab heading is a practical and decorative way to hang curtains or a wall hanging. The tabs are easy to make and attach, and, when used on curtains, they have the great advantage of providing sufficient interest in themselves to allow you to use less fabric than would be required for a more traditional style of curtain.

You can make tabs from the main curtain fabric or opt for a contrasting fabric, which is a good way of linking the curtains with other colors in your room scheme. If the fabric is lightweight, apply iron-on interfacing to stiffen the tabs.

For a wall hanging, the tabs should be made of either the main fabric or fabric used as a trimming—perhaps as a border along the lower edge.

YOU WILL NEED
❋ Decorator fabric
❋ Sewing needle and thread
❋ Fabric marker
❋ Scissors
❋ Tape measure or ruler
❋ Buttons
❋ Fusible interfacing (optional)

Making a pointed tab heading

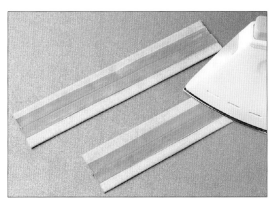

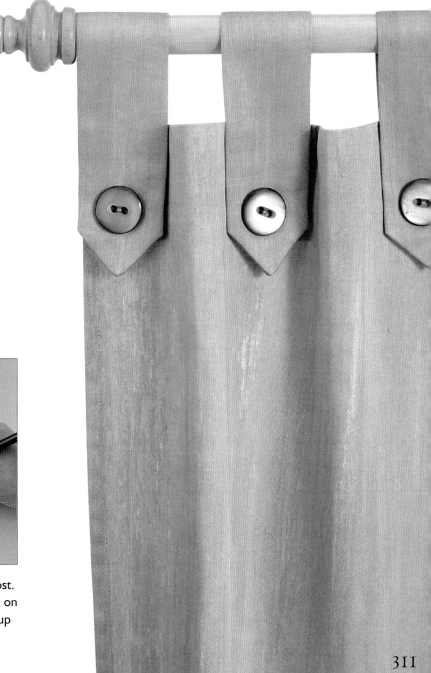

I Fold each tab piece in half lengthwise, with right sides facing. Sitch ⅝ in. (1.5 cm) from the long raw edges. Position the seam in the center of the tab as shown, and press it open. The tabs shown here have been interfaced with fusible interfacing, which is optional.

2 Lay the stitched tabs flat with the seam uppermost. Mark one tab ⅜ in. (1 cm) up from one raw end, on the centered seam line. Then mark 1⅜ in. (3.5 cm) up from the raw end on each side edge.

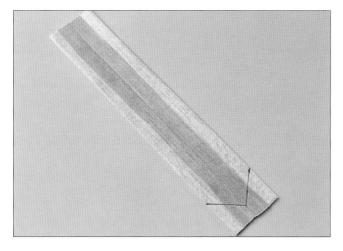

3 Machine-stitch from the mark on one side edge of the tab to the marked center point. With the needle in the fabric, pivot the tab and stitch to the mark on the other side edge. Repeat steps **2–3** for each tab.

4 Trim each tab to ¼ in. (5 mm) from the stitching, and cut away a "V" of fabric at the point to reduce bulk. Turn the tabs right side out and press.

5 Lay the curtain or wall hanging flat, right side up. Pin the tabs right side up along the top, matching the raw edges; start with the two outer tabs, and space the remaining tabs evenly between them.

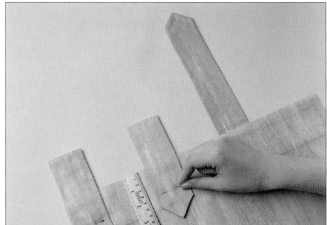

6 Attach the facing or backing so that the raw edges of the tabs are enclosed in the seam. Fold the tabs forward to lie over the right side of the curtain or hanging top. Pin them in place with the points the desired distance below the top edge. Check the fit on the rod.

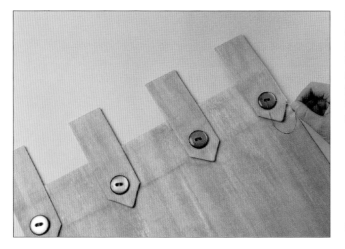

7 Using a doubled length of thread, sew a button onto each tab, stitching through all the fabric layers to secure the tabs firmly in place.

For a coordinated look, secure the pointed tabs using self-covered buttons, covered with remnants of the main fabric. Center pattern motifs on the buttons to make them more of a feature.

Tassels and Cord Trims

Tassels and twisted-cord trims are ideal for embellishing any number of items throughout the home—from embroidered cushions and drapery tiebacks to valances, shades, and lamp pulls. You can buy a wide selection of ready-made tassels and cords in a range of standard widths, but it is worth making your own. The techniques are very simple, and you can make the cord or tassel to exactly the right color and size for your decor.

The steps below show how to make a simple tassel of any size. The steps on page 314 explain how to make a plush, round-headed tassel and how to make a twisted cord trim. The cord can be as fine or as thick as you like. Finer cords can be used to edge items such as cushions, footstools, and book covers, while thick cords can be used to make sumptuous, tassel-trimmed tiebacks.

Materials

Yarn and needles Tassels and cord trims can be made from almost any type of yarn; knitting or needlepoint yarn, embroidery threads, chenille, and even raffia give excellent results. You will also need a tapestry needle with a large eye.

Molds and cardboard Tassels are made by wrapping yarn around a shape. Use firm cardboard for simple tassels. For round-headed tassels, use a suitably sized form such as a Styrofoam or papier-mâché craft ball or an empty thread spool.

Ornaments Thread on trinkets and beads to add extra interest to tassels.

Beads
Stranded floss
Card
Spool of thread
Tapestry needle
Knitting yarns
Pearl cottons
Papier-mâché craft ball
Leather strips

Making a simple tassel

1 Cut a piece of stiff cardboard the required length of the tassel and about 2 in. (5 cm) wide. Wrap the yarn evenly around the card to the required thickness. Thread a length of yarn onto a tapestry needle. Slip it under the tops of the loops, and tie them loosely together. Ease the loops off the card.

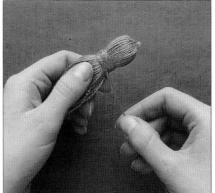

2 Cut a length of yarn about 30 in. (75 cm) long. Knot it around the tassel, about one-third of the way down from the top. Wrap the end of the yarn firmly around the tassel, covering the knot.

3 Thread the loose end of the yarn onto the tapestry needle, and take it into the center of the tassel, down into the tail. Then cut through the loops at the bottom of the tassel and trim them neatly.

Making a round-headed tassel

YOU WILL NEED

❋ Yarn in one or two colors

❋ Styrofoam or papier-mâché craft ball, 2 in. (5 cm) in diameter

❋ Pointed scissors or X-Acto knife

❋ Tweezers

❋ Tapestry needle

❋ Cardboard rectangle, 6 x 4 in. (15 x 10 cm)

❋ Small wooden or plastic bead

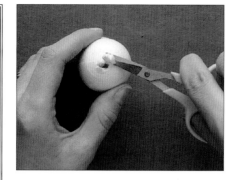

1 Using pointed scissors or an X-Acto knife, cut a hole about 5/8 in. (1.5 cm) in diameter through the center of the craft ball. Trim off any rough edges, then use the tweezers to remove the waste material.

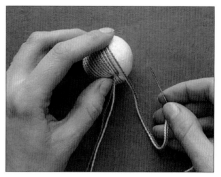

2 Thread two or three 2-yd. (2-m) lengths of yarn onto the needle. Take it through the hole in the ball, leaving 6 in. (15 cm) tails of yarn at the base. Wrap the yarn around the ball to cover it. Add more yarn as needed.

3 Wrap yarn evenly around the narrow width of the cardboard until you have the desired thickness of the tassel tail. Thread the needle with a length of yarn, then slip it under the loops at the top of the card.

4 Ease the loops off the card, and tie the thread around them. Sew the loose ends of the yarn into the middle of the tail. Cut through the loops at the base of the tail, and trim them neatly.

5 Thread the tails of yarn at the bottom of the ball onto the needle. Push the needle into the center of the tassel tail, pulling the yarn through firmly to bring the tassel and ball close together. To secure the yarn, knot it around the bead.

Round-headed tassels look particularly effective when made up of yarns in two or more different colors.

To secure a length of twisted cord to a tassel top, simply sew it neatly in place using matching thread.

Making a twisted-cord trim

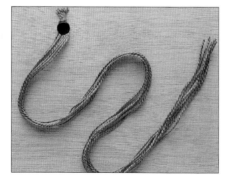

1 Cut lengths of yarn three times the desired length of the cord, and knot the ends together. Use a thumbtack to pin them to a work board or the back of a chair. Alternatively, hang them from a sturdy hook.

2 Tie the thread ends around a pencil. Rotate the pencil in one direction until the threads are very firmly twisted. Fold the twisted threads in half, and allow the strands to twist around each other. Run your hand down the threads to even out the twists. Knot and trim the ends.

Fabric Fringes

Fabric fringes are simple to make and add a charming finish to a wide range of sewing projects, including tablecloths, napkins, seat covers, and scarves and shawls.

The fringes shown here are made by removing the weft (horizontal) threads from the edge of the fabric, leaving the warp (vertical, parallel to selvage) threads as the fringe.

The fringe can be left plain, or threads can be knotted together in groups and embellished with beads for a more decorative effect.

Choose loosely woven, medium- or heavyweight fabrics for fringing; linens and heavy cottons are ideal. Lightweight fabrics are much more difficult to work with because the fringe will be too fine.

Patterned fabrics produce multi-colored fringes.

Making a basic fringe

1 Decide where the lower edge of the fringe will finish, and pull out a thread along this line to make a level edge. Measure the desired depth of the fringe, and pull out another thread to mark the top of the fringe.

2 Trim along the lower pulled thread. If the fringe is to be left plain, secure the top of the fringe with a row of machine stitching. Then use a seam ripper or a pin to pull out one thread at a time to make the fringe.

Knotted fringes

1 Make a fringe following steps 1–2 (above). Make it at least 4 in. (10 cm) long for a single row of knots or 5½ in. (14 cm) long for a double row. Measure and mark the groups about ¾ in. (2 cm) apart. On check fabrics use the different colors to space the groups.

2 Tie each group of threads together with a single knot. Tie the knots near the top if you are making a double knotted fringe. On single-knot fringes they may be placed a little lower down. Make sure that the knots are the same level on each group.

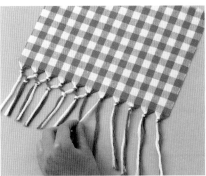

3 Divide each group into two equal halves. Knot the first half group on its own. Knot the second half with the first half of the next group. Continue knotting in this way to make a trellis effect across the fringe.

Hemstitched hem

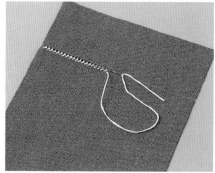

1 Prepare the fabric following Making a Basic Fringe, step 1 on page 315. Then, at the top of the fringe, draw out two or three threads to make space for the hemstitching.

2 Turn the work so that the fringe area is pointing away from you. Hemstitch across the drawn-thread panel (see page 20).

3 Turn the work again so that the fringe is at the lower edge. Pull out the threads back to the hemstitching to make the fringe.

Beaded fringe

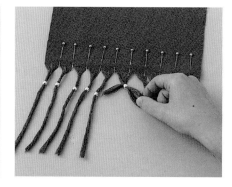

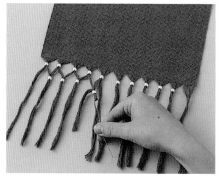

1 Prepare the fabric following Knotted Fringes, step 1 on page 315. Thread a needle with strong thread. Holding onto the ends of the thread, pass the needle through a large-eyed bead, around one group, then back through the bead.

2 Hold the bead with one hand, and gently pull both thread ends with the other hand to draw the fringe through the bead. Push the bead to the top of each group. Repeat to thread beads on each group.

3 Divide each group in half. Leave the first half group plain. Join the second half of the first group to the first half of the next group, and thread on another bead. Continue in this way.

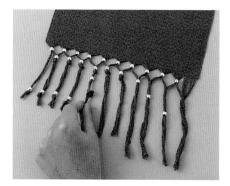

4 With the second row of beads just below the first row, knot the group under each bead to secure the bead. Add more rows of beads, if desired.

Turn a plain scarf into a coveted accessory by adding a beaded fringe (far right) or a stylish hemstitched fringe (right).

Index

Acknowledgements

Photography:
Edward J Allwright, Paul Bricknell, Jon Bouchier, Julien Busselle, Tony Chau, Alan Duns, David Garcia/ Alison Griffiths, David Garcia, Christine Hanscombe, Rob Mitchell Photography, Gloria Nicol, Lizzie Orme, Steven Pam, Lucinda Symons, Steve Tanner, Adrian Taylor, Shona Wood.

Illustrations:
Terry Evans, Coral Mula, Susan & Martin Penny.